slam

S. A. NIGOSIAN

ISLAM
Its History, Teaching, and Practices

INDIANA UNIVERSITY PRESS
Bloomington and Indianapolis

Publication of this book is made possible in part with the assistance of a Challenge Grant from the National Endowment for the Humanities, a federal agency that supports research, education, and public programming in the humanities.

This book is a publication of

Indiana University Press
601 North Morton Street
Bloomington, Indiana 47404-3797 USA

http://iupress.indiana.edu

Telephone orders   800-842-6796
Fax orders   812-855-7931
Orders by e-mail   iuporder@indiana.edu

A previous edition of this book was published in 1987 under the title *Islam: The Way of Submission* by Crucible Press, Wellingborough, England.

Library of Congress Cataloging-in-Publication Data

Nigosian, S. A. (Solomon Alexander)
  Islam : its history, teaching, and practices / S. A. Nigosian.
    p.   cm.
  Includes bibliographical references and index.
  Originally published: Leighton Buzzard, Bedfordshire : Crucible, 1987.
  ISBN 0-253-34315-1 (cloth : alk. paper) — ISBN 0-253-21627-3 (pbk. : alk. paper)
    1. Islam.   I. Title.
  BP161.3.N54 2004
  297—dc21
                              2003009549

1 2 3 4 5   09 08 07 06 05 04

To all those at Victoria College,
University of Toronto,
who encouraged and supported
my research activities

And to Debbie van Eeken
for her readiness to cooperate
with an author who often expects
the impossible.

O humanity! We created you from a single soul, male and female, and made you into nations and tribes, so that you may come to know one another. Truly, the most honored of you in God's sight is the greatest of you in piety. God is All-Knowing, All-Aware. (Qur'an, 49:13)

Contents

Maps and Illustrations

Maps

Illustrations

Preface

This edition of *Islam: Its History, Teaching, and Practices* differs from my previous edition *Islam: The Way of Submission* (1987) in several respects. The subject matter has been recast and appropriate modifications and additions have been made. But its basic character—to outline the essential aspects of Islam as a living force, not a systematic exposition of its history or philosophy—remains intact. From beginning to end, the focus is set on an overall theme: to identify a great world religion and recognize its contributions to human civilization.

In this book, seven specific issues are presented from an objective, scholarly point of view. I have sought to strike a balance between facts, traditions, current interpretation, and commentary. Consequently, these seven basic components of Islam will be treated in as much detail as possible within the scope and limitations of this book.

A quick glance at the table of contents will confirm what most readers expect to see in such a volume. The introduction offers a general understanding of the vast and absorbing aspect of Islam. This is followed by seven chapters that encapsulate and portray the unique spirit of Islam, which pervades every aspect of Muslim life and unites millions of individuals all over the world in a common bond.

Chapter 1 presents the life of Muhammad, from both the traditional perspective and in light of modern research. Chapter 2 surveys Islamic political development and territorial expansion in history. Chapter 3 discusses the formation of three main groups and various subgroups following the death of Muhammad. Chapter 4 introduces the Qurʾan, the record that contains God's message to humanity as received by Muhammad. Chapter 5 deals with Sunnah, Hadith, and Shariʿah, the body of transmitted accounts reporting on the acts and statements of Muhammad, and the compilation of Islamic canon law, considered to be divinely established. Chapter 6 deals with faith and action, the legal, theological, and moral principles as well as acts of worship that demand the performance of religious duties. Chapter 7 deals with observances and festivals. These include social practices, devotional exercises, holy days, and local feasts.

Additional features included in this volume are key dates, Muslim dynasties, the ninety-nine names of God, two maps, numerous photographs, a glossary, and an extensive bibliography for further study or research.

A few words regarding diacritical marks, the system of transliteration, translation of Qurʾanic passages, and key dates are in order. I have refrained from using any diacritical marks because the full use of diacriticals is confusing for beginners, while modified use often tends to be of little use in pronunciation.

I have deviated from the standard system of transliteration of Arabic words and names and have instead used what are in common use in English, except for the "hamza" (similar to a regular apostrophe placed between two letters to indicate a glottal sound where a new syllable is to be pronounced, such as in Qurʾan, fidaʾi, wuduʾ) and the "ayn" (a reverse apostrophe to indicate a sound pronounced further back in the throat, such as in ʿAbbasid, Kaʿbah). The translation and numbering of Qurʾanic passages are according to Arthur J. Arberry. And finally, to avoid confusion, dates are given in almost every case according to the Gregorian calendar (Western usage).

Two important points, however, need to be reiterated. First, to understand Islam properly, it is necessary to see Islam as a major universal religion, with Muhammad as the last of a series of messengers sent by God. Second, to grasp something of the spirit of Islam, it is fundamental to appreciate the Islamic emphasis on an uncompromising monotheism, with strict adherence to certain essential social, political, and religious practices, as taught by the prophet Muhammad and elaborated by tradition.

A word of thanks is due to all those who were directly involved with the preparation of this volume: to the faculty and staff of Victoria College in the University of Toronto, my alma mater, for providing me with space, time, and cooperation, without which this book would never have been written; to Dr. Robert C. Brandeis, chief librarian of Victoria University, and to the staff of the library, for their unfailing courtesy, kindness, and efficient help; to Dalia Eltayeb, a Ph.D. candidate, for taking time from her own work to read the entire draft and offer valuable suggestions for improvement; and to Jamsheed Choksy of Indiana University, who made many detailed and helpful comments on the manuscript of this book. I owe a special debt to Debbie van Eeken for her patience and cheerful cooperation. I am grateful also to Peter-John Leone, Robert J. Sloan, Kendra Boileau Stokes, and the other members of the editorial staff at Indiana University Press in seeing this book into production. Last, but not least, to my wife, whose sense of understanding is something very special to me indeed. Needless to say, I am solely responsible for whatever shortcomings the book may possess.

S. A. Nigosian
University of Toronto
Victoria College

Introduction

Islam is the second largest world religion after Christianity. Its followers today extend from Morocco to the Philippines, and it includes among its adherents different races and peoples of Asia, Africa, Europe, Australia, and the Americas. In fact, more than three-quarters of the total Muslim population in the world is found in non-Arab countries.

The word *Islam* has two meanings: "submission" and "peace"—submission to the will and guidance of God and living in peace with one's self and one's surroundings. The essence of Islam, therefore, lies in submission to God, which results in peace of mind and soul. The correct name for the religion is *Islam*, and the proper term for its adherents is *Muslims*.

The origin of Islam is ascribed to one of two points in time: creation or the sixth century C.E. in Arabia. From the Muslim perspective, the story of Islam starts not with Muhammad (c. 570–632) but shares a common biblical tradition that begins with Adam—with God's creation of the universe and human beings. The descendants of Adam are traced to Noah, who had a son named Shem. That is where the word *Semite*—descendants of Shem—comes from; like the Jews, Arabs regard themselves as a Semitic people. Shem's descendants are then traced to Abraham and to his wives Sarah and Hagar. At that point, two familiar stories about Abraham provide the cornerstones of the Islamic religion. The first story, concerning Ishmael, the eldest son of Abraham by Hagar, explains how Abraham's banishment of Ishmael and his mother led them to Mecca, where he established the family from whose descendants the prophet Muhammad emerged in the sixth century C.E. The second story tells of Abraham's attempt to sacrifice his son (the Bible specifies Isaac, the younger son of Abraham by Sarah, while the Qurʾan does not mention any names; most Muslim commentators consider it to be Ishmael, while a few think it is Isaac). The story demonstrates Abraham's submission to the will of God in the supreme test; hence the word *Islam*. The essence of Islam therefore lies in submission to God.

Those who dispute the assumption that Islam began with creation date its origin from the time of Muhammad in the sixth century C.E. in Arabia. To anyone other than an adherent of Islam, the relative merits of these conclusions are academic. No one disputes the role of Muhammad and the universal influence of Islam.

From its earliest beginnings, Islam has been a religion of action rather than of contemplation. At no time did the prophet Muhammad disdain society or politics. He made it quite clear that his mission was essentially concerned with human affairs—social, political, economic, military, and religious. He perpetuated this principle by making it impossible for future Muslim generations to divorce religious from secular affairs, to dismiss social or political issues as un-religious, or to relegate either to secondary importance. Thus, the sacred-secular dichotomy, a concept common to Westerners, is either blurred or absent in the world of Islam. The Islamic community is at once a political and a religious community. To Muslims, the notion of religion as separable from the totality of the human context is unimaginable, even detestable. All of life is sacred and must conform to the larger whole—the identity of the Islamic faith. All who belong to this great Islamic faith share a sense of identity, a sense of global com-munity. And of the various terms used to denote the Islamic "community" or "nation," the one that predominates is *ummah*.

Traditionally, the Islamic *ummah* is divided into three regions: the territory of Islam (*dar al-Islam*), the territory of peace (*dar al-sulh*), and the territory of war (*dar al-harb*). As its name implies, the first territory identifies parts of the world where Muslims predominate and in which Islam, in both its political and religious sense, governs and directs daily life and tribal or national policy. In regions such as Pakistan, Iran, and Libya, Islamic law is assumed to form the basis of government. The second territory represents regions such as India and Africa, where Muslims are in the minority but are permitted for the most part to live in peace and to practice their religion freely. The rest of the world makes up the third territory, which is viewed more as an ideological battleground con-tested by groups with conflicting values than as a literal theater of war.

Paradoxically, non-Muslims living within the territory or state of Islam (*dar al-Islam*) have been tolerated and given legal status based on their own religious perspectives. In the world of Islam, these non-Muslims belong to the *dhimmi;* that is, the people held under or protected by the dictates of the conscience of Islam.[1] The *dhimmi* may retain their own social, political, and religious status, but they are subject to certain restrictions. For instance, they may not convert Muslims to their religion or marry Muslim women.

Thus, the *ummah,* by its own Islamic measure, is a privileged community, a community of shared identity and of unity, in which cultural forms, societal patterns, and political realms all coalesce with religious and devotional aspects. Consequently, the principles of Islam dominate and regulate the whole lifestyle of the *ummah.* Indeed, the feature which most distinguishes Islam from other religious traditions is that Islam burst forth in the seventh century within the context of an Arab tribal culture and yet in less than a century became the strongest common experience of the peoples of Asia and Africa. While follow-ers of other religions suffered repression, regression, and defeat, adherents of Islam rode an unbroken wave of conquest and ruled triumphantly. Every con-quest and every victory convinced the Islamic community that God had made it invincible. Even to this day many Muslims consider the Islamic wars of ex-pansion to have been ordained by God and the warring Muslim armies to have been fighting for God's cause to bring all the people of the world under God's aegis.

Today, Muslims are intensely conscious of their decline from the great days of the past.[2] Some pious Muslim thinkers, in analyzing the causes of decline, reject any suggestion that it may be attributable to the principles of Islam. They tend instead to repudiate the new spirit of liberalism, the external influences which fuel this spirit, the exploitation of *dar al-Islam* by foreign powers, the impact of incompatible religious philosophies, and the unhealthy spirit of skepticism. Others maintain a critical view of tradition and are determined to put an end to blind obedience to authority.[3] Still others, equipped with modern historical criticism, modern philosophy, and modern science, are reinterpreting Islamic principles and proposing some far-reaching reforms in the structure of Islamic society. A few have even attempted to integrate what they see as appropriate elements from foreign thought and practice with fundamental elements of Islam.

On the issue of Islamic identity, the world of Islam is divided between two factions: the modernists and the traditionalists. The former attempt to reconcile Islam with alien concepts that nevertheless seem to have useful applications to legal systems, government structures, education, technical skills, national sentiments, self-criticism, and so on. The latter question non-Muslim constitutions and institutions, challenge the modernists' right of leadership, and view the reduced influence of Islamic people as the result of corrupting contacts with alien people and powers.

In recent years, the traditionalist view has become widespread throughout Islamic countries, assuming dramatic characteristics of what traditionalists call Islamic revivalism. As a result, imperial powers are denounced as ungodly villains outside the boundaries of normal decency. Their corrupting influence, transmitted through insidious channels, is considered to have brought about the decline of Islamic faith and practice. The only remedy for this situation is religious revivalism—the eradication of evil and a return to Islamic principles.

Religious revivalism in Islam means getting back to basics. It means the literal application in everyday life of Islamic teachings on topics such as sociology, politics, cosmology, psychology, theology, philosophy, and mysticism. The movement is not a reformation but an affirmation of ancient values. Islamic revivalism does not mean attempting to draft a blueprint of an ideal Muslim society reflecting Western or alien concepts at the expense of traditional values. An authentic revival of Islam, at least according to traditionalists, requires a renewal of the traditional framework of the Islamic faith by returning to traditional doctrines and modes of behavior.

In spite of feelings of uneasiness, especially against the West, many Muslim governments, particularly Arab rulers, purchase arms from the West, sell oil to Western industrialized countries, and buy Western products and Western expertise.

That an inherent contradiction sometimes exists between Islamic words and Islamic deeds has not occurred to many Muslim governments. Attempts to restore Islamic hegemony without recourse to modern, and therefore alien and corrupting, techniques and technologies have so far failed. In fact, Islamic proscriptions limiting freedom of thought and action in all aspects of life—private, public, and religious—have caused serious problems from Islam's earliest beginnings. Legal interpretations formulated by Muslim religious scholars frequently clashed with policy dictated by Muslim rulers in response to the needs of government, and conflict was resolved in favor of whichever faction dominated at certain times and places. By the late nineteenth century, almost all the Islamic world came under external, mainly European, domination and influence.

For the first time in its long history, Islam was exposed to the process of Westernization. Divinely ordained Islamic law, particularly as it applied to regulations codifying government, legal systems, education, and social security, was set aside in favor of man-made systems imported from Western codes. The aftermath of these experiments occurred in the post-colonial era of the twentieth century. A new generation of Muslim leaders in Pakistan and Libya, for instance, whose commitment to Islamic law was intense, attempted to re-establish the dominance of Islamic systems.

So far such efforts have met with little or no success. The reason for this is threefold. First, the conditions of modern life militate against the successful implementation of old Islamic laws. Second, a modern Muslim elite educated in Western institutions persists in supporting activities that promote the modernization of Muslim societies. And third, sectarian differences within Islam create radically divergent views on what body of regulations constitutes Islamic law.

Muslim rulers are presently torn between the conflicting views of two equally matched opponents: those who insist on a return to traditional Islamic patterns and those who demand secular reforms. Each faction is confident that its method is the only way to resolve the ills of Islam.

This adversarial relationship between theocracy and politics is also at the root of recent dramatic actions among Muslims throughout the world that provoke global attention and cause international concern.[4] For instance, Palestinian Muslim militants risk their lives by attacking Israeli settlements. The establishment of the state of Israel in 1948 has complicated matters for Palestinian Arabs,[5] who view the loss of land and holy places in Jerusalem with a sense of injustice and anger. The 1995 Oslo Accord between Israel and the Palestine Liberation Organization (PLO; established in Jerusalem in 1964) and Yasser Arafat's election as president of the executive council of the Palestinian legislative assembly in 1996 promised to open a new chapter in Arab–Israeli relations.[6] But the killing of Hamas leaders by Israel and the retaliation by Hamas suicide bombers in 1996 threatened to derail the Oslo Accord. From mid-1996 to the present, the "peace process" has been unsuccessful.[7]

In Afghanistan, Muslim fighters held out against infinitely more powerful forces, first Russian, then American. A group of Muslim religious leaders (*mullahs*) headed by Ayatollah Khomeini brought about a massive revolution in Iran.[8] Muslim zealots occupied the holy shrine of Mecca. Terrorists motivated as much by their religious convictions as by their political convictions attacked, in the name of Islam, American embassies in Libya, Pakistan, Lebanon, and elsewhere. Acts of defiance by Saddam Hussein in Iraq led to the Gulf War of 1991.[9] Twelve years later in April 2003, he and his entire regime were ousted from power by a coalition led primarily by President George W. Bush (U.S.) and Prime Minister Tony Blair (U.K.).

The growing criticism and rejection of the West led to the formation in the late 1970s of militant Islamic groups like the AMAL,[10] Hizbʾuʾllah,[11] and al-Jihad in Lebanon.[12] During the late 1980s and early 1990s, violent extremist groups such as the Islamic Jihad attacked and killed government officials, intellectuals, and foreign tourists, as well as Coptic Christians in Egypt.

Again in the 1990s, bombings carried out in Paris by radical Algerian Islamic groups such as the Armed Islamic Guard threatened France and French culture. Islamic militants bombed the American military at the National Guard Headquarters in Riyadh in 1995 and the U.S. military housing compound in Dhahran in 1996. Those bombings were regarded by many as a warning by Islamic militants to the governments of Saudi Arabia and other Gulf states about their ties to the United States and the West. Demonstrations by angry mobs in Britain against the publication of Salman Rushdie's *The Satanic Verses* regenerated the centuries-long conflict between Muslims and Westerners.[13] And most recently, on September 11, 2001, a group of Muslim terrorists destroyed the World Trade Center towers in New York and severely damaged the Pentagon in Washington, D.C. Moreover, the extreme religious and political convictions of both Osama bin Laden and Mullah Omar in Afghan politics resulted in President George W. Bush's declaration of a "war on terrorism."[14]

Revolutions (e.g., in Iran), political conflicts (e.g., the Arab–Israeli conflict), terrorist attacks (e.g., against the U.S.), and acts of defiance (e.g., Iraq) are significant examples of the resurgent militancy of Islam. The superior military, political, and economic power of non-Muslim industrialized nations is considered an alien intrusion and exploitation; indeed, a totally evil implantation that infringes on Islamic principles, which needs to be uprooted and the wounds cauterized and cleansed by whatever means possible. Thus, the current militancy in the Islamic world, as well as the popularity of overt rejection of Western modes and artifacts by some Muslims, is quite understandable.

And yet Islam has extraordinary powers of adaptation. It has succeeded in absorbing apparently incompatible systems and silently abandoning elements that are found wanting. True, the advent of Western imperialistic civilization, with its colonialist aspirations, gradually brought the greater part of Islam under Western domination in the nineteenth and early twentieth centuries. Similarly, the intrusion of modern industrialization, with all its side effects, has challenged the traditional social and religious foundations of Islam. Nevertheless, a constant transformation is taking place within many an Islamic state in order to assimilate or adapt modern technological patterns and political systems to conform with Islamic principles.

Islam

1   Muhammad, Messenger of God

Founders of Religion

Western scholars have always been fascinated by the lives of the world's religious leaders who created the faiths that have endured for centuries. Such individuals, commonly known as founders of religion, possess a unique, uncommon, or rarefied quality of the mind. They see and hear in the "mind's eye and ear" that which is hidden from the sight and hearing of ordinary people. Their vision takes the shape of an extraordinary revelation (a Western notion) or a profound insight (an Eastern notion). So powerful is this mode of thinking that the thinker's mind soars in time and space, moves beyond reason, visualizes and generates ideas, alters the course of events, and establishes another order of existence. And through the labor of several supporters or disciples, the image takes organic form and body; is realized in actions, customs, and laws; and imposes itself on millions of people.

Often it is difficult to fully understand and appreciate the nature or behavior of these religious innovators. Statements made by their disciples affirm the paradoxical character (i.e., natural-supernatural or human-divine) of these religious masters. But whatever ambiguities they exhibit in behavior or character, religious geniuses initiate radical and massive changes in civilization because their religious perception appeals to large segments of society. Such geniuses help shape the course of human history, instituting actions by which whole governments and societies are organized. They break with custom, with accepted values, with tribal and societal loyalties, with time-honored traditions, with fixed patterns. They strongly react against established religious systems, openly challenge ancient beliefs, and courageously threaten prescribed rituals. They set their own norms and lead people to another vision of truth or reality. They express their experiences in terms of the inconceivable. They make demands that are difficult and at times incomprehensible. Their influence begins immediately, during their lifetimes, because they actively proclaim their religious perceptions and experiences as eternal truths. Such was Muhammad and his religion called Islam.

But who was Muhammad, and what did he teach? Before answering these questions it is necessary to present a brief historical background of Arabia, the world into which Muhammad appeared.

Arabia

Arabia is in the southern part of the Middle East. It is the largest peninsula in the world, covering almost one and a half million square miles (about one-third the size of the United States).[1] It is bounded on the west by the Red Sea, on the east by the Persian Gulf, on the south by the Arabian Sea, and on the north by the Syrian desert. Because it is bounded by seas on three sides and by the Euphrates River on the north, the Arabs call it the "Island of the Arabs" (*jazirat al-ʿarab*). The name Arab means "nomad."

This vast landmass is mostly composed of old igneous and metamorphic rocks of the mountains along the west coast, with an accumulation of younger sedimentary rocks in the northeast, and fields of recent lava beds in the central plateau and the north. The organic matter of the sedimentary rocks under the seas has produced the world's largest accumulation of petroleum, a commodity that has been exploited only since 1932. The mountains are cut by many valleys (*wadi*), along which are caravan routes. There are oases, especially along the caravan routes, in the north. The largest continuous sandy area in the world is in the south, known as "the empty quarter" (*al-rabʿ al-khali*), while to the north is another great sandy desert.

The climate of most of Arabia is what one would expect from such a region: long and very hot summers, with little or no rain in many places, except Yemen. Because of the paucity and irregularity of rain, there are no large lakes and only one short perennial river in Aden. Water is found in the subsoil of some valleys, and various methods are used to conserve water.

In ancient times there was no single name to denote the area, nor any single name for its population. People were referred to by group or tribal names associated with various areas. Paleolithic sites exist in both north and south Arabia, but the remains reveal little about those earliest inhabitants. Precisely when Arab people appear in history is also uncertain. Numerous allusions in the Old Testament refer to peoples and places in Arabia (e.g., Isaiah 21:13; Jeremiah 25:24; Ezekiel 27:21; 2 Chronicles 9:14). A passage in the Old Testament refers to the gold that King Solomon (961–922 B.C.E.) received from the kings of Arabia (1 Kings 10:14–15). An inscription dating from as early as the period of King Shalmaneser III of Assyria (854–824 B.C.E.) mentions "1000 camel-riders of Gindibuʾ from Arabia" opposing the Assyrians.[2] And from the period of King Tiglath-pileser III of Assyria (744–727 B.C.E.) down to the reign of the neo-Babylonian king Nabonidus (555–539 B.C.E.), there are numerous references to the peoples and rulers, including queens, of Arabia.[3]

Most of the above references suggest a definite distinction between northern and southern Arab tribes. Nomadic life was dominant in the north, while organized, settled life developed in the south. The social unit of the nomad ("bedouin," from Arabic plural *badawin*) is the tribe, named after an eponymous ancestor. Love of freedom, herding, seasonal migration, and raiding has always been the lifestyle of the nomad. The traditional beast of burden is the camel. By contrast, settled people in the south developed, among other things, trade, commerce, art, architecture, and literature. A sense of difference, even antipathy, between northern and southern Arab tribes seems to have existed from the earliest times. This antipathy between northern and southern tribes caused by their differing traditions continued for a while under Islam.

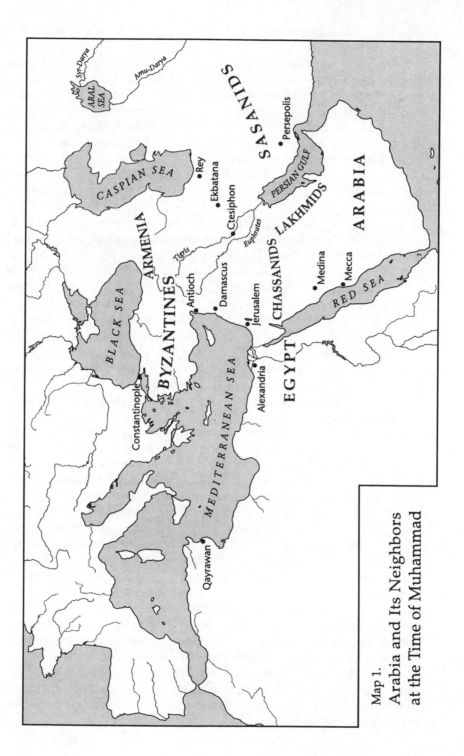

Map 1.
Arabia and Its Neighbors
at the Time of Muhammad

Arab nomads indiscriminately preyed on everyone and on each other. Trading and raiding formed the basis of their social and economic life, and their highest loyalty was to the tribe or clan, each group claiming descent from a common ancestor. Their literary heritage consisted of declamatory poems celebrating the heroic deeds of the tribe preserved through an oral tradition of recitation. Offering sacrifices and going on pilgrimages constituted their chief religious activities, and certain sites and towns considered to be holy became centers of pilgrimage and of religious ceremonies. This was especially true of Mecca, to which various tribes flocked annually.

Before the rise and expansion of Islam in the seventh century, Arabia was the scene of political instability and economic chaos.[4] By the sixth century, the thousand-year-old civilization of Yemen had collapsed. The Ethiopians (Abyssinians), Christianized by missionaries from Roman Egypt in the fourth century, launched an invasion to dominate south Arabia in the hopes of controlling the lucrative caravan trade that supplied the spices of India and the incense of Arabia to the Mediterranean world. South Arabians had appealed to their neighbors, the Persian Sasanid Empire, for help. Arabia's other neighbor, the Byzantine Empire, backed the Ethiopians. Incessant warfare between these two powerful neighbors exhausted the military strength of even the most powerful Arab chieftains. They were so drained of resources that conflict was limited to fighting among themselves.

Among the sedentary inhabitants of the peninsula, the tribe of Quraysh was relatively prosperous and enjoyed a favored position. They inhabited Mecca and controlled the caravan trade, in spite of the threat from Ethiopia, and they skillfully promoted the status of a sacred, cube-shaped shrine known as the Kaʿbah. In the shrine was a black stone traditionally believed to have been brought down to Abraham by the angel Gabriel, a stone so holy according to legend that its pure white radiance drew pilgrims to Mecca like a beacon until human wickedness turned it black. Because of this shrine, Mecca, long before the days of the prophet Muhammad, had been a sacred center to which Arabs came annually on pilgrimage. Because Mecca came to be regarded as sacrosanct territory, other Arab tribes hesitated to attack it. Instead, they came to worship and to trade, to the obvious advantage of the custodians of the holy place. In spite of its favored position, rival factions did threaten Mecca from time to time, shattering its peace with intertribal quarrels and senseless bloodshed, in the avowed interests of religion.

A few steps away from the Kaʿbah is the Zamzam well, believed to contain healing properties and reputed to be connected with the biblical Hagar and Ishmael. The Islamic story is that when Abraham abandoned Hagar, she wandered with her son Ishmael in the barren desert in search of water. In desperation, she left her exhausted son Ishmael lying on the hot ground while she ran back and forth in search of water. In the meantime, Ishmael tossed restlessly until his heels accidentally uncovered the opening to the well. Hagar and her son decided to settle there, and, in time, the children and grandchildren of

Ishmael multiplied to become the Arab race. It is for this reason that Arabs consider themselves sons of Abraham through Ishmael.[5]

Today, a building surrounds the Zamzam well. Adjacent to it is a marble tank filled with well water so that pilgrims can drink. The water is so greatly valued that some pilgrims soak their shrouds in it or carry it home in bottles.

In addition to Arab tribes, there were Jewish and Christian settlements in Arabia. Their superior knowledge of agriculture and irrigation and their energy and industry made them prosperous enough to arouse the envy of many of their Arab neighbors. In fact, their competitive presence in the social and economic life of Arabia often threatened the trade and finance of the Meccan Arabs as well as of other townsmen.

Although the influence of Judaism and Christianity extended throughout Arabia, the religion of the Arabs was by and large animistic and polytheistic. They worshipped whatever they found awesome or mystical, such as stones, rocks, trees, and stars, and they hung scraps of cloth, and other personal belongings on the branches of sacred trees, either to ward off evil or to receive some sort of divine blessing. Similar cults were associated with sources of water. Drinking, gambling, and dancing were common features of most of their religious ceremonies.

The Muslims call this pre-Islamic age the "period of ignorance" (al-jahiliyyah), the period of Arab paganism. Muslims affirm that Islam restored the pristine monotheism of Abraham that had gradually declined to decadent paganism. Islam aroused an enthusiasm for destroying all traces of the paganism of the "period of ignorance," and as a result nothing is known for certain about the pre-Islamic Arabian pantheon. Those mentioned in the Qurʾan are the gods called Allah and Hobal, the divine pair Isaf and Naʿilah, and the three goddesses al-Lat, Manat, and al-ʿUzza. Al-Lat is also mentioned in the writings of Herodotus (fifth century B.C.E. Greek historian) and in old Arabian inscriptions. She was the great mother goddess who, under various names, was worshipped all over the ancient world. Manat controlled the fortunes of people and the mysteries of life and death. Al-ʿUzza (meaning "the Mighty One") was especially important to the Meccans. When the prophet Muhammad led an armed force against them, the Meccans carried images of al-ʿUzza and of al-Lat to war.

There were probably many more minor gods and goddesses whose names and significance were forgotten under the impact of Islam, and the lack of evidence is probably no accident. Muhammad and his followers effectively put an end to all idol worship and its associated practices.

Principal Sources

The difficulty in discerning the role of Muhammad is enormous, which may come as a surprise to those who are not experts in literary criticism. But every scholar who has tried to study the available sources of information on Muhammad knows that the endeavor of sifting through the evidence to arrive at some tangible historical facts results only in the unpleasant feeling of uncertainty. Critical investigation of the material on Muhammad, both in the Qur'an and in the mass of Muslim traditions, has resulted in profound scholarly disagreements concerning his life and the part he played in the early Muslim community. In fact, the attempt to separate the historical from the unhistorical elements in the available sources has yielded few, if any, positive results regarding the figure of Muhammad or the role he played in Islam. The predicament faced by modern scholars is perhaps best stated by Harald Motzki:

> At present, the study of Muhammad, the founder of the Muslim community, is obviously caught in a dilemma. On the one hand, it is not possible to write a historical biography of the Prophet without being accused of using the sources uncritically, while on the other hand, when using the sources critically, it is simply not possible to write such a biography.[6]

Our knowledge about Muhammad's life derives from two different types of sources: Muslim and non-Muslim. The Muslim sources are written in Arabic and include (1) casual allusions in the Qur'an and (2) oral traditions collected and written down by Muslim scholars. The non-Muslim sources are preserved in the literatures of Jewish and Christian communities written in Greek, Syriac, Armenian, and Hebrew.[7]

The Qur'an is a scripture with a fixed content that was codified about twenty-five years after the death of Muhammad (more about this later in the chapter on the Qur'an). And yet it tells very little about the life of Muhammad. His name is mentioned four or five times (once as Ahmad). Two other important points that can be inferred from the Qur'an are that Muhammad spent most of his life in western Arabia, and that he bitterly resented those who opposed his claim of prophethood.

The traditional accounts of Muhammad's life derive from Muslim scholars who collected and wrote down his biographies one or two centuries after his death. The accuracy of these biographies, though unascertainable, is accepted by many, though not all, scholars. Muhammad died in 632 and the earliest material on his life derives from Ibn Ishaq (d. 768). The question of authenticity is problematic because the original work of Ibn Ishaq is lost. What is available is only an edited version of Ibn Ishaq by Ibn Hisham (d. 834). Other Muslim sources of information include Ma'mar ibn Rashid (d. 770), Sayf ibn 'Umar (d. ca. 796), al-Waqidi (d. 823), al-Baladhuri (d. 829), Muhammad ibn Sa'd (d. 843), and al-Tabari (d. 923).

In addition to the sources transmitted within the Muslim tradition, there are a few non-Muslim sources, all of which confirm the existence of Muhammad.[8] None of these materials are considered to be from before 634 C.E., and much that is of interest is from some decades later. An Armenian chronicler attests that Muhammad was a merchant and that his preaching revolved around the figure of Abraham. The Greek and Syriac materials confirm that the followers of the "new" religion are known as *magaritai* (in Greek) or *mahgraye* (in Syriac). Those terms refer to the Arabic term *muhajirun* (the "emigrants"), denoting Muhammad and his followers who migrated from Mecca to Yathrib (later known as Medina) in 622 c.e.

It must be stated, however, that the information preserved in both the Muslim traditions and the non-Muslim sources contain some essential differences. A few are chronological (e.g., the founding of Muhammad's community); others relate to Muhammad's attitude toward the Jews and Palestine.

Naturally, those diverse sources of information are not all of equal importance, even though each has a certain intrinsic value. The Qur'an stands foremost in importance. The Muslim traditions, as a rule, rank next to the Qur'an, while the remaining sources provide especially valuable corroboration of the statements in the Qur'an and the Muslim traditions.

Although this ranking may at first seem convincing, it is not free from difficulties. The difficulties become evident when an attempt is made to resolve the life and teachings of Muhammad. Does the Qur'an retain the essential features of the original teachings of Muhammad, or does it derive its authority from "faithfully preserved" later traditions? And how is one to explain the disagreements between the Muslim tradition and the non-Muslim sources?

These questions have long been the subject of dispute among scholars.[9] From among the diverse opinions, two extreme views are worth noting: those that cast doubt on the historicity of Muhammad and the integrity of the Qur'an;[10] and those that portray Muhammad based on the Qur'an and traditional Muslim biographies.[11] For our purposes, however, it will be useful to present the life of Muhammad based on the traditional Muslim accounts.

Birth of a Prophet

According to tradition, Muhammad ibn Abdullah was born in Mecca around 570 c.e.[12] His father Abdullah (ʿAbd Allah) belonged to the Quraysh tribe of the Hashim clan and died a few days before Muhammad's birth. Muhammad's mother Aminah died when he was only six years old. Two years later, his grandfather ʿAbd al-Muttalib, who was taking care of him, died too. At the age of eight, he was entrusted to his paternal uncle, Abu Talib, who was the head of the clan.

If one discounts the anecdotal details characteristic of many pious traditions, then little is known with certainty of the early life and circumstances of Muhammad. He is reputed to have accompanied his uncle Abu Talib on trading journeys to Syria. At the age of twenty-five, he was in charge of caravan transshipment of the merchandise of a wealthy widow named Khadijah, of the Asad clan. So impressed was Khadijah by Muhammad's moral qualities that she offered herself to him in marriage, even though she was fifteen years older than he was. Muhammad accepted the offer. They had two sons who died young and four daughters, of whom the best known is Fatimah, the wife of Muhammad's cousin ʿAli, regarded by the Shiʿis as Muhammad's divinely ordained successor. Until Khadijah's death in 619, Muhammad took no other wife. His marriage gave him financial independence, since by Arab custom Muhammad as a minor had no share in the property of his father or grandfather.

A traditional account in the life of Muhammad that is recounted by millions of Muslims is worth noting here. One version of the story involves Abu Talib and an adolescent Muhammad. It recounts an incident that happened during a caravan trip to Syria in which Muhammad, then twelve years old, and his uncle Abu Talib traveled. The caravan stopped at the rest house of the Christian monk Bahirah, who saw portents that led him to recognize Muhammad as the prophet to come.

Another version describes Muhammad's caravan trip to Syria, accompanied by Khadijah's slave, Maysarah. When the caravan stopped at the rest house of Bahirah, Muhammad sat under a tree in solitude. The monk wanted to know who the man sitting under the tree was. Maysarah replied that he was one of the Quraysh tribe, the people who guard the Kaʿbah. "No," said the monk, "no one but a prophet is sitting under the tree." Later, on the return journey, Maysarah, who was riding behind the Prophet, saw two angels appear above Muhammad and shield him from the sun's harmful rays. When they returned to Mecca, Maysarah told Khadijah everything that transpired during the trip.

Whichever version one tends to accept, the point of the story is quite clear: Muhammad is recognized as a prophet.

Prophetic Call

Khadijah's wealth gave Muhammad the freedom to pursue his spiritual inclinations, which prompted him periodically to wander into the hills, especially into a cave outside Mecca, for meditation and contemplation. Tradition states that on one such visit around the year 610 (when he was forty years old), Muhammad had a vision of a majestic being (later identified as the angel Gabriel) and heard a voice saying to him, "Muhammad, you are God's messenger."[13] Terrified and overwhelmed by this divine apparition, Muhammad fell prostrate. The voice commanded, "Recite!" Then Muhammad asked in terror: "What shall I recite?" And the answer came:

> Recite—in the name of thy Lord who created!
> Created man from clots of blood!
> Recite—for thy Lord is most beneficent. . . .
> who has taught man that which he knew not.
> (Qurʾan 96:1–4)

Muhammad is said to have rushed home and told his wife Khadijah that he was either possessed (mad) or had received a call to prophethood. On hearing the full story, his wife, convinced of his prophetic call, reassured him. Interestingly, according to Muslim tradition Khadijah and Muhammad turned for advice to her Christian cousin, the priest Waraqa ibn Qusayy, who reassured Muhammad that he had seen God's messenger, the angel Gabriel. "Like the Hebrew prophets," continued the priest, "you will be called a liar, and they will use you despitefully and cast you out and fight against you."[14] This marked the beginning of Muhammad's career as God's messenger, or *rasul Allah* in Arabic. From this time until his death in 632 he received at frequent intervals verbal messages (or revelations) which he believed came directly from God.

It is said that as time went on Muhammad felt physical discomfort , such as perspiring on a cold day, whenever he experienced one of these divine revelations. Muhammad, like the biblical prophets, apparently suffered the physical constraints that accompany divine messages. All his doubts must have vanished when fresh messages came to him, culminating in the command to proclaim publicly what he had been taught by God.

Those messages were sometimes written down and sometimes memorized by his followers. Ultimately, they were collected and put into writing around 650 C.E. in the form that has endured to this day and is recognized as the Qurʾan, the Holy Book of Islam.

Like the biblical prophets, Muhammad regarded himself a warner or admonisher and proclaimed his revelations to his compatriots. He emphasized four issues: the oneness of God, the goodness and power of God, the moral responsibility of humans toward God, and the judgment awaiting humanity on the day of resurrection. From the beginning, his public messages won a sympathetic audience. As he continued to preach against idolatry and advocate the worship of one God only, the number of his followers increased. Soon, his movement was called Islam and its adherents Muslims, though the Qurʾan speaks of them simply as "the believers."

Muhammad's messages were basically religious, but his preaching implied his disapproval of the conduct and attitudes of wealthy compatriots. As a result, the rich merchants of Mecca approached Muhammad to make a deal with him. They offered him a marriage alliance with one of the wealthiest families and a substantial share in the trade if he modified his criticism. Muhammad decisively rejected both offers, which invited the hostility of the Meccans.

Opposition and Threats

The opposition against Muhammad took on different forms. A person by the name of ʿAmr ibn Hisham, commonly known as Abu Jahl (literally meaning "father of ignorance"), organized a boycott against the members of Muhammad's clan that lasted for three years. Commercial sanctions were imposed on Muhammad's supporters, and some of his adherents were persecuted. He himself was publicly abused and ridiculed for his assertions about resurrection and the day of judgment. In fact, Muhammad would have been killed but for the protection afforded by his uncle Abu Talib, head of the clan, who nevertheless begged him to abandon his teaching.

The nature and extent of the persecution of early Muslims is difficult to assess. Clan loyalties, economic interests, political stability, and other issues affected the strength and the source of various kinds of opposition. A turning point came with the death of Abu Talib and Khadijah in 619, which meant the end of Muhammad's protection. Abu Lahab, another uncle of Muhammad, succeeded as head of the clan, and at the instigation of wealthy Meccans he withdrew the protection previously accorded Muhammad. This meant that Muhammad could no longer propagate his religion publicly without the risk of being attacked. He therefore sought the protection of inhabitants in neighboring towns where his fame had spread.

In 621, a delegation of twelve men came from Medina (Yathrib) to Mecca for the annual pilgrimage of the Ka°bah. But these men secretly professed themselves Muslims and returned to Medina in the hope of promoting the religion of Muhammad. The following year, a representative group of seventy-five persons came from Medina to Mecca, again for the annual pilgrimage of the Ka°bah. This second group invited Muhammad to Medina and pledged to defend him as they would their own kin. Encouraged by this unexpected turn of events, Muhammad accepted the offer and sent his faithful followers in small groups to Medina. Then, just before he was to leave, the Meccans, it is said, plotted to kill him. But he escaped by using little-known paths, and he reached safety in Medina on September 24, 622.

This emigration is known in Arabic as *hijrah* (Latin *hegira*), though its basic meaning is to sever kinship ties. All Muslim calendars are dated from the year of the *hijrah* (A.H. or *Anno Hegira*). Moreover, the *hijrah* is regarded among Muslims as the turning point not only in the development of Islam, but in world history as well.

The success of Muhammad's religion is in no little measure due to his decision to migrate to Medina. A document, known by critics as the Constitution of Medina, provides interesting information regarding the agreement made between Muhammad "the prophet" and the resident Muslims of Medina. Considered to be from the later period of his settlement in Medina, the document states, for instance, that serious disputes among the confederation of nine Arab groups (the eight clans of Medina and the emigrants of Mecca) are to be referred to Muhammad. Moreover, the revelations of Muhammad at Medina often contained religious as well as legal rules. Thus, all the evidence supports the conclusion that Muhammad quickly won the Arab inhabitants of Medina over to his faith.

Prophet and Statesman

The economic interests of Muhammad and his followers depended at first on local trade. Later, however, Muhammad approved raids, in normal Arab fashion, on caravans passing through or near Medina. He himself led three such raids in 623, all of which failed. A year later, he led some three hundred men in an attack on a wealthy Meccan caravan returning from Syria with a supporting force of more than nine hundred men. The two forces faced each other near a place called Badr, and in the ensuing battle the Meccans were badly defeated. This success appeared to Muhammad as a divine vindication of his prophethood. Moreover, it encouraged him to lead larger Muslim forces on pre-emptive raids against hostile nomadic tribes.

Meanwhile, the Meccans determined to avenge their defeat. On March 23, 625, some three thousand Meccan infantry under the leadership of Abu Sufyan arrived at Uhud, a hill outside Medina, and faced Muhammad in a battle that ended inconclusively with heavy losses on both sides. Muhammad was wounded, but the rumor spread that he had been killed. This military reverse was a blow to Muhammad's credibility, and it forced him to regain gradually the confidence of his followers. He was also committed to a war of attrition with the men of Mecca. There was no turning back.

Muhammad took the initiative once more. He forced the Medinese Jewish tribe of Qaynuqa to emigrate to Syria because they had refused to acknowledge his prophethood and probably had conspired with the Meccans. In fact, in 627, Abu Sufyan, at the instigation of the Khaybar Jews and with the help of nomadic tribes, raised an army of ten thousand men in the hope of occupying Medina. Muhammad ordered the digging of ditches (or trenches) to defend exposed approaches to the city before the Meccan cavalry arrived to lay siege. Unsuccessful attempts to cross the ditches, dissension among the besiegers, and one final disastrous night of wind and rain forced the Meccan army to withdraw after only a two-week siege. In the aftermath of the withdrawal, Muhammad attacked the Medinese Jewish clan of Qurayzah because they had plotted against him. All males were executed and women and children were sold as slaves.

Next, Muhammad devised a strategic plan to take Mecca without bloodshed and to convert its inhabitants to Islam. Based on a carefully calculated risk (or as tradition states, in response to a dream), Muhammad ordered his followers to march to Mecca to perform the annual rite of pilgrimage. But he was disappointed that only sixteen hundred men would accompany him. Nevertheless, he proceeded to execute his plan with his faithful group. The date was March 628 (A.H. 6), a date celebrated in Islamic history as the "Treaty of al-Hudaybiya."

Muhammad and his followers halted at al-Hudaybiya, near Mecca, since some Meccans were determined to prevent, by force if necessary, the entrance into Mecca of this formidable and suspect force of pilgrims. Fortunately, this critical standoff did not last long. The Meccans sent a delegation to negotiate a treaty with Muhammad. According to the pact, hostilities were to end and Muslims were to postpone the performance of the pilgrimage rite to the following year. Muhammad's farsightedness as a statesman is evident in his immediate acceptance of these conditions, even though some of his followers did not agree.

To compensate disaffected followers for the withdrawal from the gates of Mecca, Muhammad led them two months later against the Khaybar Jews, then settled in the territory north of Medina. When the Khaybar Jews surrendered, Muhammad allowed them to remain in their settlement on the condition that they pay a tribute of half their total produce. He followed this profitable precedent at one neighboring Jewish settlement after another without meeting much resistance. Muhammad's policies resulted in more converts and in substantial material gain, and his fame spread far and wide as his political power grew.

Meanwhile, a number of factors helped Muhammad succeed in his ultimate aim: the taking of Mecca. Abu Sufyan was replaced by several new, weak leaders who accomplished little for the Meccans. The treaty of al-Hudaybiya lifted the threat to Meccan caravans of further retaliatory raids from Muhammad's Medinese and swung the pendulum of opinion in favor of Muhammad. Several leading families emigrated to Medina and became Muslims, and Muhammad married a widowed daughter of Abu Sufyan, thus strengthening his ties with the Meccans. This new relationship led Muhammad to plan with his father-in-law, Abu Sufyan, for the peaceful surrender of Mecca.

In March of the following year Muhammad, accompanied by a large force of devoted followers, entered Mecca according to the provisions of the treaty. He circumambulated the Kaʿbah seven times and touched the cubical black stone with his staff. Then followed the offering of sacrifices and the call to prayer. In accordance with the treaty, he was allowed to remain three days, during which time he married the sister-in-law of his uncle, al-ʿAbbas, after being reconciled with him.

This truce did not last long however. In November 629 (A.H. 7) the Meccans attacked one of the Arab tribes that had made an alliance with the Muslims. In response to this attack, Muhammad, after two months of secret preparations, encamped outside Mecca with some ten thousand of his men. The Meccans, represented by Abu Sufyan and other leaders, negotiated for a peaceful surrender. A general amnesty was promised by Muhammad if the Meccans would formally submit. Virtually no resistance was offered and Muhammad entered Mecca in triumph, both as a statesman and as the prophet of God.

Muhammad spent about three weeks in Mecca settling various matters of administration. All idols in the Kaʿbah and in neighboring shrines were destroyed. He then entrusted the sacred territories to their traditional hereditary custodians and confirmed others in their old offices. To the poorest among his followers, he invited wealthy Meccans to grant loans. Many adopted his religion, even though he himself did not insist on their becoming Muslims. Soon, a large force of Meccans fought side by side with his faithful Medinese companions in the face of new threats and opportunities. Indeed, Muhammad shared the spoils of every fresh success so generously with the Meccans that his Medinese complained of unfair treatment.

Militarily, Muhammad was the strongest man in Arabia. Many nomadic chiefs pledged their allegiance to him and offered their men for his raids. Several tribes sent representatives to negotiate alliances. Poets who had once ridiculed him praised his actions in laudatory verses. His armies reached northwards to Byzantine areas occupied by Christianized Arabs. Though it is difficult to know how much territory was unified under the banner of Islam, the evidence suggests that Muhammad moved quickly and effectively against armed opposition in Arabia on the one or two occasions when it was offered.

Muhammad devoted the last years of his life to consolidating the nascent Islamic community. Various observances, such as fasting, pilgrimage, the veiling of women, and providing alms tax, were all institutionalized and given the sanction of Qurʾanic revelation. Moreover, he firmly prohibited his followers from fighting each other. He developed a confessional pride and communal solidarity that has hardly been surpassed by other religious founders. He insisted that the Islamic community accept the social and moral obligation of permitting "the people of the book" (those who believed in God, revelation, and scripture, such as Jews and Christians) to live freely among them and under their protection provided they accepted the Islamic social system and paid their taxes. Muhammad thus secured their allegiance and their skills as farmers, merchants, and artisans.

Muhammad also put Arabia on the map. Internally he strove for the unification of all Arabs under the banner of one religion and one Holy Book; externally he provided an outlet for energies previously dissipated by internecine strife, directing those energies instead to expansion beyond the borders of Arabia. Whatever truth lies behind this assumption, the undeniable fact is that the momentum initiated by Muhammad became the driving force behind the formation of the caliphate (from the Arabic word *khalifah,* meaning "successor") and the development of the Islamic empire.[15]

The date assigned to the founding of the Islamic community is usually 622, the year of the *hijrah.* The agreement made between the eight clans of the Medinese and the expatriates from Mecca established the nucleus of the Muslim community.

Although at first Muhammad was simply the head of one of the component groups existing in Medina, ten years later, by the time of his death in 632, an astonishingly large number of Arabs who professed Islam acknowledged him as leader. In fact, from a mere city-state in Medina, the Islamic community had become a "supertribe," a confederation of Arab tribes bound by their Islamic faith rather than by blood kinship.

Muhammad went on pilgrimage to Mecca for the last time in March 632. When he returned to Medina he made preparations for an expedition to the Syrian border. Before he could leave, his health gave way and he lay sick for several days. On June 8, 632, he died, leaving the entire Muslim community in mourning. The dispute over the succession to leadership eventually resulted in the most important schism in the history of Islam. This development will be discussed later. Here it need only be pointed out that Muhammad's Islamic movement had become, to an increasing degree, not a local, regional, or tribal force, but an Arab force.

Muhammad's focus of interest during all these years had been the training, education, and discipline of the Muslim community. His moral, social, and political influence remained long after he left the scene. It is not always easy to distinguish with confidence genuine tradition from later accretions. Though Muhammad has suffered greatly both from critics and from apologetic writers,

The Prophet's Holy Mosque in Medina, Saudi Arabia

The site of the first mosque built in Medina by Muhammad when he migrated from
Mecca in 622. Several restorations and expansions have been made through the centuries. The dome indicates the place where Muhammad's house stood and where he is
buried. *Courtesy of the Royal Embassy of Saudi Arabia.*

nobody who studies the life of Muhammad can fail to be impressed by two of
his most dominant characteristics: spiritual leadership and political acumen.[16]

An Assessment

A balanced understanding and interpretation of the nature, role, and
contribution of Muhammad or of any of the many religious leaders of genius
is not an easy task. The view that he was both a political genius (or a great statesman) and a spiritual guide (or a religious leader) is testified in the Qurʾan, in
the Islamic Traditions, and in historical sources. Certainly, Muhammad partici-

pated in social life in its fullest. He married, had a household, judged, ruled, raided, fought many battles, and underwent painful ordeals. He was human enough to become engrossed in the solutions to social, economic, and political problems. But Muhammad was also a pious, contemplative person. He spent long periods in solitude and meditation, seeking peace and divine revelation, and he was commissioned specifically to propagate God's message to humanity. He possessed the spiritual qualities of serenity, inner peace, charity, mercy, generosity, and magnanimity. He sought constantly to perform the will of God, and in fact his participation in social and political activities was precisely to integrate those areas into a spiritual whole.

In addition, assessors of Muhammad by and large agree on his tremendous achievements in developing the dual religious and social character of Islam. It is said, for instance, that as the founder of a state and of a religion, Muhammad made the religion of Islam the basis of Arab confederation and unity. Again, one reads that from the very beginning, Muhammad inculcated among his followers a sense of brotherhood and a bond of faith unmatched in any other religious or social group.

A number of qualities, therefore, make Muhammad exceptional by any standard: his compelling personality, which gained the support and affection of his compatriots; his moral qualities, his religious teachings, and his political directives, which became the exemplars of virtuous character; his courage, impartiality, resoluteness, and generosity, which attracted the admiration of many.

Thus, from the Muslim point of view, those who aspire to the sanctity of life emulate Muhammad, at once a spiritual guide and a socio-political leader. In fact, generations of devout Muslims have considered Muhammad to be the prototype of human perfection in all social, political, and spiritual spheres. There is no better evidence for this than the Qurʾanic statement: "Truly, you have a good example in the *rasul Allah*" (Qurʾan 33:21).

Three basic epithets are used to symbolize the three characteristics of Muhammad: *rasul, nabi,* and *ʿabd.* These can be seen in the formula of benediction upon Muhammad: "Oh God, bless our Lord Muhammad, Your servant (*ʿabd*) and Your Messenger (*rasul*), the unlettered prophet (*nabi*), and his family and his companions, and salute them." Muhammad's role as messenger is further emphasized in the Islamic proclamation of faith (*shahadah*): "There is no god but God (*Allah*), and Muhammad is the Messenger of God (*rasul Allah*)." Hence, Muhammad as the messenger of God embodies the harmonious integration of human qualities (sensual, social, economic, military, and political) and the divine.

If Muhammad is the prototype of all human perfection, then how can human beings emulate him? The answer, according to millions of devout Muslims, lies in following the words and deeds of Muhammad. These are found in the Holy Book (Qurʾan), in the collection of oral traditions, or narrations, memorized and transmitted through succeeding generations (Hadith), and in the body of transmitted actions (Sunnah). These are the sources and guides of all

Islamic thought and life. In them one finds what the messenger of God prescribed regarding every situation in life, be it domestic, social, political, or religious.

Indeed, for more than thirteen hundred years Muslims all over the world
have modeled their lives after Muhammad the messenger of God.[17] The following quotation from Sayyed Abuʾl-Aʿla Mawdudi represents the great reverence
attributed to Muhammad:

> He is the only example where all the excellences are blended together into one
> personality. He is a philosopher and a seer and a living example of what he teaches.
> He is a great statesman as well as a military genius. He is a legislator and also a
> teacher of morals. He is a spiritual luminary as well as a religious guide. His vision
> penetrates every aspect of life and there is nothing which he touches and does not
> adorn. His orders and commandments cover a vast field, from the regulation of
> international relations to the habits of everyday life like eating, drinking and clean-
> liness of the body. On the foundations of his theories, he established a civilization
> and developed a culture. And here he produced such a fine equilibrium in the
> conflicting aspects of life that one cannot find even the slightest trace of any
> flaw or defect. Can anyone point out any other example of such a perfect and
> all-around personality?
>
> This is why, after him, there is no need for new prophethood and the Qurʾan
> describes Muhammad as the last in the chain of true Prophets.[18]

Traditionally, every mention of Muhammad by name or title is followed by
the invocation "peace be upon him." This practice is also observed with the
names of Jesus, other prophets, and the archangel Gabriel. Tradition assigns two
hundred names to Muhammad, including "the Prophet," "the Messenger," "the
Trustworthy," and so on. According to Muslims, the Bible also gives him a
name: Shiloh. The passage in question reads:

> Then Jacob called his sons and said: "Gather around that I may tell you what will
> happen to you in days to come. . . . The sceptre shall not depart from Judah, nor
> the ruler's staff from between his feet, until Shiloh comes, and the obedience of the
> peoples is his." (Genesis 49:10)

The word *Shiloh* is of uncertain meaning. Muslims regard it as a reference to
Muhammad, while Jews and Christians regard it as a reference to the Messiah.

To be sure, Islamic tradition states that 124,000 prophets were sent by God
to every nation and people in the world.[19] The Qurʾan asserts also that God sent
a messenger to every nation in the world according to the language spoken by
each people (Qurʾan 10:48; 14:4). And yet Muhammad stands apart in a unique
way from his predecessors. He is considered as the "seal" of the messengers, the
last of the messengers God sent. He integrates and culminates in himself the
function of prophethood.

Such claims may challenge traditional definitions of what is meant by a messenger or a prophet. Numerous volumes written by Western Islamicists and
Muslim authorities discuss at length the centrality of this issue to Islam. Here,
one can only summarize the views of scholars by saying that, according to

Muslims, prophets or messengers are those whom "God has chosen because of certain perfections in them by virtue of which they become the instruction through whom God reveals His message to the world." In other words, Muhammad, like other messengers and prophets before him, received his message directly from God. Twenty-eight such messengers are mentioned in the Qurʾan. Five of these are Arabs, three are identified only by epithets, and the remaining twenty are Jews, all biblical figures such as Adam, Noah, Abraham, Moses, Zechariah, Jesus, and John the Baptist.

According to Islam, the quality of divine revelation given to all prophets and messengers is essentially the same, though in matters of detail there has been a gradual evolution toward a final, perfect revelation. Muhammad's message, therefore, is considered the completion, culmination, and perfection of all previous revelations. That he is the last of the prophets or messengers is emphatically stated in the Qurʾan: "Muhammad is not the father of anyone among you; but is the Messenger of God and the seal of the prophets" (Qurʾan 33:40). It is declared furthermore that the coming of Muhammad was foretold by Jesus (under the name of Ahmad) and that his name was specifically recorded in the Torah (Jewish scripture) and in the Gospel, but later generations willfully perverted these passages (Qurʾan 7:157).

Be that as it may, the Qurʾan repeatedly disclaims all superhuman characteristics for Muhammad. He is like all human beings, a mortal person. Yet, unlike most individuals, he is commissioned with the sole duty of conveying God's final message to all humanity. Since prophethood comes to a complete end with Muhammad, future generations will not and need not have prophets, only pious thinkers and reformers. Also, his pronouncements on all matters in life are to be accepted as divine revelation and in one sense "infallible." Obedience to his message is submission to God. Thus, the Muslim ideal is based on the life of Muhammad and the Qurʾan.

2 Islam in History

The Caliphate

Serious differences arose within the Islamic community immediately after Muhammad's death in 632. The critical issue was the designation of a political successor only, since a religious successor to Muhammad, the "seal" of the prophets, was unthinkable.

While Muhammad's closest kinsmen were preparing his body for burial, one faction insisted that the Prophet had designated no successor and that therefore they were free to elect a leader. Another faction insisted that the Prophet had designated ʿAli, his cousin and son-in-law, to succeed him.

Muhammad's preference at the time of his death may have been general knowledge, but several of his highly respected companions prevailed upon the Medinese to elect a single leader from among two of Muhammad's fathers-in-law. The aging Abu Bakr was chosen. ʿAli and his kinsmen were dismayed, but for the sake of unity they agreed to accept the decision.

Abu Bakr became the first caliph (Arabic for "successor") and survived for two years, 632–634. This leadership was maintained by three succeeding caliphs, ʿUmar (634–644), ʿUthman (644–656), and ʿAli (656–661), after which the office of the caliphate devolved upon two powerful dynasties who claimed descent from Muhammad and the Quraysh tribe: the Umayyad dynasty (661–750) and the ʿAbbasid dynasty (750–1517). The Ottoman Turks then assumed the office of the caliphate and retained it until its abolition in 1924.[1]

The First Four Caliphs (632–661)

The first four caliphs, in crushing the power struggles that followed the death of Muhammad, were at first able to conceal internal disunion, but this only produced a festering schism that persists even now. Ad hoc solutions to the question of the caliphate finally plunged the neophyte Islamic community into civil war, which left a legacy of permanent political divisions.

Consolidating both the political hegemony and the religious heritage inherited from Muhammad proved difficult from the beginning. Abu Bakr's first task was to discipline rebel tribesmen who reasoned that their allegiance to Muhammad and their obligation to pay an alms tax ended with their leader's death. The success of his action against the rebels led Abu Bakr next to organize and direct several military campaigns against Roman Syria, all of which were spectacularly successful. On his deathbed in 634 Abu Bakr nominated as his successor ʿUmar, another father-in-law of Muhammad and also a member of the Quraysh clan.

ᶜUmar improved on the precedents set by Abu Bakr, particularly in the areas of political administration and military organization. During his ten-year reign, Islamic conquest and expansion outside Arabia spread into territories controlled by both the Persian Empire and the Roman Empire.[2] His military expeditions into the Roman Byzantine Empire led to the conquest of Syria in 636, Jordan and Israel (Palestine) in 638, and Egypt in 642. At the same time his campaigns against the Persian Empire gave him control in 637 of the territory now known as Iraq and of the Iranian plateau in 642.

ᶜUmar's plans for further conquest came to an abrupt end when he was stabbed to death in 644 by a Persian slave. But by then he had firmly established the foundation of an Islamic state—one which would express both Arab culture and Islamic characteristics. He had also devised two policies, one for the conquered non-Muslim people and the other for the victorious Muslim Arabs. The former were to pay taxes in return for protection and for the freedom to maintain their separate cultural and religious identity. The latter were to occupy newly constructed quarters supported by the taxes of the former.

ᶜUmar's death marked the end of the first phase of Islamic territorial conquest, and a period of consolidation and civil war followed. Again, the choice of a new caliph became a point of dispute between two contenders: ᶜAli and ᶜUthman. Six of Muhammad's leading companions were appointed to elect a new caliph. The choice of leadership fell on ᶜUthman, one of several sons-in-law of Muhammad and a member of the Umayyad. Again ᶜAli and his supporters conceded defeat, but this time discontent within the Islamic community against Caliph ᶜUthman's rule was general.

From the very beginning ᶜUthman instituted policies that antagonized many devout Muslim tribes. First, he placed Meccans, particularly relatives and members of his own family, in key positions such as provincial governorships to strengthen and control the Islamic state. The result was internal dissension and opposition to any policy he initiated. Next, he appropriated for his own use some of the money collected from conquered lands, especially the income from property taxes, which was supposed to be divided equally among his armed followers. This created resentment among Muslim troops and warriors. Then, he seemed to favor the interests of the Quraysh aristocracy, which had done well out of the wars and conquests by exploiting opportunities for trading and slave dealing. This created jealousy, particularly among followers who had done the fighting and saw themselves cheated out of a fair return on their commitment. And finally, in order to avoid complications caused by variant texts, ᶜUthman ordered a definitive compilation of Muhammad's messages and the production of an authoritative text of the Qurᵓan. Abu Bakr and ᶜUmar, the previous caliphs, may have made collections of Muhammad's revelations, but ᶜUthman produced a definitive text, determined by a commission headed by a secretary of the prophet Muhammad. The outcome was religious discontentment among the pious, since oral tradition varied and no authoritative text was likely to please everyone.

ᶜUthman's unpopularity came to a predictable end. Disenchantment grew

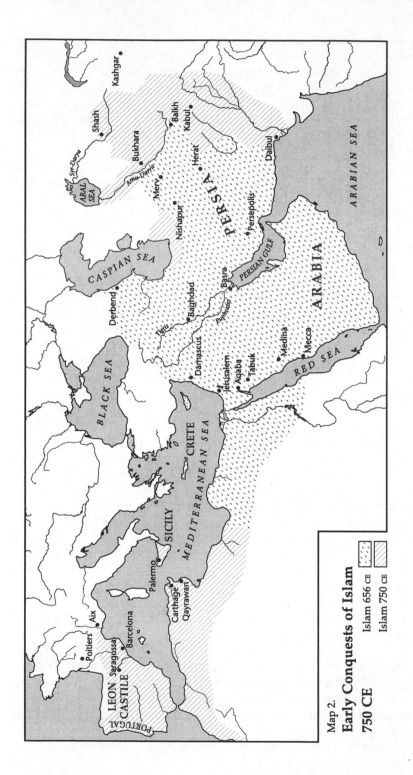

Map 2.
**Early Conquests of Islam
750 CE**

Islam 656 CE
Islam 750 CE

ARABIAN SEA

PERSIA

Kashgar

Shash

Balkh

Kabul

Bukhara

Herat

Amu-Darya

Syr-Darya

ARAL
SEA

Merv

Nishapur

Daibul

Persepolis

PERSIAN GULF

ARABIA

CASPIAN SEA

Derbend

Baghdad

Basra

Tigris

Euphrates

Mecca

Medina

Damascus

Tabuk

Aqaba

Jerusalem

RED SEA

BLACK SEA

CRETE

SICILY

MEDITERRANEAN SEA

Palermo

Carthage

Qayrawan

Barcelona

Aix

Saragossa

Poitiers

LEON

CASTILE

PORTUGAL

to such an extent that in 656 ʿUthman's own army demanded his abdication. When he refused to step down, the insurgents burst into his palace and assassinated him. For the first time Muslims had killed their caliph, leader of their own Islamic community. This disregard for Muhammad's (and Qurʾanic) injunction not to shed a believer's blood had momentous consequences. It opened the door to civil violence and resulted in a schism which has never healed.

At the time of Muhammad's death, his cousin and son-in-law ʿAli (from the Hashim clan) had hoped to secure the caliphate for himself. For the best part of twenty-four years in the course of three successive caliphates, these aspirations had lain in abeyance. Now, with the death of ʿUthman, it seemed natural to the people of Medina to hail ʿAli as the next caliph. But a number of leading Meccans, along with ʿAʾishah, daughter of the late Caliph Abu Bakr and Muhammad's surviving widow, contested ʿAli's leadership by accusing him of playing a part in the assassination plot. The result was a bloody battle that broke the unity of the Islamic community forever—a battle usually remembered as the Battle of the Camel, because it took place around the camel upon which ʿAʾishah sat to lead her allies.

ʿAli won this battle but was destined to lose the war. ʿAʾishah was exiled to Medina, while ʿAli disestablished the center of the caliphate at Medina, in Arabia, in favor of Kufah, a garrison town in Iraq. However, the caliphate of ʿAli was again challenged, this time by Muʿawiya, the governor of Syria for twenty years, a cousin of ʿUthman, a brother-in-law of Muhammad, and the son of Abu Sufyan of the Umayyad clan. With a large army of Syrian Arabs, considered at the time to be the best in the entire Islamic state, and with the support of Meccan generals, administrators, and traders who had backed ʿAʾishah, he set out in 657 to avenge ʿUthman's assassination. ʿAli deposed Muʿawiya, but the latter ignored him.

The confrontation that took place at Siffin, on the Euphrates River, was indecisive. Muʿawiya got the worst of the fighting, but he persuaded ʿAli to accept a truce on condition that ʿAli submit the question of the caliphate to arbitration. ʿAli accepted, but the concession infuriated a group of his supporters who asserted that no individual who held the caliphate could submit his claims to arbitration. They immediately withdrew from ʿAli's army and formed a separate, hostile group known as the Khariji (pl. Khawarij, meaning Seceders). ʿAli's efforts to suppress them were fruitless. They survived to evolve into a violently radical egalitarian sect that advocated piety rather than kinship as the sole qualification for Islamic leadership.

Meanwhile, the arbitrators ruled against ʿAli, who refused to abide by their decision. Soon his power was curtailed and his sphere of authority reduced, and his prestige dwindled. In 661 he was assassinated by a Khariji; and anyone brave enough to advertise his allegiance to ʿAli thereafter was marked for death. ʿAli's followers were regarded as apostates and infidels whose blood, the Khawarij maintained, it was lawful to shed.

From the very beginning the Khawarij were a fanatical, rebellious, nomadic group who could not compromise their basic principles. Their wars were holy wars (*jihad*) directed mainly against Muslims, including all the women and children related to their victims, and waged with terrifying and systematic ferocity. Their pious fanaticism made them as indifferent to their own lives as to the lives of their victims. Overt opposition by the Khawarij against Mu'awiya, however, proved fruitless. Action required a degree of consensus. More often disagreement led to further fragmentation of the sect and to uncoordinated guerrilla warfare by small groups. Against overwhelming odds, they were prepared to fight to the last man, and sooner or later most of them were wiped out. Only one sect, the Ibadis (Abadis), survived into modern times.

After 'Ali's death, his partisans transferred their allegiance to his eldest son Hasan, who was easily persuaded to resign all his rights to Mu'awiya.

The Umayyads (661–750/1031)

The Islamic community now recognized Mu'awiya of the Umayyad clan as the rightful successor to the caliphate. His accession heralded the end of succession by nomination or election. Instead, Mu'awiya established the Umayyad dynasty in Syria, which monopolized the caliphate for ninety years (661–750) and restricted the succession mainly to family members. The Umayyads then ruled from Spain (756–1031), which under a succession of rulers became an autonomous Islamic state. Under the Umayyads, the Islamic community reached its greatest expansion, from the Atlantic shores of Portugal and France across to India's border with China.[3]

Mu'awiya I (661–680) was a superb statesman. His first move was to set up the caliphate in Damascus, Syria, his own power base. Under his leadership, internal feuds, opposition, and revolt were stamped out and Islamic unity restored. He skillfully organized and centralized the administration. His efforts to systematize the legal and ethical teachings of Muhammad showed his sensitivity to and deep concern for the religious differences that pious leaders struggled to reconcile. And yet several ambitious and disappointed non-Umayyad tribesmen bent on overthrowing his dynasty remained a constant threat. The storm broke during the short, turbulent reign of his son Yazid I (680–683).

Enemies and pietist circles (as well as later historiographers) have stigmatized the Umayyads as temporal kings who had usurped the office of succession to the Prophet. The Quraysh aristocracy in Medina, the partisans of 'Ali and of his progeny, and the Khawarij all expressed, in open revolt, their religious grievances and their contempt for the privileged position and policies of the Umayyads in Syria.

'Ali's son Hasan had died, and his partisans now swore fealty to Husayn, Hasan's brother. Husayn and his followers repudiated Yazid I as the legitimate caliph and rallied disaffected factions in revolt against him. The first major action of the rebels ended in disaster. Husayn and his supporters were ambushed and Husayn was killed by a pro-Umayyad force at the Battle of Karbala in Iraq. However, this defeat, far from merely dispossessing one faction to the advantage of another, was a significant event in the annals of Islam. The rebels exploited Husayn's death by declaring him a martyr to the apostate forces that had usurped the Prophet's mantle. ʿAli was declared the only rightful successor to the Prophet. The rebels branded all previous caliphs as usurpers and confirmed the descendants of ʿAli as the true *imams* ("leaders"; for Shiʿi, religious head of community; for Sunni, merely a prayer leader) and the true caliphs, who alone were capable of receiving the transmissible divine light of ʿAli. Thus was born the Shiʿi (partisan) faction of Islam.

Both the Shiʿi and the Khawarij, with the support of several nomadic tribes, persisted in armed if sporadic rebellion against the Umayyads and later against the ʿAbbasids, but with limited success. Though many distrusted Umayyad rule and were sympathetic to the cause of the Shiʿi and the Khawarij, they were not ready to organize a civil war and endanger the unity of the Islamic community.

Under the leadership of Yazid I, uprisings at Mecca and Medina were swiftly suppressed by the Umayyad Syrian army. Medina was plundered while Mecca was besieged and the Kaʿbah, the sacred shrine, was damaged.

Meanwhile, in the vacuum created by Husayn's death at the Battle of Karbala, the Quraysh ʿAbd Allah ibn az-Zubayr rallied the forces of rebellion for another attempt against Yazid I. Before he was ready to move, the news arrived that Yazid I had died. An ambitious Syrian general, Husayn ibn Numayr, nominally loyal to the caliph, now offered to recognize az-Zubayr as caliph, provided he established his authority in Syria. Uncertain of the Syrian general's motives and perhaps wary of opportunists, az-Zubayr decided to retain his base of opposition in Arabia. His authority was soon recognized in Iraq and Egypt without seriously threatening the Syrian power base of the Umayyads. Nine years later the Umayyad Syrian army dislodged him.

The years following the death of Yazid I were filled with violence and crisis. His eldest son Muʿawiya II (683–684) died within a year without leaving an heir. Rather than appointing his brother to succeed, leaders of the Syrian Umayyads chose an old man as the next caliph, Marwan ibn al-Hakam (684–685), former advisor and secretary to Caliph ʿUthman. It was a decision that invited further tribal rivalry and warfare until finally the caliphate passed after Marwan's death to his son ʿAbd al-Malik.

The goals of ʿAbd al-Malik (685–705) were to reorganize his administration and finances, to increase the dominance of Islam and the strength of Arab nationalism, to crush rival caliphates supported by the Khawarij, Shiʿi, and other insurgents, and to renew his attack against the Byzantine Empire. Under his rule, the Islamic community enjoyed cultural, political, and religious fame and splendor. The magnificent mosque known as the Dome of the Rock in Jerusalem was built during his reign in 691. Poets and scholars flourished under his patronage. Agriculture and irrigation were restored while peace and prosperity prevailed throughout his empire.

Al-Walid I (705–715), the eldest son of ʿAbd al-Malik, succeeded his father, and under him the prestige and reputation of the Islamic empire reached its climax. The three holiest cities, Mecca, Medina, and Jerusalem, were enhanced by a construction boom of beautiful new buildings. Tight security and rest

Dome of the Rock in Jerusalem, Israel

The Dome of the Rock, also called Mosque of Omar (Qubbat al Sakhrah al Musharra-fah), was built by Caliph ʿAbd al-Malik in 691 over the traditional site of Solomon's Temple and the rock where, reputedly, Abraham prepared to sacrifice his son. Muslim tradition identifies the rock as the spot from which Muhammad ascended to heaven on his nocturnal journey from Mecca. The mosque is the earliest remaining Islamic monument and one of the most beautiful examples of Islamic architecture in the world. It is covered with blue, green, and white mosaics and topped by a dome of gold leaf. *Courtesy of Israel Government Tourist Office, Ministry of Tourism.*

houses were provided along pilgrimage routes across Arabia. The inflow of revenue from raids, plunder, and new conquests filled the treasury.

This new wave of conquest gathered momentum in about 710 and carried the Arabs westward along the coast of north Africa through Libya, Tunisia, Algeria, Morocco, and across the Straits of Gibraltar into Spain and Portugal. The Visigoth state of King Roderick collapsed and the Muslim Arabs overran the peninsula, crossed the Pyrenees, and occupied what is now southern France. The surging flood of their advance was finally contained in 732 by Charles Martel at a decisive battle at Tours, near Poitiers.

Expansion eastward into Asia was as spectacular as the westward campaigns. Muslim Arab troops marched across the Caucasus beyond the Iranian plateau into Georgia, Armenia, Uzbek, Bukhara, Samarkand, Kandahar, Baluchistan, Afghanistan, and through India up to the borders of China.

In less than a century after the Prophet's death, the Islamic religion had spread from Europe to China, spanning the entire world, or as much of it as was known then. Only the European kingdom of Byzantium, founded by Greek and Roman settlement, barred Islam's passage into eastern Europe.

Sulaiman (715–717), the brother of al-Walid I, succeeded as caliph. He must have seen that his resources were stretched to the limit and his lines of communication overextended. He acted to consolidate Islamic conquest and to reduce the risk of dissension provoked by factional and tribal rivalry and jealousy. To these ends Sulaiman recalled his troops from distant garrisons and released political prisoners. He replaced Arab governors and Quraysh leaders in high office with Yemenite and other tribal leaders and moved swiftly to execute anyone who opposed him. He even ignored the wishes of his family and designated the cousin of his father, ʿUmar ibn ʿAbd al-Aziz, as the next caliph, perhaps making this unorthodox choice of a successor on the basis of competence rather than traditional bloodlines. Sulaiman anticipated that ʿUmar had the strength to reconcile the social, economic, and religious differences that seemed to plague the Islamic empire as soon as its armies were idle.

Before his accession, ʿUmar II (717–720) was the governor of the Hijaz region of Arabia. He was a deeply religious man and realized that the Islamic empire urgently needed religious reforms. He used state policy to create a balance between religion and justice. For instance, he ended overt discrimination against non-Arab converts to Islam; he reduced, as far as he could, sources of resentment that divided Muslim against Muslim, including the distrust of the government and its supporters against the followers of ʿAli; he asserted that the prime duty of the state was to extend the Islamic religion, not to exact taxes; and he insisted on the responsibility of every Muslim to pay an alms tax (*zakat*) for the benefit of the less privileged in the Islamic community. This pious and ascetic man earned a lasting reputation despite the brevity of his reign and the short-lived consequences of his reforms.

When ʿUmar II died, the caliphate returned to an heir of ʿAbd al-Malik— Yazid II (720–724), brother of al-Walid and Sulaiman. Slowly and quietly the reforms of ʿUmar II were dropped and the powers of the conquerors over their vassals and servants were re-established. But before he was able to reappoint family members to all government posts, his policies were cut short by his untimely death—allegedly of grief at the death of his favorite slave girl.

Hisham (724–743), the fourth son of ʿAbd al-Malik, became the next caliph, and his twenty-year tenure compares favorably with his father's prosperous rule. His strong religious convictions were made explicit by his preference for the company of religious scholars and by his direct intervention in religious affairs. The first executions for heresy as an offense against Islamic doctrine occurred during his administration. In spite of sporadic revolts throughout the empire, peace and security prevailed for the greater part of his reign. To maintain and consolidate his power over vassals from Europe to China, Hisham followed the traditional Umayyad pattern of rule, appointing trusted family members, friends, and followers to key posts and rewarding them for competent and loyal performance.

However, the demands made on the caliphate required strong and unambiguous direction, and disintegration was never more than one weak or ineffectual administration away. All the signs after the death of Hisham in 743 pointed to the end of the Umayyad dynasty, as three weak caliphs came to power within a year. The decline of Arab control in subject lands, the cost of maintaining state properties, internal and external defense, and local developments, as well as the taxation of non-Muslims, all led to chaos and civil strife. The last of the Umayyad caliphs was Marwan II (744–750), a grandson of Marwan I. But the tide of discontent now ran too strongly to be countered.

Factional grievances that had been brewing for years finally came out into the open. The blow that ultimately toppled the Umayyad dynasty came in 749 from the ʿAbbasids, a group claiming descent from al-ʿAbbas, uncle of the prophet Muhammad.[4] In the conflict that ensued between the Umayyads and the ʿAbbasids, Marwan was killed in Egypt, where he had fled for refuge. Members of the Umayyad clan who were not able to escape were mercilessly hunted down and exterminated by the ʿAbbasids.

Several surviving supporters of the Umayyads, including ʿAbd ar-Rahman, grandson of Caliph Hisham, managed to escape the grisly vengeance of the ʿAbbasids and make their way across northern Africa to Spain. There, Arab troops hailed ʿAbd ar-Rahman I (756–788) as the first ruler of the Moorish state of Spain, which under a succession of Umayyad rulers became an autonomous Islamic state.

This surviving branch of the Syrian-based caliphate (usually known as the Caliphate of Córdoba) became so well-established in Spain that one of them, ʿAbd ar-Rahman III (912–961), declared himself caliph in open defiance of the then impotent ʿAbbasid caliphs in Iraq. However, by the end of the reign of Hisham II (976–1009), the Umayyad dynasty in Spain was in decline. Internal revolt, racial and religious separatism, and civil war brought about the collapse of the Umayyads in 1031. Then, for almost five centuries, Islam's dominion of Spain was reduced to several Muslim states governed by a score of petty warlords. Of those, two dynasties made a lasting impression: the Almoravids (1056–1147) and the Almohads (1130–1269). Islamic rule in Spain was permanently extinguished by King Ferdinand of Spain, who drove Islam out of the peninsula into north Africa in 1492.

Most historians agree that modern Western thought is the direct result of the intellectual culture of Spanish Islam. Scholars from medieval Christendom visited Spain to learn philosophy, mathematics, astronomy, and medicine. In fact, some of the oldest European universities owe an enormous debt to scholars who brought the academic excellence of Islam from the Arab universities of Spain.

The ʿAbbasids (749–1258/1517)

The downfall of the Umayyad caliphate and the establishment of the ʿAbbasid caliphate ushered in a new climate of thought and administration. There had always been new faces and new ideas, but now the caliphate itself had changed. The original hegemony of early caliphs ruling an empire through Arab appointees had begun to break down under the Umayyads. What the ʿAbbasids inherited was only part of the action centered on their own power base, Baghdad, and the idea of an Islamic empire was already history. Under the ʿAbbasids, converts to Islam and former vassals were recruited to defend and extend the power of Islam.

First, the ʿAbbasids moved the capital of the empire, and hence the caliphate, from Damascus in Syria to Baghdad in Iraq, making heavy use of the Iraqi and Persian bureaucratic class, which had converted to Islam. This meant that Persian traditions predominated in the court and in day-to-day administration. The office of the Islamic caliph came to resemble ancient Oriental royalty, ruling in pomp and ceremony far removed from subjects whose only purpose was to serve their masters.

Next, the ʿAbbasids asserted the importance of religious scholars and leaders, emphasizing the religious character and authority required of a caliph. They compared the authority of the caliph to the "shadow of God on earth." The ʿAbbasids equated the caliphate with Islamic orthodoxy, appointed religious scholars and teachers as judges and legal advisors, and channeled political dissent into various religious sects which could be watched and contained. Under the ʿAbbasids the caliphs came to be recognized as "Commanders of the Faithful," and as such they had a double responsibility: to be both secular heads and religious leaders (*imams*) of the Islamic community. No better evidence can be cited for the theocratic rule of the ʿAbbasid caliphs than their innovative use of throne names to express dependence on God: al-Mustaʿin ("one who seeks help"); ar-Rashid ("one who is rightly guided"); al-Mutawakkil ("one who depends").

Since religion rather than race became a more significant factor in distinguishing members from non-members of the Islamic community within the ʿAbbasid empire, Islam was now open to people with a variety of cultures and traditions. The ʿAbbasids were thus in a position to select the most useful elements from a variety of cultures. Soon, the idea of the Arabs as a privileged class was abandoned and recruitment for the ʿAbbasid army was thrown open to Muslims of all races.

Meanwhile, the Shiʿis, who had sided with the ʿAbbasids to topple the Umayyads, were bitterly disappointed by the ʿAbbasids, who either ignored their claim to descent from ʿAli or found it irrelevant. The Shiʿis, along with other extremist groups, rebelled but to no avail. The ʿAbbasids were too well entrenched and they snuffed out the rebellion. The dissent represented by the Shiʿis was suppressed and driven underground, where it continued to fester for centuries.

Abu al-ʿAbbas (nicknamed as-Saffah, meaning "the Lavisher," 749–754) owed his rise to power and his position as the first ʿAbbasid caliph to the Shiʿis, to various political conspirators, and to military uprisings, all of which combined to topple the Umayyads. However, by skillful maneuvers, al-ʿAbbas speedily removed those individuals he considered potential rivals, even though some of them had contributed to his rise to power. At the same time, he relentlessly executed surviving members of the Umayyad family and desecrated the graves of past caliphs.

Al-Mansur (754–775), brother of Abu al-ʿAbbas and his successor, is considered the real founder of the ʿAbbasid dynasty. He consolidated the shaky new empire and adopted policies which, during his twenty years of leadership, stabilized the caliphate and assured its survival. He moved the capital of the caliphate from Kufah to Baghdad and stamped out resistance from the Shiʿis and other dissidents. When he died, he left to his son and successor, al-Mahdi, a treasury amounting to several million dinars. This earned him during his lifetime the reputation of a miser.

Al-Mahdi (775–785) is noted for his improvements to communications throughout the empire, his fortification of important centers, his encouragement of the arts, and his founding of towns and schools. His attempts to win over dissenters failed. Unrest among the Shiʿis and adherents of ancient Persian religious movements, such as Manichaeans and Zindiqs, combined with those who held extreme messianic ideas, continued to plague his empire. After his death his son al-Hadi reigned for only a year, to be succeeded to the caliphate by Harun, another son.

Historians credit Harun (called al-Rashid, meaning "the rightly guided," 786–809) with attaining "one of the apogees of caliphal splendor." His fame in the West stems from *The Arabian Nights* (or *The Thousand and One Nights*). But unrest and rebellion in several regions, including Persia, Syria, Egypt, Tunisia, and Morocco, marked his reign. To assert his caliphal authority he established two policies as key duties of leadership: holy war (*jihad*) and inquisitorial tribunals. He personally initiated and executed both policies by invading the Byzantine territories in Turkey and by hunting down religious dissidents.

Before his death, Harun settled the potentially contentious issue of his succession. His son by an Arab wife, al-Amin, was to inherit the caliphate and the western lands, while al-Maʾmun, another son born of a Persian slave, was to govern under his brother's suzerainty the eastern half of the empire and be next in line of succession. But al-Maʾmun was more Persian than Arab. He fretted under his brother's dominion until his resentment erupted in rebellion and civil war. He laid siege to Baghdad with his Persian army, deposed and murdered al-Amin (809–813), and became the caliph of a united empire.

The reign of al-Maʾmun (813–833) is considered by most historians to be the golden age of Islamic civilization. His triumph over al-Amin marks the ascendancy of Persian interests and cultural influences, while Arab influence declined in both administrative and military affairs in favor of Persian protocol and practice. Al-Maʾmun quelled rebellion in various parts of his empire and led further expeditions against the Byzantines. He built two observatories, one in Syria and the other in Iraq, and encouraged the study of astronomy and geometry. He founded a "house of knowledge" (*bayt al-hikmah*) in Baghdad, where scientific, literary, and philosophical works from Greek, Syrian, Persian, and Sanskrit sources were translated.

Caliph al-Ma'mun also had visions of healing the deep rift between the Shi'is and the Sunnis (traditionalists). His attempts at religious unity, however, were no more successful than similar efforts made in the past, even though at one point he proclaimed the Shi'i 'Ali ar-Ridah (a descendant of 'Ali and the eighth imam) as heir apparent. The result was a sharp reaction from the Sunni *ulama* (scholars of Islamic law and theology), led by Ahmad ibn Hanbal, founder of one of the Islamic law schools. Their firm and vigorous response resolved this difference of opinion in their favor, proving that the religious leaders, not the caliphs, were the final authority on Islamic faith and practice.

Another son of Harun al-Rashid, al-Mu'tasim (833–842), succeeded to the caliphate. Though he is remembered for his military and political acumen, prerequisites for survival in the caliphate, he may have been the unwitting architect of his dynasty's dissolution. He introduced the Turkish connection—a military corps of Turkish slaves and mercenaries with no allegiance more compelling than political power. In other respects, al-Mu'tasim followed firmly in the tried-and-true tradition of his predecessors. He resumed attacks on Byzantium, finally crushed a twenty-year-old rebellion led by the heretic Babak, and transferred the capital of the empire from Baghdad northward to Samarra.

Al-Wathiq (842–847) accelerated the practice of replacing large numbers of Arab and Persian forces with Turkish troops. His reign marks the beginning of the decline of the 'Abbasid caliphate. He was succeeded by his brother al-Mutawakkil (847–861), who belatedly attempted to get back to basics of traditional Islamic law and theology. This policy was the antithesis of the liberalism introduced by the 'Abbasids in the eighth century. It resulted in discrimination against the "people of the book" (primarily Jews and Christians, who were required among other things to wear distinctive dress) and in persecution of the Shi'is and the pro-Mu'tazilites, a group committed to the defense of Islam by rational argument rather than repression of heresy and infidelity. Al-Mutawakkil was murdered by one of his Turkish guards and was succeeded by his son al-Muntasir (861–862), who plotted the assassination. He survived for six months before he himself was deposed by Turkish guards.

A period of anarchy followed during which the dominant general, a Turk, appointed, deposed, and murdered three caliphs in rapid succession between 862 and 870: al-Musta'in (862–866), al-Mu'tazz (866–869), and al-Muhtadi (869–870). In the end, the Turks chose al-Mu'tamid (870–892), the eldest surviving son of al-Mutawakkil, as caliph. He and his next two successors, al-Mu'tadid (892–902) and al-Muktafi (902–908), successfully checked the power of their Turkish guards and suppressed a threatening rebellion of slaves from the agricultural region of southern Iraq. But it was only a holding action. In the meantime the caliphate lost ground as one provincial governor after another declared independence and established an autonomous dynasty.

Religious dissent also surfaced. A group of Shi'is, claimants to the inheritance of Zayd, a descendant with a direct link to 'Ali's grandson, established in 864 around the Caspian provinces the first of a series of local independent dynasties, and a second independent Shi'i state was established in Yemen in 901. In the interval, during Caliph al-Muʿtamid's rule, the twelfth Shiʿi imam disappeared in mysterious circumstances, precipitating retaliatory acts of terrorism by certain Shiʿi groups against Sunni institutions. Among the terrorists were the Qarmatians in Syria and Arabia and the Fatimids in North Africa. The Qarmatians were bold enough to raid the holy city of Mecca and carry away the sacred black stone from the Kaʿbah. Subversive Shiʿi elements had also infiltrated the caliphate itself.

The increasing instability of the ʿAbbasid caliphate became glaringly obvious in the reign of al-Muqtadir (908–932). Viziers and their factotums were all that kept the caliphate from total collapse. Factions competing for influence, military conspiracies, and succession plots became the order of the day. Three of the caliphs of this period, al-Qahir (932–934), al-Muttaqi (940–944), and al-Mustakfi (944–946) were deposed and blinded. Caliph ar-Radi (934–940) was forced to hand over political and military power to military commanders (*amirs*), two of whom gave themselves the title of supreme commanders. The only function left for the caliph to perform was to exercise his moral authority as spiritual head of Sunni Islam.

Rival Dynasties (945–1925)

Divested of their power and their control of the state, the ʿAbbasid caliphs were reduced to puppets of military commanders. By the end of the tenth century, local governors and military officers made themselves masters of the ʿAbbasid caliphs, dethroning them at will and appropriating imperial revenues. More provincial governors, some of them rough tribesmen recently converted to Shiʿi Islam, took advantage of the disorders in the caliphate and set up their own dynastic emirates or confederations. Their rise to power helped the Shiʿis develop their own distinctive theology and law and threatened the existence of the ʿAbbasids. Henceforth, provincial governors and commanders allowed the caliphs to retain their honors and titles as the moral and spiritual heads of Islam, and to survive as pensioners.

Some of these provincial dynasties, such as the Buyids, the Samanids, the Ghaznavids,[5] and the Fatimids, acquired widespread prestige within the Islamic world.[6] For instance, the Ghaznavid Empire (977–1186) was the achievement of a Turkish guard hired to oversee slaves of the Samanids. It was his son, Mahmud of Ghazna (998–1030), who led one of the most powerful military forces ever assembled in the Islamic empire, which conquered northern India in his great expansion of Islamic territory. He was the first Muslim ruler to be called *sultan* ("authority") by his contemporaries. His court bargained with the caliphs to legitimize his power in exchange for treasures plundered from India.

Similar opportunists exploited the collapse of the central government to establish dynasties in western areas of the ʿAbbasid empire. A successful revolt among the Kabylie Berbers in Tunisia in 909 created a dynasty of rival caliphs claiming descent from Ismaʿil, the seventh imam, whose bloodlines reached back through Husayn to ʿAli and his wife Fatimah, the Prophet's daughter. These Isma'ili Fatimids laid claim to the caliphate as the only true heirs of 'Ali's line, appropriated the petty fiefs of local dynasties such as the Aghlabids, the Rustamids, and the Idrisids, conquered most of north Africa, and built a new Islamic capital in Cairo, Egypt, in 973.

The Fatimid caliphate (910–1171), founded by 'Ubaydallah al-Mahdi, and the Spanish Umayyad caliphate (928–1031), declared by 'Abd ar-Rahman III in defiance of Baghdad, coincide with the decline of the 'Abbasids and the rise of minor dynasties. The Spanish Umayyad caliphate, with its capital in Cordoba, became the most cultured civilization west of Byzantium. Similarly, the Fatimid caliphate, with its capital in Cairo, created a brilliant Islamic civilization in the Middle East that rivaled any culture in the region since the pharaohs.[7] Both of these caliphates were active in denouncing and campaigning against the 'Abbasid caliphate. The Fatimid caliphs and their agents were determined to replace the 'Abbasid caliphate by an Isma'ili one, and for over a century they pursued their ambition by disseminating propaganda through agents and by force of arms.

One group of Shi'i Isma'ilis, the Nizaris, became specialists in planning and carrying out political assassinations from their mountain strongholds in Syria and Iraq. They spread terror throughout the Islamic empire, attacking and holding strategic strong points from time to time to give them a bargaining advantage. They became known in history as "Assassins" (in Arabic *hashashin* meaning "users of hashish"), a European term assigned to them by the Crusaders to suggest the source of their courage.

Although famine, civil disorder, and foreign invasions plagued the Fatimid caliphate in its decline, its cultural and economic splendor far overshadowed that of the weak and poverty-stricken 'Abbasid caliphate. To this day, the University of al-Azhar in Cairo, founded in 970 by the Fatimids, is recognized as a major center of Islamic culture, learning, and leadership.

Meanwhile, a group of nomadic Turks, led by a tribe known as the Seljuks, began to identify themselves with Sunni Islamic rule, order, and the protection of property. By 1044 they had occupied most of the Iranian plateau, and by 1055 they had raided the territories of Armenia, Byzantium, south of the Bosphorous (modern Turkey), Syria, and Iraq. In their role as enthusiastic Sunni Muslims, the Seljuk Turks released the 'Abbasids from the tutelage of the Buyids, a group of political opportunists who had adopted the Shi'i form of Islam because it represented the disloyal and dominant opposition. In return, the 'Abbasid caliph al-Qa'im (1031–1075) crowned the Seljuk leader Toghril Beg as "King of the East and the West," investing him with the sultanate and the responsibility for protecting the Islamic community (*ummah*) and for fighting the holy war (*jihad*) against all infidels.

The spread and dominance of the Seljuk Turks over the greater part of the 'Abbasid empire in the Middle East crystallized the division between secular and religious power, a division that had started a century earlier when the caliphs had been stripped of all but religious or moral authority. Henceforth, the Islamic constitution recognized the caliphs as spiritual heads and the sultans as state rulers. The Seljuks took control of the empire, assigned land grants to military chiefs for their service, initiated the spread of Sunni Islamic centers of learning (*madrasah*), and directed repeated incursions into Byzantium.

The triumph of the Seljuk Turks over the Byzantine emperor Romanus Diogenes at the Battle of Manzikert (north of Lake Van in modern Turkey) in 1071 virtually destroyed Byzantine power in Asia Minor, though not north of the Bosphorous. Christian Anatolia (modern Turkey except for the fortified stronghold of Constantinople) was gradually lost to Islam, and the Byzantine government still operating from Constantinople appealed to the pope and the Latin West for aid. The response was a series of Crusades that started in 1096 and continued for almost two centuries.

Much has been written about the Crusades, particularly as they affected Christian Europe.[8] Less has been written about the effects on Islamic countries. Because of the Crusades and the military defeat of the Muslims, Islamic strongholds and large Muslim populations had to submit to Christian rule for the first time since the Islamic conquests of Christian territories (632–733).

For a while the triumphant Crusaders managed to maintain their bridgeheads in the Middle East, thanks to repeated reinforcements from Europe. But they were invaders barely surviving on extended cobweb lines of communication, too weak to sustain successive Muslim attacks. Ultimately, the Muslims regained the initiative, launched a holy war (*jihad*) to restore and defend their faith, and repossessed from the infidel usurper what they considered to be Islamic territory. Eventually, all the lands briefly overrun by the Crusaders were repossessed by Muslims.

Beyond the eastern border of the Mediterranean, the Crusaders had little if any impact on the Islamic world. In fact, during the twelfth and thirteenth centuries (the age of the Crusades), the ʿAbbasid caliphs reasserted their political power, the arts flourished, and Islam spread into new territories in central Asia and Indonesia.[9] The establishment of a sultanate in Delhi in 1206 created a permanent base for Islamic civilization in the heart of India.

However, the effective rule of the Seljuk Turks began to disintegrate during the twelfth century. Increasingly, one military dynasty replaced another until the power of the Seljuk sultans grew weak and vulnerable to a new menace: the Mongols.

Originally, Mongols consisted of loosely organized nomadic tribes in Mongolia, Manchuria, and Siberia.[10] Sometime before the 1200s a Mongol chieftain by the name of Temujin (1162–1227), later known as Genghis Khan (meaning "Mighty King"), unified and organized scattered tribes into a superior fighting force. As the undisputed master of Mongolia, he and his successors set out on a spectacular career of conquest, spreading terror and destruction everywhere.[11]

Under the leadership of Genghis Khan, the Mongol armies swept over northern China, conquered Beijing (Peking), and in 1220 advanced to the northeastern borders of Iran. One by one the cities of Azerbaijan, Georgia, Samarkand, Bukhara, Khorasan, Merv, and Nishapur were captured, ravaged, and devastated by fire and the sword. After their victory the Mongols returned to east Asia.

For almost a century, succeeding generations of Mongol leaders sustained their rampaging and devastating campaign from the Pacific Ocean to the Danube River, sweeping across China, India, the Middle East, and Europe. In 1243 they forced the Seljuk sultan in Syria to become their vassal. In 1256 they destroyed the fortresses of the Nizari Isma‘ilis, and in 1258, under the leadership of Hulaga Khan (grandson of Genghis Khan) they invaded and sacked Baghdad and Syria. The ‘Abbasid caliph al-Musta‘sim (1242–1258) was executed together with his kinsmen. A few years later, the Mamluk sultan Baybars I of Egypt invited Ahmed Abul-Qasim, one of the few surviving scions of the ‘Abbasid family, to establish the caliphate in Cairo.

Baybars I is considered the real founder of the Mamluk Turkish sultanate of Egypt. Though he was a ruthless usurper, he was also talented and farsighted. To add luster and legitimacy to his reign, he revived the ‘Abbasid caliphate and acknowledged the caliph as the spiritual head of Islam. Descendants of this cardboard caliphate retained their shadowy silhouettes until 1517, when the Ottoman Turks invaded Egypt and permanently extinguished the ‘Abbasid line.

Meanwhile, the establishment of the sultanate in Delhi in 1206 created a permanent base for Islamic civilization in India. To be sure, Muslims had come to India from Arabia during the eighth century and later from Persia and Afghanistan during the eleventh century, but the Delhi sultanate provided a focus for and a stimulus to the Islamic community in India that lasted for more than three hundred years (1206–1526). In 1526 Babar (1483–1530), a descendant of Timur (Tamerlane, the Mongol), established the Islamic Mughal Empire in India. (The Persian term "Mughal" is the same as the Indian term "Mogul," both meaning "Mongol.")

The Mughals (1526–1858)

India flourished under a succession of remarkable Muslim Mughal emperors. The first five to follow Babar extended their territory often at the expense of other Islamic and Indian kingdoms. Akbar the Great (1556–1605), the grandson of Babar, is recognized as the greatest of the Mughal emperors. He reigned for forty-nine years and conquered all of northern India and Afghanistan. He was a religious personality who ruled wisely and won the loyalty of many native Indians through a policy of religious tolerance, which was condemned by detractors. Conservative Sunnis accused him of trying to displace Islam with a new syncretistic religion. Akbar and his supporters countered that they were only emphasizing the universal aspects of Islam. Their policy seems to have been justified by events. In time, great numbers of native Indians converted to Islam. One of the emperors, Jihan I (1628–1658), built in memory of his favorite wife the most beautiful and costly tomb in the world: the Taj Mahal.

Daratagaha Mosque in Colombo, Sri Lanka

The Daratagaha Mosque squeezed between commercial buildings, in the vicinity of the town hall, seen in the background. *Courtesy of British Airways/BOAC.*

Situated at Agra, south of Delhi, its construction took twenty-one years (1632–1653). Most of those who see it believe that it justified the effort.

With the passing of time the power of the conservative Sunni element grew to such an extent that the Mughal emperor Aurangzeb I (1658–1707) was prompted to impose conformity to traditional Islamic values.[12] He tried to force non-Muslims to convert to Islam, levied a special tax on Hindus, and destroyed many Hindu temples. He then moved against Bijapur and Golconda, two Shiʿi kingdoms in southern India, in a campaign that proved disastrous. His policies alienated the Hindu Rajput military, which formed a vital part of his army, and because of this, internal troubles and costly wars developed during his reign, which in turn sapped the economy of the ruling class and the morale of the army. He left a troubled inheritance to his descendants.

Within decades the Mughal Empire had broken up as several groups gained control in central and western regions of India and founded their own kingdoms. By 1757 the British East India Company became one of the leading powers in India, and in 1803 it placed the Mughal emperor under its "protection." A Muslim-led rebellion in 1857 against the British failed and brought the Mughal Empire to its end. Emperor Bahadur II (1837–1858) was banished and control of India was assumed by the British crown.

Ninety years later, in 1947, India's Muslim population established the separate Islamic state of Pakistan. But social, political, and cultural differences among the Muslims of India triggered yet another split, culminating in 1971 in the formation of a second independent Muslim state, Bangladesh.

The Safavids (1501–1722)

A close contemporary of the Mughal dynasty that ushered India into the nineteenth century was the Safavid dynasty of Persia.[13] It emerged gradually as the Mongol leaders became anxious to secure for themselves, by subtlety or the sword, a rich Islamic slice of the Persian pie. Factional rivalry, open conflict, and political instability gave way to a semblance of order under Isma'il I (1501–1524), the first of the Shi'i Safavids. He proclaimed himself shah (a Persian term meaning "king" or "prince"), and, despite his Kurdish antecedents, he was able to document family connections traceable to 'Ali, the fourth caliph. For 250 years, he and succeeding Shi'i Safavid shahs exerted a potent influence in reversing centuries of conservative Sunni dominance across Persia and southeastern Turkey.

Shah 'Abbas I (1588–1629) is recognized as the greatest of the Safavid rulers. His kingdom included nearly all of present-day Iran, with Isfahan directly south of modern Teheran as its capital. Under the Safavids, Shi'i Islam became the state religion, resulting in the execution of members of the Sunni and other Islamic sects. Despite serious internal weakness and repeated invasions by Uzbeks and Ottomans, Persia held firm as a Shi'i state. Then, for half a century after Shah Nadir's death in 1747, civil wars between Zand and Qajar dynasties plagued Persia. In the end, the Qajars won control of the country and governed it under a number of capable leaders until 1925.[14]

The Qajars (1779–1925)

During the entire period of the Qajars, Persia came under the power and influence of Russia and Great Britain,[15] and by the 1900s both powers controlled the Persian government and dominated its trade. This was the state of affairs until after the First World War, when Reza Pahlavi, an army corporal, led a military coup in 1921. In 1925, Reza became Shah of Iran, the first of two rulers who represented the short-lived Pahlavi dynasty. He lasted until 1941 when the British and the Russians forced him to abdicate in favor of his son, Muhammad Reza (1941–1979), who ruled for thirty-eight years.

The rejection of age-old Islamic convention, the introduction of Western, non-Islamic values, and a regime that was seen by many Iranians as fascist and repressive provoked a major revolution that overthrew the monarchy in 1979 and restored Qur'anic law under the leadership of Ayatollah Khomeini. How successful the regime of authoritarian religious leaders is likely to be is a matter for speculation. There is no doubt, however, that the Islamic revolution of the Shi'is created and will continue to create worldwide repercussions. It perpetuates ancient rivalries, traditions, and values; it is resistant to change; and it resists modern influences, particularly non-Islamic influences.

The Ottomans (1281–1924)

The Ottoman Turks were the last leading power in Islam and the final dynasty to claim the office of the caliphate. The origin and history of the Ottomans before 1300 is shrouded in legend.[16] They may have been a nomadic group who came to Asia Minor from the east during the great wave of Turkmens. Founded by Osman I (also written 'Uthman) in the eastern vicinity of the Byzantine Empire, the Ottoman forces eventually threatened the Byzantines. Soon their prestige as champions of Islam spread far and wide, and their empire lasted more than six hundred years, ruled by a series of competent successors.[17]

When Osman I died in 1324, his son Orkhan (1324–1360) succeeded and immediately organized the Ottoman forces in Asia. In 1345 the Christian Byzantine emperor, John Cantacuzene, called on Orkhan to aid him in a civil war instigated by Empress Anna. The result was a threefold victory: the triumph of Cantacuzene; the marriage of Orkhan to Theodora, daughter of the Byzantine emperor; and an Islamic bridgehead in eastern Europe to match the one in western Europe, in Spain. Repeated calls on Orkhan by the Byzantine emperor to aid him against invasions by Serbians and other European people contributed to the settlement and spread of the Ottomans and Islam into eastern Europe.

During the reign of Murad I (1360–1389), the Ottomans captured Adrianople (Edirne) in 1365 and made it their capital the following year, replacing the old capital of Bursa. In the years 1371 to 1372 the Ottoman forces of Murad I conquered Macedonia, Bulgaria, Serbia, and parts of Hungary, and they raided Greece and Albania. Both Genoa and Venice made treaties with Murad I in 1387. Finally Murad I was assassinated by a Serb just after the Battle of Kossovo in 1389, having defeated a coalition of Serbs, Bulgars, Bosnians, and Albanians.

The years following the death of Murad I were critical ones for the Ottoman Empire. The Mongols, under the leadership of Timur (Tamerlane), invaded Anatolia and routed the Ottoman Turks at the Battle of Angora (Ankara) in 1402. The Ottoman ruler Bayazid I (1389–1402) was captured and the complete defeat of his army threatened the dissolution of the Ottoman Empire. However, Muhammad I (1403–1421) regained control of the empire after Timur retreated in 1403 and after two other contestants, Sulayman and Musa, were eliminated.

He devoted most of his energy thereafter to consolidating the Ottoman Empire and his authority.

During the reign of Murad II (1421–1451), a Crusade, instigated by Pope Eugene IV and composed of troops from Hungary, Poland, Bosnia, Wallahia, and Serbia, was launched to drive the Ottomans out of Europe. At first, Murad II negotiated a ten-year truce, but when the Hungarians broke the truce and renewed their Crusade, he responded swiftly, completely defeating the Crusaders at Varna in 1444.

When Muhammad II (also called Mehmet II, the Conqueror, 1451–1481) succeeded his father Murad II, he devoted his attention to the capture of Constantinople, the capital of the Byzantine Empire. His great triumph followed on May 29, 1453, when Muhammad II and his militant Ottoman army forced an entry through the fortifications of Constantinople. In the ensuing bloody battle the Byzantine emperor Constantine IX was killed, along with thousands of his forces. Near midday, Muhammad II ordered his troops to halt the fighting while he took ceremonial possession of the Christian church of Saint Sophia in the name of Islam. Later, he accorded the Greek patriarch considerable civil and religious authority over the Christian Orthodox inhabitants. Soon churches were transformed into mosques, new palaces were built, and the Ottoman capital was transferred to Constantinople, now called Istanbul. Thus, the once mighty Christian empire of the Byzantines was permanently conquered by the Ottoman Muslims.

The establishment of Istanbul as the capital of the Ottoman Empire was the beginning of the Imperial age. Now the Ottomans spoke of their empire as "a great tent" supported by the high officers of the state. They referred to the government of the sultan (a title of honor adopted by Muslim princes and rulers since 900) as the "Sublime Porte," meaning the sublime entrance to the sultan's imperial palace. The extent of their empire, though constantly changing, stretched from India to Europe, including north Africa, Cyprus, Crete, Greece, the Balkan states, and Russia. All non-Muslim citizens within the Ottoman Empire were subject to the dictates of Islam, although they were treated as separate groups who could retain with certain restrictions their religious and cultural identity. No such latitude was permitted within Islam. Internal Muslim dissent or revolutionary movements were met with severe and often fatal punishment.

Selim I (1512–1520), grandson of Muhammad II, overcame his two brothers before succeeding to the throne. In 1517 he overran the Mamluk rulers of Egypt, assumed the title of caliph, and secured control of the holy sites in Arabia. His son and successor Sulayman II (1520–1566) was a proud and ambitious ruler who concentrated his efforts on Islamic expansion in Europe. He made an alliance with France, invaded and occupied Belgrade, Yugoslavia (in 1521), and Hungary (in 1526), laid siege to Vienna (in 1529 and 1532) and to Malta (in 1565). He incited the newly converted Protestant princes of Germany against the pope and the ruling emperor and made occupied Hungary a stronghold for Protestant groups, particularly the Calvinists. This support of Protestantism,

Aya Sofya Mosque in Istanbul, Turkey

The great sixth-century Byzantine church of Saint Sofia was transformed into Aya Sofya Mosque in 1453. The Ottoman Turks added the four minarets and the royal tombs, seen in the foreground. *Courtesy of Turkish Tourism and Information Office.*

along with the alliance with France, remained the official policy of the Ottomans for almost two centuries.

A series of inferior leaders followed Sulayman's death, heralding years of progressive decline.[18] The sultans gave less and less attention to government and left day-to-day administration in the hands of viziers, most of them court favorites rather than men of ability. Corruption, cliques within the government, and intrigue hatched in the harem led inevitably to the decline of the military organization. Soon the Janissary corps (an elite corps of Turkish infantry storm troops) made and unmade sultans, most of whom were mere puppets in their hands.

By the eighteenth century the Ottoman Empire and the well-being of the Islamic community were sagging. By the nineteenth century they were near collapse. The Ottoman Empire lost territory by default and mismanagement. Several European powers kept the Ottoman Empire, now considered "the sick man of Europe," from total disintegration. Islamic communities in Africa, western Asia, and India found themselves being partitioned among aggressive European powers. Those that retained some vestiges of autonomy questioned the authority of the Ottoman sultans and the claim that their authority derived either from God or from a general Muslim consensus. The Ottoman religious establishment was even branded as un-Islamic by some and rejected in favor of a vague pan-Islamism by others.

Alien international forces, tensions, and problems created by modern technologies, the rise of nationalism, and the longing to restore consistent and rational leadership prompted a group of reformers who called themselves Young Turks to revolt against the Ottoman sultanate in 1908. Sultan Abdul Hamid II (1876–1909) was deposed in spite of a counter-revolution mounted by his supporters. The Young Turks took over the government, initiated measures of reform, and took steps to eliminate corruption, all in the hope of restoring the greatness of the Ottoman Empire. But groups in all parts of the empire had already had enough. They demanded independence from Ottoman rule.

On November 1, 1922, the Ottoman sultanate was abolished, to be replaced a year later by the Republic of Turkey. Few Muslims mourned the passing of the Ottomans, but that was not the case with the caliphate. On March 3, 1924, the centuries-old institution of the caliphate was abolished too. To many Muslims, the words of Mustafa Kemal Attaturk, then president of the Turkish Grand National Assembly, were little short of apostasy: "The idea of a single caliph, exercising supreme religious authority over all the peoples of Islam, is an idea taken from fiction, not from reality." Thus, the concept promulgated by Muhammad's followers in Arabia in 632 ended in Turkey in 1924.

In the course of its turbulent history, the caliphate had survived despite numerous modifications, despite counterclaims of rival caliphs, and at times despite powerful resentment against individual caliphs. But throughout Islamic history the institution survived without a break and was recognized among Muslims both as a moral link as well as a symbol of solidarity. Muslim dynasties, political factions, and religious sects might come and go according to the vicissitudes of the moment, but the institution of the caliphate, the highest office reserved for each mortal successor of the prophet Muhammad, continued as the justification for claiming the allegiance of all people, either as adherents of the Islamic religion or as subject people paying tribute. Indeed, rival dynasties ruled and dominated vast territories, fought others and each other, organized revolts, founded institutions, and raised buildings, all in the name of the caliphate by virtue of their status as "successors" and "defenders" of Islam.

The abolition of the caliphate offended Muslims everywhere, and various attempts were made to restore this fundamental institution. Three congresses were held, one in Cairo in March 1926, another in Mecca in July 1926, and a third in Jerusalem in 1931, but they met with little or no success. Another attempt by King Faruk of Egypt in 1939 to revive the institution of the caliphate met with vigorous opposition, especially from the Turkish government.

To date, no office has replaced the institution of the caliphate, but this does not necessarily mean that Muslim opinion is finally resigned to justifying Islam without it. Evidence suggests that many Muslims are far from resigned. The abolition of the caliphate has proved to be a self-inflicted wound that has left a scar on the Muslim consciousness. The idea of an unbroken succession linking the present to its source and fountainhead is still cherished by many Muslims and is likely to survive for many generations to come.

Recent Developments

Muslim states that yearned for independence from the Ottoman Turks soon found that their countries were being partitioned among European powers after the First World War. They had neither the military nor the technological resources to resist these alien international forces, so instead they tried to manipulate European powers to keep them on each other's backs, but off the backs of Muslims. The strategy had only partial success, and relations with Europeans deteriorated even more after the Second World War.

Since the Second World War, the political independence of many Islamic countries has led to the creation of several forms of Islamic nationalism, calculated to give a particular state or nation an Islamic identity. Islamic principles and national sentiments created the development of several movements such as pan-Arabianism, Islamic socialism, and lately Islamic Marxism.

The relationship between Islam and contemporary Muslim governments is multi-dimensional. It involves both individual piety and public affairs. The most far-reaching changes for modern Islam lie in the legal sphere, particularly as they apply to measures aimed at the reinstatement of Islamic law (Shariʿah). Whereas Western nations base their social and political systems on secular laws, Islamic countries are bent on eradicating such alien distinctions. Their goal is to bring their social order and political aspirations in line with the body of Islamic law because it provides guidelines for every sphere of life. In one sense, then, Islamic law stands above the state, since it represents the will of God, while Muslim rulers are merely its executors.

Today, Muslim communities in virtually every region of the world, except China, live free of non-Muslim domination. Though political rivalry, industrialization, and population growth have created severe problems for Muslim states, those states remain loyal to Islamic principles, however they may interpret them—as Shiʿi or Sunni. The Muslim masses, however, are haunted by the age-old desire for a deliverer who will bring peace, social justice, and improvement to their status quo.

Another recent development is the rapid expansion of Islam in sub-Saharan Africa. Undoubtedly, African religion was most affected by its contact with Islam, although the interaction of that religion did not mean a total abandonment of African religious traditions. Islam reached north and northwestern Africa (Egypt, Ethiopia, Sudan, Libya, Tunisia, Algeria, and Morocco) immediately after its inception in the seventh century C.E. From then on, Islam's expansion in other parts of Africa was relatively slow until the colonial period which started in the 1400s, when it once again spread south of the Sahara, establishing various important centers both inland and along the entire coast of Africa.[19]

The relationship of colonial Christians to the peoples of Africa was based on the assumption that Africans were "savages" with an inferior culture that needed the Christian faith and European "civilization" before they could take their place proudly with the Western world. Similarly, cultured Muslims were disdainful of the masses of African tribes.[20] But the steps to become a Muslim were easier than those necessary for Christian conversion and baptism. Moreover, Muslim converts had more freedom to achieve religious status or leadership roles than their Christian counterparts, who had to acquiesce to the demanding requirements of ordination and strong moral discipline. Islam was readily able to accommodate a wide range of African practices, such as polygamy, certain forms of magic and divination, and traditional male dominance. Yet Islam rejected certain African traditions, particularly the representation of divinities by images and the secret societies that challenged the prerogatives of the Islamic *ummah,* or unitary community.

In spite of those restrictive features, Islam took root and expanded in sub-Saharan Africa as well as in industrialized countries. One such interesting development is the growth of Black Muslims in the United States of America.[21] Another is vigorous proselytization. Until recently, Islam had no organized missionary movement, but today students are trained to work as missionaries throughout Asia, Africa, Europe, and the Americas.[22]

Today, Muslims are found in significant numbers in the United States and in European countries, particularly Germany, France, and Britain.[23] Here, Muslims share common concerns regarding the practice of their faith, the retention of Islamic identity, particularly for their children, and the preservation of family life and Islamic values. Hence, the issue of assimilation is acute among Muslims residing in the West. Membership in mosques and Islamic centers in Western cities and towns often incorporates and reflects religious, ethnic, and racial distinctions. Most Muslims living in the West are second- and even third-generation, and they participate in professional and civic life. And yet they face issues of identity and faith as a religious minority.

Issues of adaptation and change are causing tremendous difficulties both for Muslim governments as well as Muslim individuals wherever they happen to live.[24] These changes present Muslim thinkers with some severe problems, if not imminent threats, that demand critical assessment.[25] For instance, is modern Islam fragmenting unified elements of life and dividing Islamic statehood into separate socio-political entities? Is nationalism undermining the great resilience of Muslim culture and institutions? Have modern scientific views challenged religious dogmas and even threatened faith in the reality of God or truth?

Various responses have been suggested as solutions to these critical questions, and yet none seem to close the yawning chasm that separates modernity from traditional Islamic culture, with its hallowed associations. Muslim rulers everywhere find themselves increasingly dependent on alien international forces that can neither be evaded nor controlled. Although this demanding political and social condition plagues them, they have not lost adherents. On the contrary, new Muslim intellectuals are just beginning to distinguish lasting, perennial Islamic truths from archaic cultural traditions that obscure them. Given time, Muslims are capable of successfully resolving the present-day challenge.

Mosque in Washington, D.C., U.S.

One of the many mosques built by recent Muslim settlers in the Western world. *From the private collection of the author.*

Indeed, the potential for adapting Islamic principles to meet the challenges and tensions of modern technology and alien culture is inherent in the character of Islam. Islamic civilization was once intrinsically superior to Christendom. Its leading thinkers were innovators in postulating theories on how society and government might be improved by applying Islamic principles. Today, this determination to implement the command of God in a secular and material world has not been abandoned. Even now, individuals in the Muslim world are slowly attempting to integrate genuine Islamic culture. In this way, the eternal values of Islam may yet be resurrected to affect not only Muslims but the entire human race.

3   Muslim Groups

Like all other religions, Islam is split into many different groups, and this sub-division of Islam is similar to other religions in two ways. First, Muslims form one religious community and their differences do not impair their basic sense of solidarity as adherents of Islam. In fact, Muslims tend to regard different Islamic groups as making a positive contribution to the overall development of Islam. Second, Muslims, like Christians (Catholic, Orthodox, and Protestant) or Buddhists (Mahayana, Theravada, and Tantric), classify various Islamic sects or factions under three major groupings, namely Sunni, Shiʿi, and Sufi. In order to understand the differences it is necessary to recall the disagreement over ʿAli's right of succession that split Muslims into two groups. Those who were loyal to ʿAli came to be known as Shiʿis (partisans or legitimists), questioned the legality of earlier elections, and denounced the claims of the first three caliphs as spurious. Those who accepted the legitimacy of the first three appointments to the caliphate in accordance with established custom came to be known as Sunnis (traditionalists or orthodox). They accused ʿAli of complicity in the assassination of Caliph ʿUthman and dismissed his claim to succession as having no legal justification. As to the origin of Sufi, the earliest use of the term in literature occurs in the early ninth century, though later Sufis claimed the name to be as old as Islam. The following discussion considers the basic views held by the three major branches. A few of their subgroups will also be mentioned.

Sunni

The largest group of Muslims (making up more than 85 percent of the total Muslim population) are the Sunni, who recognize the first four caliphs and attribute no special religious or political function to ʿAli or his descendants. Those who claim to follow what the prophet Muhammad laid down either by word, deed, or tacit approval came to be known as "the people of the *sunnah* and the community" (*ahl al-sunnah wʾal-jamʿa*). The term *sunnah* means a "well-trodden path," a "custom," or "practice." In the religious terminology of Islam, the term signifies the example set by the prophet Muhammad. It distinguishes this group from Shiʿi adherents, who view descent by birth in direct line from the prophet Muhammad as crucial. In a modern context, the term Sunni indicates the traditional way of the consolidated majority of the Islamic community as opposed to the Shiʿi ("partisan") dissenters.

The issues raised by the early schismatic groups and the positions they adopted culminated in the formulation and subsequent general acceptance of a set of principles which became Sunni, or "orthodox," doctrines. The foremost and fundamental element emphasized by Sunni orthodoxy was the primacy of tribal or community consensus (*ijma*). This concept gained such strength that it became the main distinguishing feature between Muslims who accepted the views and decisions of the majority and those who did not. The Sunnis, then, considered themselves a privileged community protected by God's hand and endowed with infallibility, while dissidents were condemned as heretics.

This doctrinal proscription against dissent, however, soon gave way to more tolerant and liberal views that recognized the coexistence of diverse sects and schools of thought, and these views quickly gained wide currency among the Sunnis. This tolerance ultimately made it possible to embrace within the Muslim community any member who did not formally renounce Islam, deny the oneness of God, or deny the prophethood of Muhammad. This broad-mindedness saved the integrity of the Sunni community.

The two names that are associated with formulating Sunni doctrine are al-Ash'ari and al-Maturidi. Despite certain theological differences between the two, their doctrines merged in the course of time and gained wide currency, particularly after the eleventh century. Later, Sunni theologians placed increasing emphasis on divine omnipotence, projecting a deterministic outlook on life at the expense of credence in the freedom of human will.

Meanwhile, several Sunni theologians, between the ninth and twelfth centuries, began provocative explorations of inquiry. Their works came to fruition in the comprehensive system of Ibn Sina (980–1037), popularly known to the West by his Latinized name of Avicenna. Unfortunately, the powerful impact of natural theology these scholars brought to bear on Islamic thought posed a threat to Sunni orthodoxy. Soon these philosophers became the target of suspicion and attack by those who tolerated no argument against revealed theology.

Abu Hamid Muhammad al-Ghazali (1058–1111), the famous Muslim scholar and mystic, openly attacked these philosophers in a book called *The Incoherence of the Philosophers* (*Tahafut al-Falasifa*).[1] He began by asserting that the decay of Islamic faith in his lifetime was due to two important factors: the respect shown by Muslim thinkers to Greek and other philosophers, and the faulty Arabic translations of original works of philosophy. He then explained the failures and incoherency of their arguments, asserting at one point that a system of philosophy is not as sound as the discipline of mathematics. Abu-l-Walid Ibn Rushd (1126–1198), known to the West by his Latinized name of Averroës, responded with a rebuttal to al-Ghazali that denounced his arguments, but he failed to satisfy Sunni orthodoxy. Islamic Spain's brilliant movement of philosophical inquiry survived among European scholars, but it died within the Islamic community.

One other characteristic distinguishes Sunni from Shi'i theology. The Sunni doctrine of infallibility differs sharply from that of the Shi'is. Infallibility, for the Sunnis, is not a quality inherent in all prophets; rather, it is a special grace received from God. Consequently all prophets may sometimes commit mistakes, but they are exempt from minor and grave sins, from unbelief, and from sordid deeds. Superhuman knowledge is given from time to time by God to his prophets or messengers, who are commissioned to deliver God's message. Not so with the Shiᶜis. Prophets and imams are sinless and infallible and therefore cannot err. In fact, the imams possess an inherited superhuman knowledge that enables them to anticipate every event in the world until the day of resurrection and judgment.

The Sunnis also differ from the Shiᶜis in matters of law. The Sunnis reject the practice of temporary marriages (*mutᶜa*) as sanctioned by the Shiᶜis. Moreover, in contrast to the Shiᶜis, the Sunnis have a more lenient attitude toward matters of custom and tradition. This attitude, however, has led to several backlash reformist movements. The most violent, a reaction that took the Muslim world by surprise, occurred in Arabia in the eighteenth century among reforming zealots commonly known as the Wahhabis.[2]

The movement owes its origin to Muhammad ibn ᶜAbd al-Wahhab (1703–1792) of north Arabia, who advocated the purification of the Islamic faith by ridding it of degrading accretions and who insisted on the right to independent thought. Despite strong opposition, his condemnation of the "authority" (*taqlid*) of the medieval schools proved to be a greater liberating force than any other single factor in the shaping of modern Islam.

ᶜAbd al-Wahhab recognized only two authorities: the Qurᵓan, and the Sunnah (Tradition) of the prophet Muhammad with the precedents of the Companions of the Prophet. He denounced allegorical interpretation of the Qurᵓan, upheld the doctrine of predestination, and insisted that good works follow a sound faith. He made attendance at public prayer an obligation, stripped mosques of every ornament, and prohibited the use of the rosary. Invoking or seeking the intercession of prophets, saints, or angels was strictly forbidden. Anyone caught smoking tobacco was to be punished by a maximum of forty stripes.

This new sect soon became involved in warfare, expanding its influence all over north Arabia into Iraq and Syria. ᶜAbd al-ᶜAziz, commonly known as Ibn Saud, captured Riyadh, in Saudi Arabia (in 1920), and the twin holy cities of Medina and Mecca (in 1925). By arming the people and creating agricultural colonies, he soon controlled almost the entire Arabian peninsula.

Modern Wahhabis retain their puritanical reforming zeal and are committed to restoring Islam to a semblance of its original form in the Prophet's time. Their chief contribution has been to rid Islam of medieval teachings and practices that were not part of its original doctrine. Their territories have profited greatly from the application of Western technology and the sale of oil, factors which may inhibit an early return to ancient ways and values.

Another leader who longed to reform Islam was Mirza Ghulam Ahmad (1835–1908) of Qadian, Punjab.[3] After spending years studying Islam and other religions, he claimed to have received revelation, giving him the right to receive homage. He held that the statement in Qurᵓan 61:6, which foretells the coming of a messenger called Ahmad, speaks of him. Soon he started and administered the Ahmadiyyah movement, claiming to be the Mahdi—a messiah expected by Muslims, Zoroastrians, Hindus, and Buddhists. In fact, he claimed to be an *avatar* (incarnation) of Krishna (Hindu deity) and a spirit of the prophet Muhammad.

Ahmad's teachings were anathema to orthodox Muslims. The claim which gave orthodox Muslims the most offense was that revelation had not ceased with the prophet Muhammad and that the Prophet's personality had merged with Ahmad's, making him a prophet too. He also taught that Jesus was crucified but taken down from the cross and resuscitated, after which he went to preach in Kashmir, where he died and was buried at the age of 120.[4]

Less than half a century after Ahmad's death, the Ahmadiyyah movement split into two groups. The issue that divided them was Ahmad's claim to be a prophet. Followers who were able to accept Ahmad as a reformer but not as a prophet distinguished themselves from the original sect by establishing their own splinter group in Lahore. During the partition of India in 1947 the original group that accepted all Ahmad's claims—known as Qadianis, a reference to Ahmad's birthplace—moved to Rabwah in Pakistan.[5]

The Qadianis are a close-knit society but possess a strong missionary orientation. Their aggressive propagation of their faith has often caused trouble; nevertheless they have spread to many parts of the world and have gained thousands of converts in southeast Asia and Africa. In 1967 their khalifa (a title meaning caliph assumed by their leader), Hafiz Mirza Nasir Ahmad, paid a visit to Europe, including Copenhagen, The Hague, Oxford, and Glasgow.

The members of the Lahore group, by contrast, are more moderate both in their doctrine and in their missionary activities. Unlike the Qadianis, who have cut their ties with the general Islamic community, the Lahore group prefers to remain within the Islamic fold. Both groups, however, insist that Islam, as they each interpret it, is the only rational religion that suits contemporary society.

Shi'i

The Shi'i branch of Islam (making up about 10 percent of the total Muslim population) differs significantly from the orthodox Sunni majority. Shi'is themselves are divided into groups and subgroups, some of which are discussed later in this section.

When 'Ali was deposed and assassinated in 661, his followers proclaimed his eldest son Hasan (and grandson of Muhammad) as 'Ali's legitimate successor. But Mu'awiya I persuaded Hasan to renounce his claim to the caliphate in exchange for a large pension and retirement in Medina. Eight years later, Hasan died—of natural causes according to the Sunni (Mu'awiya's faction), of poison according to the Shi'is ('Ali's supporters). Now 'Ali's inheritance fell to 'Ali's second son, Husayn, Hasan's younger brother and the only surviving grandson of the Prophet.

For a while Husayn lived quietly in Medina, but when Yazid I succeeded his father Mu'awiya I to the caliphate in 680, Husayn refused to acknowledge him as caliph. A superior force of Yazid's men caught up with Husayn and encircled him and his band of two hundred men at Karbala in Iraq. After refusing every invitation to surrender over a period of ten days, Husayn's band was cut down to the last man, and his head was sent to Yazid in Damascus. Yazid is said to have reacted with something a little short of gratitude. Delivering Husayn's head was hardly calculated to please any Muslim who stopped to think how the prophet Muhammad might have reacted to the dismemberment of a grandson. Most Muslims felt shame rather than satisfaction. Husayn's head was later buried with his body in Karbala, now a great sanctuary of the Shiʿis.

As one might anticipate, Shiʿi opposition did not end there. Husayn's death fueled the lambent flames of ʿAli's martyrdom and strengthened all Shiʿis in their consuming hatred of the established Umayyad caliphate, which they were instrumental in destroying centuries later. Even then, their victory was short-lived. The Sunni ʿAbbasids who had engineered the downfall of the Umayyads liquidated their Shiʿi supporters as soon as they had served their purpose. They were after all traditional enemies and never to be trusted beyond the limits set by mutual expedient, something the Shiʿis should have known. The ʿAbbasid rulers overthrew and killed their leaders, destroyed the grave of Husayn, and hunted down for extermination anyone who had ever claimed or boasted of direct descent from ʿAli. But those events were still centuries away.

What had begun as a political, regional, and tribal faction soon acquired a religious significance. The Shiʿis appeared to be impotent politically, but they attracted malcontents (who for various reasons were dissatisfied with the ruling house of the Umayyads) like a magnet attracts iron filings. The Shiʿis insisted that ʿAli's rights had been grossly infringed upon and that the headship of the Islamic community, the caliphate, belonged legitimately to ʿAli and his descendants. This claim led to social struggle and political revolt. A certain Mukhtar ibn-Ubayd mobilized a large group of discontents and installed Muhammad ibn al-Hanafiya, another son of ʿAli by a wife other than Fatimah (the Prophet's daughter), as the Mahdi (the "rightly guided"). The attempted revolt failed, but the movement left an important legacy. After Muhammad ibn al-Hanafiya's death, a belief began to circulate that he had retired into "concealment" and that the faithful must expect his return to restore peace and justice to the world.

Thus, in the early history of Islam, the politically motivated Shiʿis developed into a religious sect with a unique dogma based on their own theological premise. This premise derived basically from two sources: the violent death or martyrdom of Husayn, who became the central figure in the "passion" plays performed to this day, and the belief in the return of the Mahdi, now recognized as a divine person. Repeated political defeat and persistent persecution in their early days did not in any way deter Shiʿis from promoting and exploiting their best interests or from developing their own doctrines.[6]

First of all, they rejected the Sunni principle of *ijmaʿ* (the consensus of the community). Instead, they substituted the doctrine of the *imam* (spiritual head directly descended from ʿAli), who is the infallible embodiment of Islam and around whose authority the entire Shiʿi religion revolves. In every age God entrusts the guidance of his obedient servants to these infallible imams. Thus, all faithful Shi'is believe that the imam is, through his relationship to Muhammad, the divinely appointed ruler and teacher who has succeeded to the prerogatives of the Prophet himself. Moreover, the imam possesses superhuman qualities, more particularly a "divine light" (i.e., superhuman knowledge), which is transferred to him from Adam through Muhammad and 'Ali.

Among the Shi'i masses there still survives the popular belief that the imam cannot be physically harmed and that his body casts no shadow. In fact, most Shi'is hold to the belief that 'Ali and succeeding imams assume divine attributes and powers and as such they are both sinless and absolutely infallible in their pronouncements in all matters. They possess an inherited divine knowledge by which they know all that will happen. They are incapable of error. They are the source of all truth, the sole and ultimate authority for interpreting the Qur'an, and the only individuals to whom absolute obedience is a religious obligation.

According to the Shi'is, the third cardinal article of faith, after the belief in God and in his messenger the prophet Muhammad, is the belief in the imam and submission to him. Also, Shi'is make greater allowance for the doctrine of free will than do the Sunnis, holding that God has foreknowledge of all human action but does not predestine it. On matters of law, the Shi'is differ from the Sunnis in certain details, the most conspicuous being laws or conventions regarding (a) prayer, (b) marriage, (c) the veneration of tombs of imams, and (d) dissimulation of faith—the opposite of a proclamation or of a witness to faith.

In matters of prayer the Shi'is differ from the Sunnis in the form of the "call to prayer," and in the ritual of ablution accompanying prayer.

For marriages, the Shi'is permit a temporary marriage (mut'a) contracted for a specific period of years, months, or even days. This type of marriage is claimed on the basis of Qur'an 4:28, which states: "You are permitted, in addition, to seek wives using your wealth in wedlock but not in license; such wives as you enjoy thereby, give them their apportionate wages, for there is no fault in your agreeing together after the due apportionment."

Visiting and worshipping holy places, particularly the tombs of the imams, occupies a central place in Shi'i religion. In fact, pilgrimages to Karbala and other Shi'i holy sites far outweigh in importance any pilgrimage to the holy city of Mecca.

To avoid courting suffering, danger, and death, Shi'is justify the concealment of their beliefs (taqiyya, meaning "dissimulation") on the basis that belief is in the heart, known only to God.

Since the sixteenth century, Shi'i worship and doctrine have formed the official Islamic faith of Iran. Shi'i communities also survive in Iraq, Afghanistan, Pakistan, India—especially in Uttar Pradesh and Lucknow—in south Asia, Lebanon, Syria, Saudi Arabia, Yemen, the Gulf states, and elsewhere throughout the world. Despite the centrality of the doctrine of the imam, Shi'is have split into several subgroups, three of which are considered important: Imami, Zaydi, and Isma'ili.

Imami

The Imami (the Twelvers) are numerically the largest of the Shi'i sects.[7] They recognize twelve imams in the 'Ali-Fatimah line of descendants, ending with the disappearance of Muhammad the Mahdi.[8] These twelve imams are, in chronological order:

1. 'Ali (d. 661)
2. Hasan (d. 669)
3. Husayn (d. 680)
4. Zayd ibn 'Ali (d. 740)
5. Muhammad al-Baqir (d. 731)
6. Ja'far al-Sadiq (d. 765)
7. Musa (d. 799)
8. 'Ali ar-Rida (d. 818)
9. Muhammad al-Jawad (d. 835)
10. 'Ali al-Hadi (d. 868)
11. Hasan al-'Askari (d. 874)
12. Muhammad al-Mahdi (d. 878)

The belief in the return of the disappeared or hidden imam is characteristic of all Shi'i sects, though there is no agreement as to his identity. The Imamis hold that the twelfth imam is still alive, guiding human affairs, and will return some day. Indeed, there is an extensive apocalyptic literature devoted to calculations related to the date when he may be expected to return.[9]

Theologically, the imams believe that the Qur'an is created, that God is good and therefore cannot do evil, and that humans possess free will—that they may know and obey God or reject him. Since God desires the welfare of humanity, he has sent his prophets to give proper guidance. However, God recognizes that to err is human, a conclusion amply demonstrated by divisions in the Islamic community.

Consequently, God has sent, in addition to his prophets and messengers, the imams—the infallible guides in religious matters. The true imams are the direct descendants of Muhammad through the union of 'Ali and the Prophet's daughter Fatimah—members of the "holy family." That is to say, the choice of true imams is divinely determined by birth, not left to human error. The twelfth imam did not die, as his enemies assert, but was removed by God from human sight (i.e., made to disappear), just as Jesus was, according to the statements recorded in the Qur'an. The return of the twelfth imam to earth will herald the triumph of Islam and God's last judgment.

In addition to asserting this theology, imams insist that the prophet Muhammad announced 'Ali as his successor, but that Abu Bakr, 'Umar, and 'Uthman all deliberately subverted the Prophet's intention and deprived 'Ali of his legitimate right. Generations of sinful Muslims defrauded the true and divinely appointed imams, who willingly accepted their tragic destiny for the sake of God's truth.

In the course of time, the degree to which the Imami system of doctrine and law diverged from the Sunni increased rather than diminished. Various attempts were made to reduce the schism between them, each attempt frustrated by long memories and hatred nurtured from one generation to the next by tales of Sunni perfidy. Thirteen hundred years of embittered controversy have so far proven to be an insurmountable obstacle to any positive results. In modern times the stronghold of the Imami sect is in Iran, though small communities exist in Iraq, Syria, Lebanon, and India. The parliament of Iran, it is stated, has been established under the auspices of the "hidden" imam.

Zaydi

Another branch of the Shiʿis which has survived to this day is known as the Zaydis. Their name is traced to Zayd ibn ʿAli, the fourth imam and a grandson of Husayn, who was killed leading an armed rebellion in 740. Although at one time Zaydis spread far and wide and established a powerful state in the vicinity of the Caspian seacoast, today their communities are restricted mainly to the highlands of Yemen.

The Zaydis are the most broad-minded of the Shiʿi adherents, reflecting in their customs and beliefs elements from both Sunni and Shiʿi traditions. They do not dismiss caliphs Abu Bakr and ʿUmar as usurpers, but acknowledge only as imams the descendants of ʿAli. The imams of Yemen, for instance, have included descendants of both Hasan and Husayn. In no way are their imams considered infallible or impeccable. In fact, they can be, and have been, deposed, and Zaydis may acknowledge, as they have acknowledged, more than one imam at a time.

Furthermore, they reject the idea of the hidden or disappeared imam and demand that their imam be learned and able to lead his forces into battle. His leadership in battle sanctions any causes in which they take up arms against Sunnis, Sufis, or any foe of Islam in a *jihad* ("holy war"). Their imam is held to be a human being whom God guides, not one who possesses a divine light, as asserted by the rest of the Shiʿis. Thus, Zaydi doctrine concerning the imam lies midway between the Sunnis and the Shiʿis.

In matters of law and theology the Zaydi have their own law books and follow the consensus of their own scholars. They differ also in some ritual matters, such as ablution and the call to prayer. They forbid mixed marriages and the eating of meat slaughtered by a non-Muslim, with strictures that allow for no exceptions. They regard the Sunnis as a rebellious group rather than as apostates, but they are hostile to Islamic Sufi orders (mystical groups), which they have banned in Yemen. In this and other respects Zaydi observances verge on the puritanical. They have endured for almost ten centuries since they first established their imamate in Yemen in 901, making it the oldest surviving Muslim state.[10]

Isma'ili

The Isma'ilis (the Seveners) are another interesting and historically important sect within Shi'i Islam.[11] Their break with other Shi'is occurred in 765 over the succession of the sixth imam, Ja'far al-Sadiq. Instead of recognizing Musa as the seventh imam, as did other Shi'is, the Isma'ilis upheld the claims of his elder brother Isma'il and after him Isma'il's son Muhammad. This son is said to have disappeared in much the same circumstances as the twelfth imam of the Imami sect. Some Isma'ilis closed the series of imams with Isma'il, the seventh imam, and they await the return of Isma'il's son, Muhammad. Hence, they are called the Seveners. Other Isma'ilis, however, believe that the imamate continues in the line of Isma'il's descendants. They have no dogma related to the return from the past of a disappeared imam.[12]

In matters of theology, the Isma'ilis have absorbed ancient systems of thought, extreme esoteric principles, and various theosophical elements. The universe is viewed as a cyclic process and each cycle follows a septennial pattern, with the advent of seven messengers of God marked by revealed scriptures (*natiq*). The beginning of each of the seven segments is introduced by the following seven messengers: Adam, Noah, Abraham, Moses, Jesus, Muhammad (the Prophet), and Muhammad (son of the seventh imam, Isma'il). The series of seven segments represents a progression that culminates with the advent of imam. Between each *natiq* lies a series of seven messengers of God without revealed scriptures (*wasi*), who consolidate the work of the previous *natiq* by interpreting the will of God to humanity.

Naturally such a view destroyed the fundamental Islamic doctrine of the finality of the prophethood with Muhammad. To state that seven messengers or interpreters followed the prophet Muhammad is to reduce Muhammad to an intermediate member of a series and to assert that these seven are, in a sense, higher than the Prophet. Little wonder that even other Shi'i groups and all Sunni Muslims condemn Isma'ilis as extremists (*ghulat*).

Isma'ilis claim that their teachings derive from a hidden source and must be obeyed without question and without exception. Members are divided into grades according to their capacity to understand the sects' complicated theology. The lowest grades receive simple instruction while the highest delve into esoteric teaching.

Nizari

A subgroup of the Isma'ili is the Nizari. When Caliph al-Mustansir of the Fatimid dynasty in Egypt died in 1094, the Isma'ili Shi'is split over the ques-

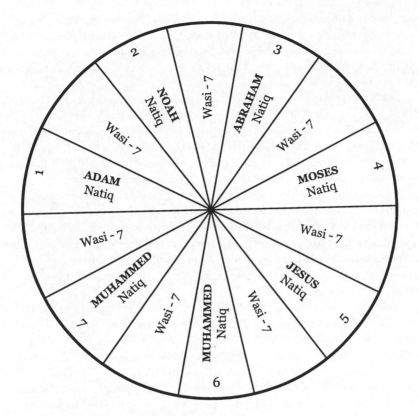

Septennial Cyclic Pattern of Universe

tion of succession. The eldest son of al-Mustansir, al-Nizar, was imprisoned and his younger brother al-Mustaʿli was hailed as caliph. Many Ismaʿilis refused to accept this departure from precedent and rallied in support of al-Nizar (hence the name Nizaris) as the rightful successor.

The founder and leader of the Nizaris was al-Hasan ibn al-Sabba, who occupied the fortress of Alamut in northwest Qazwin and other strongholds in Lebanon, spreading terror all over the Islamic world. He and his followers were known as Assassins (*hashashin*, meaning *hashish* smokers, or Indian hemp smokers). They are remembered especially for their careful planning of the assassination of opponents and the high success rate of their operations. Their well-known practice involved smoking hashish in order to induce ecstasy, which would make them ready to commit any act of murder.[13]

Little, if anything, is known about their teachings or doctrines. The general assumption is that they probably conformed to the general principles of the

Ismaᶜilis. For instance, there were, it seems, various degrees among their ranks, with the grand master at the head of the group. While their hierarchy is not clear, there were headmen of districts, propaganda agents, initiates, and fanatic suicide squads (the *fidaᶜis*) who were ready to risk their lives to assassinate targets marked for death.

The Nizaris spread from Egypt to India, including Iran, Iraq, and Syria. Their strongholds were destroyed in the thirteenth century by the Mongols and by the Baybars, the Mamluk sultanate of Egypt. In 1834 the Qajar shah of Persia gave to Hasan ᶜAli Shah, the imam of the Nizaris, the title of agha khan. When trouble developed in 1840, Hasan ᶜAli Shah fled to India and settled in Bombay, which to this day is the headquarters of the movement.[14]

Succession to the title of agha khan is closed to all but family members and usually falls to the eldest son of the deceased agha khan. As leader and supreme head of the movement, the agha khan exerts tremendous influence both within and outside his community, often taking an active part in politics and social reform. Huge contributions are made to him, enabling him to fund cultural and charitable activities. His followers, mostly Nizaris, live today in India, central Asia, Iran, Syria, and East Africa.

From the ninth century to the eleventh century, Ismaᶜili teaching spread from Africa to India. For instance, the Mustaᶜlis survive today mainly in India, where they emigrated from Yemen in the sixteenth century. They represent the group of Ismaᶜili who broke off their association with the supporters of al-Nizar (the Nizaris) when al-Mustaᶜli succeeded al-Mustansir, the Ismaᶜili Fatimid caliph. They hold to the view that their imams ended when al-Amir, son of Mustaᶜli, died in 1130. Al-Amir is said to have left a son, the infant al-Tayyib, who disappeared and is therefore invisible. Little is known about the development of the Mustaᶜlis, except that they have fragmented even further into several small factions during the course of their history.

The Khojas are Hindu converts to Islam who generally follow Ismaᶜili doctrine. As might be expected, most of them live in central Asia, on the west coast of India, in the Punjab, and in East Africa. Most of them owe allegiance to the agha khan, but subdivisions have occurred. One group claims affinity with Imami Shiᶜis. Khojas in the Punjab do not recognize the agha khan as leader; instead they follow certain Sufi orders.

Several prominent Ismaᶜili thinkers are also credited with forming in the tenth century a secret society called the Brethren of Purity. This group published an encyclopedia entitled *The Epistles of the Brethren of Purity* in the hope of promoting a universal spirituality. The Persian Omar Khayyam (1050–1123), whose long poem the *Rubbaᶜiyyat* (Quatrains) brought him lasting fame, is said to have been an Ismaᶜili.

Though Ismaᶜilis made significant contributions to the literature and culture of the Islamic community, they do not now enjoy the power or influence they had in the past. But they still claim a number of adherents throughout the Islamic world.

Sufi (the Mystics)

The term *Sufi* is derived from the Arabic word *suf,* meaning "wool," and is applied to ascetics and mystics who once wore rough wool (as some still do) against their skin. The Sufi (mystical) movement developed as a reaction against dry Islamic legalism and the worldliness of an expanding and increasingly wealthy Muslim community.

The history of the Sufi movement is largely a history of individual mystics, though they share a number of characteristics. The movement is characterized by the scrupulous observance of divine law as stated in the Qur'an and, in the course of time, as specified in the traditional sayings of the prophet Muhammad. In addition, Sufis are credited with large-scale missionary activity all over the world, educating the masses and deepening the spiritual concerns of Muslims everywhere. The influence of the Sufis in the formation and development of Islamic society, particularly in the area of Muslim piety, is incalculable.[15]

The purpose of the Sufi is to seek union with God through ecstasy.[16] They specify two prerequisites: passing (*fana'*) from the conscious experience of passion and desire to the arrest of conscious thought; and then arriving (*baqa'*) to a conscious state of a continuous union with God. Sufis further distinguish between the "state," their avowed goal, and the "station," the means to the ends they seek. The former identifies divine gifts such as meditation with God; contemplation of God; tranquility in God's presence; love, fear, hope, and longing for God; intimacy with God; certainty of God; and nearness to God. The latter represents qualities to be applied "on the path" in arriving at a state of union. Such qualities include repentance, renunciation, poverty, abstinence, patience, contentment, and trust in God.

A Sufi master (*shaykh*) is an obligatory adjunct to an individual's search for union with God. A neophyte cannot begin without a master to guide him. The master, who must be absolutely obeyed, assists the individual seeker to pass through the stations and to arrive at a state of awareness of permanent union with God. Having arrived at this highest stage, the master invests the individual with the Sufi's patched cloak in recognition of his becoming a full-fledged member of the Sufi order.

The earliest Sufi members were ascetics who, during the expansion of the Islamic empire, looked back nostalgically to the simplicity of Islam in the days of the prophet Muhammad. As a form of social protest, they wore rough woolen clothing and renounced all worldly pleasures.

Early Sufi ascetics traveled far and wide within the Islamic empire laying the foundations of fraternal orders—groups centering on the teachings of a leader-founder. The religious ferment often associated with the founding of such orders was particularly strong in Basra, Iraq, and no single figure is more typical of it than Hasan al-Basri (642–728), who is regarded by Sufis as one of the first leading exponents of their sect.[17] Another Sufi of similar stature is Rabi'ah al-ʿAdawiyyah (d. 801), the famous woman saint of Basra, Iraq, whose ideal of love of God, detached from hope of heaven and fear of hell, developed into a mystical doctrine of love and grace fused into one.[18] Her sentiments are found in the often-quoted verses:

> I love Thee with two loves: love of my happiness and perfect love—to love Thee as is Thy due.[19]

All Sufis are ascetics insofar as they believe in the purification of the soul. But some of them began making a distinction between the process of attaining purification and its achievement: ecstatic emotional experiences, that is, a heightened awareness of God. During the ninth and tenth centuries, such Sufis attracted a notoriety which began to set them apart. Their heightened sensitivity resulted in ecstatic trances, which led them to attest that their souls had merged with God. In other words, the contemplation of God transcended and excluded all awareness of themselves so that they became conscious only of the reality of God. Music, chanting, dancing, or the recitation of poems were used to induce these experiences of sublime religious transcendence.

Friction between Sufis and legalist, orthodox Muslims culminated in the execution of the Sufi saint al-Hallaj (c. 857–922) in Baghdad, Iraq.[20] Al-Hallaj even succeeded in offending some fellow Sufis, not on account of his beliefs but because he ignored the Sufi tradition of secrecy or discretion and publicly proclaimed his ecstatic transcendental relationship and experience with God.

Al-Hallaj's offense, as far as traditional, legalist Muslims were concerned, was less related to Sufi beliefs (because they were already familiar with them) as it was to articulating them publicly. Orthodox Muslims accused al-Hallaj of heterodoxy. But what finally scandalized them was his ecstatic claim that "I am the truth" (*anaʾl-haqq*), a claim based on one of the ninety-nine names ascribed to God (see Qurʾan 20:114, and the claim of Jesus in John 14:6). He was publicly scourged for uttering such blasphemy, and when he refused to recant he was crucified and a series of persecutions against the Sufis followed. It is likely that al-Hallaj was unpopular among contemporaries, but later Sufis venerated him as a holy martyr whose only fault lay in his inability to keep secret the truth about reality.

Some Sufis who had been sympathetic to al-Hallaj fled to central Asia, where they were chiefly responsible for the conversion of the Turks to Islam. Sufis who submitted to persecution under Shiʿi or Sunni rule violated all the norms of Islamic society, rejected orthodoxy, and accused orthoprax Muslims of executing "God's lovers."

The intervention of al-Ghazali (1058–1111), a scholar who distinguished himself in all the legal, philosophical, and other studies of his time, occurred in the middle of all this confusion and hostility.[21] Considered one of the greatest figures in the religion of Islam, al-Ghazali was able to justify Sufism (mysticism) and to show that it was true in spirit and in form to orthodox Islamic faith and practice. In his great work *The Revival of the Religious Sciences* (*Ihyaʾ ʿUlam al-Din*), he interpreted orthodox Islamic law and theology with Sufi emphasis on religious experience, sincerity, and inner devotion. In the years that followed al-Ghazali's exegesis of Sufi theology, the administrators of Islamic law (*ulama*) and the Sufis drew closer together, though they never fully united. Each side conceded the important and necessary role that the other contributed to the Islamic community.

This courtship, however, was temporary. It ended when the Spanish Muslim Sufi Ibn ᶜArabi (d. 1240) expressed his monistic view that there is nothing but God, and the universe is merely his outward aspect.[22] His prolific writings express strange imagery which is basically antinomian (i.e., amoral or lawless) and asserts that if everything is God, then evil is only an illusion. Though the administrators of Islamic law again resisted his teachings, Ibn ᶜArabi made an extraordinarily lasting impression on later Muslims and non-Muslims (e.g., Dante, Ramon Lull, St. John of the Cross, and possibly Baruch Spinoza).

By the thirteenth century, the basic ideas of Sufism had fully permeated the entire world of Islam. The thirteenth century is usually identified as the golden age of Sufism, even though the Mongol invasions and the fall of the ᶜAbbasid dynasty had thrown the Islamic political scene into complete chaos. The figure that towers above all other Sufis during this period is Jalal al-Din ar-Rumi (1207–1273) of Bakh (in modern Afghanistan).[23] His greatest work is his didactic work of poetry, the *Masnavi* (or *Mathnavi*), an encyclopedia of mystical thought, second in importance only to the Qurᵓan. While it has little artistic unity, it contains poems of unquestioned genius, erudition, and profound religious feeling. Ar-Rumi's disciples formed the Mawlawi (or Mevlevi) brotherhood, an organization of "whirling dervishes" who sought ecstasy through sedate gyration (an elaborate dancing ritual) accompanied by music that was intended to represent the order of the heavenly spheres.[24]

Membership in this mystical community was at first restricted to a number of masters, each with a few disciples. The foundation of monastic establishments, or rather Sufi orders (*tariqa*), was laid by the Persian ᶜAbd al-Qadir al-Jilani (1077–1166) in Baghdad, Iraq.[25] Others soon followed, and during the thirteenth century different orders proliferated, some representing regional and some empire-wide constituencies with local chapters. Thus Sufism ceased to be the path of the few and instead influenced the masses. Now there were two kinds of membership: the initiates or the inner circles, and the associates or laymen, who occasionally visited centers of Sufi activity. Rules, initiation ceremonies, and prescribed orders of ritual, particularly the practice of repetitive formulas of prayer (*dhikr*, meaning "remembrance"), were elaborated for initiates. Rigorous training, spartan accommodation, and long periods of seclusion preceded the ceremony of investiture by the master. The ceremony represented a culmination of events by which the adept became part of the *silsilah*—the chain of mystical succession and transmission leading back to the Prophet himself.

Each Sufi order developed unique characteristics of initiation, period and method of instruction, performance of ritual practices, social obligations, missionary activities, and political affiliations. Some perfected techniques they claimed induced states of ecstasy unmatched by any other order, though detractors might argue that the ends did not always justify the means. Some induced ecstasy by concentration upon fixed parts of the body, others through contemplation only, and still others through music and dance.

Casual observers might conclude that such rituals had more in common with abnormal psychology than with religion. Scholars of Islam, however, unless they are totally unsympathetic to emotional expressions, do not fail to note that descriptions of Sufi ecstasy suggest forms of worship that exemplify the highest order of absolute love and devotion. Whatever the verdict of modern analysts, the historical evidence suggests that no matter what the form to which they subscribed, Sufi orders were responsible for bringing together different shades of spiritually interested Muslim members, giving them an emotional outlet otherwise denied by the strict orthodox elements of the community.

The number of individual Sufi orders throughout the Muslim world is so large that it is impossible to list them all here.[26] Only a few of the more important ones are mentioned here. The most widespread and probably the oldest of all existing Sufi orders is the Qadiri, named after ʿAbd al-Qadir al-Jilani (1077–1166), a native of Iraq. His adherents are scattered all over the Islamic world from west Africa to India, while his tomb in Baghdad is still considered a holy site for pilgrimage.

Another important but far less widespread Sufi order is the Suhrawardi, named after the mystic ʿUmar al-Suhrawardi (d. 1236) of Persia. His strict and rigorous spiritual discipline did not attract a large following, but near the end of the fourteenth century it inspired a related order, known as Khalwati, founded by ʿOmar al-Khalwati (d. 1398). This order spread into Turkey and Egypt, and later a disciple of the order of Khalwati introduced his own version of it, the Tijani order, in northwest Africa.

Discipleship in the Sufi world is often based on a purely spiritual experience, unrelated to a historical evolution of concepts or a tradition passed on from one generation to the next in a documented sequence of genealogical links. Such was the case with Ahmad al-Badawi (also called Sayyid al-Badawi) (1199–1276) of Egypt, founder of the Ahmadi or Badawi order.[27] He has been venerated among Egyptian Muslims as the greatest saint, for no apparent reason except that he enjoyed stargazing and meditating in absolute silence for long stretches at a time. Still other Sufi orders were associated with the name of a disciple of a well-known master, or even the disciple of a disciple of a famous master.

Throughout the centuries most Sufi orders also performed useful social services in the Islamic community. In some areas they fulfilled functions such as civil defense, public security, and public relief. In others they organized political revolutions, spiritual revivalism, and social rehabilitation. Few religious groups among the religions of the world have attempted to teach what the Sufis succeeded in communicating to ordinary people: mysticism. As a result, almost every male Muslim feels himself to be a link in the spiritual chain of the Sufi orders, attempting to implement its ideals in modern society.

The heyday of the Sufi movement lasted for six centuries, from the thirteenth to the nineteenth, but from the start it was subject to conservative elements within Islam that placed limits on its most extreme practices and unorthodox principles. Throughout the long history of the Sufis, these practices were subjected to severe criticism and in some regions were strictly banned. Then, at the turn of the twentieth century, Sufi orders faced two new and threatening challenges: the rise of Islamic puritanical movements and the introduction of modern technology. Today, Sufi orders in many Islamic countries are on the decline and those individuals who persevere in preserving the spiritual heritage of each surviving order do so by justifying mystical experience on the grounds that it conforms to modern science and to pristine Islam.

Other Groups

Besides the three major Muslim groups and subgroups, there are other groups throughout the Muslim world that significantly differ from the rest in their beliefs and practices. Some, for instance, assert doctrines that are in sharp contrast to Islamic values. Others have their own collection of sacred writings and adhere to their own legal systems. Still others perform religious duties that are quite distinct from established Muslim principles. Some include elements from other religions, while a few consider their leaders to be divine beings. But they all derive from one common source: Islam.

Here an important question arises: Should such groups be considered part of the worldwide Muslim community, the *ummah*? If yes, then they should be mentioned in books like this one. If not, then they should be omitted.

The opinion of Western scholars is sharply divided on this matter. So too is the opinion of Muslim leaders. Some countries victimize such groups, others tolerate them, a few ignore them. In order for the reader to judge, we shall briefly survey seven of these groups that share a common Islamic heritage but at the same time drastically diverge from established Islamic principles. These seven are: Murjiʾah, Khariji, Nusayri, Druze, Yezidi, Bahaʾi, and Black Muslims.

Murjiʾah

The Murjiʾites have long since passed into history, but their influence on Islamic thought has been great and lasting. Originally they were a political group that considered the Umayyads as usurpers, but their members refused to fight over the issue. Moreover, Murjiʾites argued that a Muslim remained a Muslim no matter what the individual did. To them, profession of the Islamic faith was justification enough for accepting individuals to the Islamic community. They preferred to defer or postpone (Murjiʾah means "one who postpones") judgment on fellow Muslims in the conviction that such pronouncements were God's prerogative on the day of judgment. This meant that they refused to judge anyone guilty of grave sin (polytheism being the exception) or to consider a ruler unworthy of his office. Anyone who affirmed his faith in Islam by confessing belief in God and of his prophet Muhammad was considered by the

Murji'ah to have an indelible faith, even if his deeds did not confirm it. The sect did not survive into the twentieth century.

Khariji (pl. Khawarij)

Few Khawarij exist in the world today. They are distinguished from other Muslims by the strict puritanism that is as much a part of them now as it has always been. They denounce celibacy, mysticism, music, gambling, the use of tobacco, and concubinage except with the express permission of a wife or wives. In addition, intermarriage with Muslims outside their sect is discouraged. They have their own collection of sacred writings and their own Tradition (Hadith), they maintain their own legal system, and they adhere to a set of principles steeped in antiquity. They assert that mere profession of faith (shahadah) does not make a person a Muslim unless it is accompanied by good works and righteous deeds. They insist, furthermore, that anyone found guilty of grave sin is considered an unbeliever, an apostate, who needs to sincerely repent and perform public penance. Failure to make restitution places the guilty beyond the pale. They cease to be Muslims and the duty of a Khariji is to vindicate the truth by killing them.

Khawarij believe that all Muslims have absolute equality in the eyes of God. The conclusion they draw from this premise is that the only prerequisites required for leadership of the Islamic community are righteous character and piety regardless of color, race, or sex. It is a notion that stands in sharp contrast to the positions held by both the Shi'is and the Sunnis, who eventually hunted them down to virtual extinction. Self-destructive policies of confrontation have given way in recent times to moderate forms of self-discipline and dissent expressed through the publication of works of scholarship and their own journals.

The 'Ibadi Khawarij represent one of the moderate forms. The Berber 'Ibadis once maintained a separate state in central Algeria from 761 to 908, when it was destroyed by the Fatimids. Today, descendants of the 'Ibadi survive in Algeria, Libya, Tunisia, Oman, east Africa, and Zanzibar Island.

Nusayri

The Nusayris are another Shi'i sect found mainly in Syria. They are named after Abu Shu'ayb Muhammad ibn Nusayr, who announced in 859 that he was the bab ("gate," signifying "forerunner") of the tenth Shi'i imam 'Ali al-Hadi. Their belief is based on a triad of concepts which are extensions of Isma'ili doctrine.[28] This triad consists of belief in a "divine essence," identified with 'Ali; belief in a "name," identified with the prophet Muhammad; and belief in a "door," identified with Salman—a Persian slave who converted to Islam through the prophet Muhammad and is venerated by Shi'is, Sunni, and Sufi alike.

Nusayris also believe in a doctrine that is quite foreign to Islam: metempsychosis or the transmigration of souls, which is the belief that souls enter a different body at death. The doctrine excludes women (who are presumed to have no souls) with the exception of Fatimah (the Prophet's daughter), to whom Nusayris give the masculine name of Fatir (creator).

In matters of ritual, Nusayris observe strict secrecy, degrees of initiation, and certain Christian festivals and saints' days. They follow the practice of dissimulation or concealment of faith, since they are often targets of persecution.

Druze

The name Druze is associated with a Persian Muhammad al-Darazi, about whom little is known except that he lent his name to a group of sectarian Shiʿis. The movement, however, dates from the rule of Fatimid caliph al-Hakim, who in 1021 proclaimed that he was a divine incarnation, then disappeared shortly after a palace coup. (He is still believed to be in occlusion; that is, hidden with the promise of return.) However, the mastermind behind the Druze organization was Hamza ibn ʿAli, a Persian whose teachings are incorporated into several letters that along with other writings represent Druze scriptures.

The Druzes now occupy mountainous regions of Lebanon and Syria, with an estimated population of 200,000. Intermarriage with outsiders is strictly prohibited, and new adherents are not actively sought. The sect has remained for centuries a close-knit community and has developed a distinct racial identity.[29]

Two main classes may be distinguished among the Druzes: the learned (or knowledgeable) and the ignorant (or inexperienced). High moral character, daily religious exercises, and distinct clothing featuring white turbans distinguish the former group. The most learned and pious among them are considered spiritual chiefs (shaykhs), from whom each district or village appoints its head. The latter are subordinate to the learned group.

Druzes do not observe the Islamic injunction to fast and make pilgrimages. Perhaps because these are basic Islamic doctrines, the Druze practice dissimulation, disguising their identities whenever there is danger of persecution. Within their ranks they demand recognition of al-Hakim as lord, and submission to his orders. They also hold to the idea of the transmigration of souls. Severing contaminating contact with unbelievers and infidels, speaking the truth, and mutual defense are the cardinal principles to which every Druze faithfully adheres.

Yezidi

The Yezidi (Yazidi) are mainly a Kurdish sect spread across western Asia, the area presently occupied by Turkey, Syria, Iraq, and Iran.[30] They are often called devil worshippers by their detractors, but they call themselves worshippers of God. They use their own Kurdish language in worship, but possess two sacred books in Arabic: *The Black Book* and *The Book of Revelation*. Their religion is an Islamic adaptation incorporating Jewish, Zoroastrian, Christian, and Manichaean elements. They believe that God is the creator of the universe and that the Peacock Angel (*Malak Ta'us*) carries out God's will as his active agent. This angel is represented by bronze and iron peacocks, seven of which are connected with seven angels who assisted God in creation.

Yezidis invoke the Peacock Angel in prayer. They also perform the rituals of circumcision and baptism, though the former is optional. The ritual of fasting is observed for three days in December. The rite of pilgrimage is made in September by visiting the tomb of ʿAdi ibn Musafir (d. 1162), who is considered to have become divine. In matters of belief, the decisions of their chief spiritual leaders (*shaykhs*) are considered infallible. Marriage outside the sect is strictly forbidden and adultery is punished with death. One becomes a Yezidi only by birth.

Baha'i

In 1844, an Iranian Shiʿite Muslim named Mirza ʿAli Muhammad (1819–1850) declared that he was the long-awaited twelfth imam and assumed the title of Bab. Gathering around him a group of disciples who called themselves Bab'is, the Bab launched a movement for religious and social reform. Within a short time, the movement had gained so much momentum that both religious and political forces in Iran took drastic counteraction. The Bab was publicly executed on July 9, 1850, and many of his followers were eliminated through either imprisonment or execution. Before the Bab died, however, he foretold of the appearance of a leader greater than he to carry on the work of establishing a universal religion. Thus, his remaining disciples were sustained by the hope that all was not lost.

Among the group of survivors was a man named Mirza Husayn ʿAli Nuri (1817–1892), the eldest son of the minister of state, who, by virtue of his family connections, was spared the fate of many of his companions. He had abandoned his family name and assumed the title Baha'u'llah ("Glory of God").

In 1852, an event occurred that affected the future course of the movement. One of the Bab's followers attempted to assassinate the Iranian shah, an act that provoked further persecution against the Bab'is. Baha'u'llah was imprisoned and later exiled to Baghdad, then under the jurisdiction of the Turkish government. During that period, which lasted approximately ten years, Baha'u'llah made an unexpected announcement: the one whose coming had been foretold by their master, the Bab, was none other than he, Baha'u'llah. All those who recognized him as the chosen of God, the promised one of all the prophets, were to follow him. Except for a few who remained unconvinced, the company of Bab'is recognized him as the fulfillment of the prophecy and from that day called themselves Baha'is.[31]

Baha'u'llah appointed his eldest son, Abbas Effendi, as his successor. In assuming leadership of the movement, Abbas Effendi changed his name to Abdul Baha ("Servant of Baha," or "Servant of Glory"). He invoked all Baha'is to spread Baha'u'llah's message—the unification of humankind through the medium of Baha'i—to the four corners of the world. Baha'u'llah's grandson, Shoghi Effendi, assumed leadership of the Baha'i faith, and he was the last in the direct line of succession from Baha'u'llah. Today, the Baha'i movement seeks converts throughout the world, irrespective of race, color, language, or religion.

The written works of the Bab, Baha'u'llah, Abdul Baha, and Shoghi Effendi make up the sacred literature of the Baha'is. Among the hundreds of writings of Baha'u'llah, two books are regarded as especially important by Baha'is: the *Kitab-i-Aqdas* (*Most Holy Book*) and the *Kitab-i-Iqan* (*Book of Certitude*). Baha'is consider both books to be no less divinely inspired than the sacred writings of other religions.

In matters of faith, the Baha'i teaching assimilates beliefs and practices from other previous faiths, Eastern and Western, extant and extinct. In addition, it adumbrates elements of modern science. Prophets such as Abraham, Moses, Zoroaster, Krishna, Buddha, Jesus, Muhammad, and Baha'u'llah are considered by the Baha'is to be "manifestations of God." Few obligations regulate the lives of the Baha'is. One duty is to pray. Another obligation is to fast. A third obligation relates to marriage. Monogamy is the rule, and a couple may marry only after the consent of their parents. Finally, Baha'i parents are under a religious obligation to educate their children. The use of narcotics and intoxicants of any kind, except for medicinal purposes, is strictly prohibited.

Black Muslims

The Black Muslims are a Muslim group among blacks in America whose original name was Nation of Islam. The founder was Elijah Muhammad (originally Elijah Poole), but the dynamic leadership of Malcolm X (originally Malcolm Little) brought the organization to international prominence. Another person who was instrumental in the development of the group was Wallace D. Fard, who spoke of the "lost-found" nation of Islam. Before his disappearance in 1953, he had established an effective organization called the Black Muslims of America.[32]

Elijah Muhammad's teachings reflect Muslim and Christian elements.[33] He stated that God had come to the United States in the person of Fard, who appointed him as a prophet. God is the only eternal being; hence, humans do not attain immortality. Heaven and hell are simply two conditions on earth which reflect one's state of mind, moral condition, and actions. The human race was originally black, but a genius called Yakub created people of all shades, including whites. White races are inherently wicked and will be overthrown by the blacks when they usher in their new civilization by the year 2000.[34]

Black Muslims are obligated to attend temple meetings twice weekly unless permission has been granted to the contrary. Whites are excluded. Prayers are in English and occasionally in Arabic. Worship includes readings from both the Qur'an and the Bible. Members are also expected to observe the Muslim rite of prayer five times daily, though it is not strictly enforced. Cleanliness, personal dignity, and the respect of males for females are strongly emphasized. Alcohol, tobacco, drugs, cosmetics, sexual immorality, dancing, gambling, and similar frivolous abuses of leisure are strictly prohibited. Certain dietary laws are also followed.[35]

Malcolm X was a well-known exponent of the movement and Elijah's second-in-command.[36] After visiting Mecca and experiencing Islam in Islamic lands, he returned to the United States to found his own movement. He was not able to reconcile his newfound insights into Islam with Elijah's teachings and was embarrassed by the non-Muslim practices in Elijah's movement.[37] Malcolm X was murdered in 1965, but Black Muslims in the United States are still active and membership is showing signs of growth.

Wallace Warid Deen Muhammad assumed the leadership after the death of his father Elijah Muhammad in 1975. He renamed the movement the American Muslim Mission and persuaded its members to abandon all eccentricities and adopt "authentic" Islam in its entirety. To this end, members of the American Muslim Mission have gone to study at traditional Islamic learning centers, such as al-Azhar in Cairo and the Islamic University of Medina.

A small group still retains the previous name of "Nation of Islam" and maintains its old policies.

4 Qur'an

Divine Revelation

The Qur'an (also written Koran, meaning "Recitation") is, for Muslims, the final revelation of God (Allah) and as such contains his divine message to humanity as revealed to his prophet Muhammad. This divine communication is seen as the final stage in a long series of divine messages conducted through specific messengers or prophets chosen by God, starting with Adam and ending with Muhammad. In other words, God addressed humanity through chosen individuals to proclaim to them the happy consequences of worshipping and following him and to warn them against the terrible consequences of disobeying him. In each case, however, the message was altered and falsified by the perversity of later generations. Finally, God revealed his message in a definitive form to the prophet Muhammad through the archangel Gabriel. The Qur'an, then, is the infallible message or speech of God.

Besides the Qur'an, Muslims believe that four other books (external to the Qur'an and not part of it) also originated from God and are to be regarded as holy scripture.[1] These four Holy Books are inscribed on eternal tablets in heaven, the exact copies of which have been sent down by God at different periods to different prophets. In chronological order of divine revelation, these four Holy Books are:

- *The Scrolls* (*Suhuf*) Ten scriptures (now lost or untraceable) revealed to the Prophet Abraham (Qur'an 2:129; 53:39).
- *The Torah* (*Taurat*) The Holy Book revealed to the prophet Moses (Qur'an 2:50; 3:2; 5:72).
- *The Psalms* (*Zabur*) The Holy Book revealed to the prophet David (Qur'an 4:163).
- *The Gospels* (*Injil*) The Holy Book revealed to the prophet Jesus (Qur'an 3:2; 5:72; 57:26).

Except for the first book, which has been lost, all the others, including the Qur'an, have the same purpose: to reform humanity. Whenever the faith of people wavered or lapsed, God sent a fresh message or revelation through chosen prophets. On each occasion the message or the divine revelation contained in the message or book was adulterated by human imperfections. The Qur'an, therefore, restores the eternal truth for all time and for all humanity. That is to say, the imperfections contained in the previous books are all resolved and cleared up in the Qur'an once and for all. In a sense, then, the Qur'an is God's final revelation—the perfection and culmination of all truth—sent through his angel to Muhammad for all human beings. This is the cardinal Islamic view regarding the Qur'an.

Consider the following quotations from the Qur'an:

He [God] has sent down to you [Muhammad] the Book (Qur'an 3:5)

This Qur'an could not have been invented apart from God (Qur'an 10:37)

Behold We [God] have revealed to you [Muhammad] an Arabic Qur'an (Qur'an 42:5; 43:1)

Muslims have never questioned the authenticity of the Qur'an as the speech of God, though controversies have raged among Muslims as to whether the Qur'an is the created or uncreated words of God, and also whether every letter or only the message as a whole is the speech of God.[2] Again, Muslims insist that the Qur'an was revealed in Arabic (Qur'an 43:1); according to pious Muslims, therefore, the words and chapters are inimitable. Consequently, Muslims have deprecated, if not prohibited, any attempts to render the Qur'an in any language other than Arabic, since to translate it is tantamount to profaning the sacred language God chose as his instrument of communication.

Arabic, then, is an integral part of the Qur'anic revelation. It is a sacred language whose very sounds and utterances play a positive role in the ritual acts of Islam. And yet there are many translations of the Qur'an in various languages done by Muslims and non-Muslims, all of which are considered by pious Muslims to convey the meaning of the Qur'an, but are not in any sense the speech of God itself.[3]

Muslims and even non-Muslim scholars of Islam universally acclaim the Qur'an as representative of the purest and most elegant forms of the Arabic language. The Qur'an is, in fact, the language model for teaching Arabic. It may be emulated but it cannot be matched. The belief of orthodox Muslims that the Arabic in the Qur'an is inimitable by any human pen justifies their conclusion that the Qur'an constitutes a permanent miracle so conclusive that it cannot fail to convince the world of its divine origin. The prophet Muhammad himself, it is said, cited this miracle as evidence of the authority of his mission, and publicly challenged the most eloquent men of his time to write even a single chapter comparable to the beauty and clarity of Qur'anic Arabic (Qur'an 2:23).

Among adherents, the unexcelled literary style of Qur'anic Arabic is one of the proofs of its divine origin (Qur'an 12:2). Another is its form and substance, the reiterated tradition that God "sent down an Arabic Qur'an" (Qur'an 12:2; 20:112; 41:1; 42:5; 43:1). Incomparable style and an indisputable tradition confirm the conviction of all Muslims (as they did the prophet Muhammad himself) that the Qur'an is a faithful and unalterable reproduction of an original preserved in heaven, sent down in sections of manageable length and in relation to the circumstances of the moment (Qur'an 17:106).

Fixed Scripture

The Qur'an in comparison with more voluminous accretions of sacred writings is short. It is slightly shorter than the New Testament and is divided

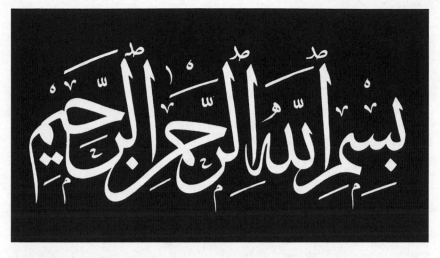

Inscription from the Qur'an

The inscription in Arabic reads: "In the name of God, the gracious, the merciful." This statement, which is found in the opening line of every chapter in the Qur'an, is inscribed in many mosques. *Courtesy of MSA Services.*

into 114 chapters, arranged in order of length from the longest to the shortest, except for a short opening prayer in chapter one—a chapter not only held in great veneration by Muslims but also regarded as the quintessence of the entire Qur'an itself. Here is its content:

> In the name of God, the beneficent, the merciful.
>
> Praise be to God, Lord of all the universe; the most merciful, Master of the Day of judgment. We worship Thee only and to Thee we beg assistance. Direct us in the right way, in the way of those whom Thou hast been gracious—not of those against whom Thou art incensed, nor of those who go astray. (Qur'an 1)

Pious Muslims accept the tradition that the Qur'an is a record of what the prophet Muhammad said while in a state of ecstatic seizure, which, also according to tradition, induced severe physical pain.[4] It was a record that was transcribed over years rather than days. The divine revelation known as the Qur'an transmitted through the prophet Muhammad took some twenty years to deliver. Starting some time between 610 and 612 Muhammad received periodic divine revelations, or messages from God, until his death in 632. At first they alarmed him, but some of his relatives took him seriously and soon he attracted a small following of adherents. They memorized and documented the divine messages delivered to Muhammad on makeshift material, such as palm leaves, fragments of pottery and, according to traditional accounts, on the shoulder blades of camels. Muhammad's death closed the era of the revelations. To this day Muslims regard Muhammad as the "seal of the prophets," that is to say, the last prophetic voice to close the series of revelations with final authority.

After 632, people who had been close to Muhammad began collecting whatever revelatory materials had survived. Such collections may have been made during the caliphates of Abu Bakr and ʿUmar, but the definitive editing of the Qurʾan was carried out during the reign of Caliph ʿUthman (644–655). A committee was set up to gather all documents and check all oral traditions related to the Prophet. This work resulted in an official version of Muhammad's teachings consisting of the collection of different texts into one single corpus, henceforth called the Qurʾan, and regarded as the speech of God, or the Holy Book.

The structure of the book, like the Bible, comes in chapters, each of which is called a *surah* (a "row"). The *surahs* are composed of verses, each of which is called an *ayah* (a "sign"). The verses often rhyme, but they are not the verses of poetry. The chapters are arranged in roughly descending order of length and are usually named by some catchword appearing in the text. Thus, the second chapter is called "The Cow" because of a reference to a sacrifice of a cow which Moses demanded of the Israelites; chapter three is entitled "Ali Imran" because the family of Imran is mentioned; chapter four is called "Women," and so on.

There are some puzzling features: cases of interpolation; trivial dislocations; omissions that render the sense unintelligible; material in more than one style; alternative versions of the same passage in different parts of the Qurʾan; and God appearing in the first and third persons in the same sentence. Whatever those phenomena mean, they indicate some kind of editing.

Memorization and Recitation

The head of every chapter in the Qurʾan (except the ninth, which is considered a continuation of the eighth) is prefaced by the following auspicatory statement: "In the name of God, the beneficent, the merciful." This represents a distinguishing characteristic of all books and writings by Muslims and is placed at the beginning as a duty of piety.

The following statement made in a letter by Zaka Ullah, an Indian Muslim leader, to his Christian friend Charles Freer Andrews illustrates what the Qurʾan means in terms of simple, contemporary piety. "You will never understand this power and warmth of religion among us [Muslims] until you can feel in your heart the poetry and music of the noble Qurʾan." Indeed, the chanting of the Qurʾan is the primary music of Islam. It is the soul of Islam and is reflected in the speech of all faithful Muslims. Muslim piety and even scholarship demand memorization and recitation of the Qurʾan. The reason for this is simple. The Qurʾan is, first and foremost, a scripture to be confessed by rehearsing its contents. Of course, the Qurʾan is also a storehouse for theology and law, a blueprint for society. But the fundamental characteristic of Muslim piety and faith is vocal participation in the articulation of Qurʾanic content. Indeed the divine injunction is "Recite the Qurʾan" (Qurʾan 73:20f.). Hence, the pledge of true dis-

Illumination of the Qurʾan

Calligraphy and text illumination of the Qurʾan are considered by many Muslims as pious acts. *Courtesy of Turkish Tourism and Information Office.*

cipleship lies in recruiting the memory and the voice. Silent assent is not a witness to Muslim piety or faith.

There are several forms of Qurʾanic recitation, each determined in measure by the demands of Arabic vowel forms, and yet there is a single tonality in any recitative pattern. In fact, like a virtuoso singing an aria, a skilled reciter of the Qurʾan can reduce an Arabic-speaking audience to helpless tears.[5]

The primacy of recitation is based both on divine injunction and on the experience of the prophet Muhammad himself. Tradition states that on the night God was to honor Muhammad with his mission, the angel Gabriel appeared to Muhammad with an inscribed brocade and said:

"Recite!"

"What shall I recite?" replied Muhammad.

In reply, the angel only pushed the brocade more closely under his eyes and repeated, "Recite!"

"But what shall I recite?" asked Muhammad.

For the third time the angel pushed the brocade into his face so violently that it almost smothered him and said, "Recite!"

Overtaken by fear, Muhammad replied again, "But what shall I recite?"

Then the angel said, "Recite! In the name of your Lord who created; created man from blood clots. Recite! Your Lord is the most Beneficent; who taught by the pen, taught man what he knew not!" (Qur'an 96:1–5).[6]

The divine command to Muhammad was to "recite." Since then, Muslims have obeyed this divine command by reciting the contents of the Qur'an, which literally means "recitation."

"Recitation" of the Qur'an in Islam is equivalent to a statement of "faith" in Christianity. Hence, the primary sign of a true Muslim is recitation of the Qur'an. Tradition ascribes the following sayings to the prophet Muhammad, sayings that serve as a reinforcement to the habit of recitation:[7]

> If any man recites the Qur'an and memorizes it, God will cause him to enter Paradise and will grant him the right to intercede successfully for ten people of his household, all of whom deserve Hell Fire.

> The best man among you is he who learns the Qur'an and teaches it.

> Learn the Qur'an, recite it and sleep.

> The most excellent act of worship is the reciting of the Qur'an.

Contents of Divine Message

Besides providing a rich, varied, and abiding source for strict memorization and recitation, the Qur'an is warning, guidance, criterion, and mercy. Its subject is human beings; its theme is the exposition of reality; its aim is an invitation to humanity to accept God's guidance in the "straight" path (Qur'an 1:5). Unlike the multiple authorship of most other scriptures, the Qur'an is the product of one man's revelations. Though references to topics such as theology, jurisprudence, science, and history are scattered throughout the Qur'an and appear incoherent, the sense of divine claim and authority, the dignity of human existence, the folly of human perversity, the impending day of judgment and destiny, the eternal condition of bliss or doom, and the reality of God's mercy are all dominant themes.[8]

Attempting to trace the sources and development of the religious ideas expounded in the Qur'an seems like a rational and apposite task to non-Muslim scholars. They have postulated some Jewish and Christian (mainly Nestorian Syriac) sources with some Arabian additions, and they have identified problems that so far defy clear solutions. To Muslim exegetes, such questions are not only meaningless but blasphemous, because the Qur'an is God's word.[9] A search for sources or the channels through which Qur'anic ideas reached Muhammad is regarded as sacrilegious, not simply futile. The Qur'an is the repository of God's ultimate teachings and demands. As such, it proclaims the existence of the one and only God, Lord and creator of the universe, the all-wise, the all-just, the all-compassionate, the all-merciful, the all-benevolent, the omnipotent, the omniscient, and the omnipresent. Consider the following statement:

God is He that created the heavens and the earth, and what between them is, in six days, then seated Himself upon the Throne. He directs the affair from heaven to earth, then it goes up to him in one day, whose measure is a thousand years of your counting. He is the knower of the unseen and the visible, the All-Mighty, the All-Compassionate, who has created all things well. And He originated the creation of man out of clay, then He fashioned his progeny of an extraction of mean water, then He shaped him, and breathed His spirit in him. (Qurʾan 32:4–5)

Next, the Qurʾan confirms the impending day of reckoning, an affirmation that was received by Muhammad's fellow citizens with profound disbelief and scornful sarcasm. The attraction of paradise and the fear of hell are graphically described in the Qurʾan because, within the cosmic order, the moral order of human beings assumes a central point of divine concern. According to the Qurʾan, the moral dualism in human nature gives rise to moral tensions and struggles (Qurʾan 91:8; 70:19–35). "Seek honor and reject dishonor" (Qurʾan 3:106) is the ethical injunction of the Qurʾan for all humanity. In fact, the one and only demand in the entire Qurʾan enjoins the exercise of moral and ethical judgment. Social and economic justice follow as a result of human moral order.

In pursuance of this moral order, the Qurʾan emphasizes the abiding importance of five duties: confession of faith, prayer, almsgiving, fasting, and pilgrimage. More will be said about those religious duties later. Here they are mentioned to indicate what measures the Qurʾan prescribes for the implementation of moral law and spiritual values.

This paramount emphasis on moral law and order leaves some Christian readers with the impression that the Qurʾanic God is watchful, frowning, and punitive, an interpretation similar to the view of some Muslim legalists who think of God as chief judge demanding socio-political justice. Regardless of the relevance of these assessments, the Qurʾan, with the same insistence that it enjoins disciplined adherence to a moral order, also condemns lack of trust in the mercy of God as a cardinal infidelity.

Apart from its doctrinal message, the Qurʾan also contains a narrative or historical content. The trials and vicissitudes of human beings—be they kings, prophets, people, or tribes—serve to illustrate essential themes: the moral dualism in human nature and God's interest in the betterment of human actions. Human beings, according to the Qurʾan, in spite of a legacy of ignorance and foolishness, are endowed with the most immense potential, with a "spirit from the *amr* [i.e., order, will, command] of God." The Qurʾan explains this human paradox in a characteristic way: humans are frail and falter, but as vice regents of God they possess an innate strength to transcend all evil.

An analogy in the Qurʾan illustrates this point vividly (Qurʾan 33:72). God offered "the trust" (i.e., the faith of Islam) to the heavens and the earth and the mountains, but creation rejected it. Only humans volunteered to receive it. And yet they are unable to fulfill their commitment and obey the law which they accepted. Thus, human beings are foolish and unfaithful in not considering the consequence of their disobedience and indifference. Nevertheless, the nature

and content of God's *amr* with reference to humanity is such that it can trans-
form moral tensions into creative action. In other words, the *amr* that is with
God is so sure, so definite, and so powerful that it imbues selected human beings, who are charged with and impelled by messages influencing the destiny
of humanity. Such select human beings are considered prophets. Muhammad
is the final prophet and the Qur'an the ultimate, definitive message of God to
humanity.

The Qur'an also contains some important legal proscriptions. For instance,
drinking alcohol and gambling are banned on the grounds that both "are the
works of the devil" (Qur'an 5:93). Polygamy is strictly regulated to a maximum
of four wives, provided that husbands can do justice to all. If they cannot, they
may marry only one woman (Qur'an 4:3). Marriage has no sacramental status
in Islam; it is simply a contractual relationship or agreement. The rights of the
bride require due status, contract, and provision before any sexual relations are
legitimately sanctioned.[10] Sexual relations outside marriage (except with slaves)
are prohibited. Fornicators and adulterers are to be punished (Qur'an 14:19–20;
17:34; 24:2–3). Incest is absolutely forbidden (Qur'an 4:26–28). Divorce is possible only after certain requirements are met (Qur'an 2:226). Inheritance laws
require that male inheritors receive twice as much as female inheritors (Qur'an
4:11–13, 175).

The list of legal injunctions and prohibitions is lengthy and includes the care
and honor of parents, prohibition against infanticide, rules governing murder
and vengeance, rights of orphans, property rights, trafficking, usury, and so on.
The most complete Qur'anic summary of these codes is Qur'an 17:22–39. In
the end, integrity, humility, and kindness are advocated as the attitudes that
should govern everyday living.

Like all scriptures, the Qur'an includes a great diversity of material and
touches on many themes. But it has but one essential message to humanity: be
pious. Over and over again and in a variety of ways, the Qur'an exhorts its hear-
ers to "command what is good and forbid evil" (Qur'an 3:110, 114; 7:157; 9:71,
112; 22:41; 31:17).[11] This Qur'anic injunction on piety has both a positive and
a negative mandate. Followers of Islam are to do good works in this world and
to engage in pious thoughts of the world to come. But they must also try to stop
or intervene any evil acts or thoughts executed by others in this world. To adopt
this activist or militant stance with regard to piety enshrines the pious ideal
among many followers of Islam.

The depth of the religious feelings inspired among pious Muslims by the
Qur'an and the veneration in which it is held are difficult to communicate to
non-Muslims. In some countries, even children under ten years of age are required to memorize the whole book, containing 6,239 verses, or 77,934 words.
In other places, it is common to require children to memorize selected passages
rather than the entire book. Adult Muslims frequently quote verses from the
Qur'an not only before performing a religious duty, but also before starting any
undertaking, including eating, entering a home or vehicle, traveling, or writing.
Some Muslims carry a copy of the Qur'an with them always as a reminder of

the existence of God so they will refrain from acts of disobedience. Others carry a copy of the Qur'an as a talisman against misfortune. Still others cite Qur'anic verses because of their proverbial nature. For instance, a favorite proverbial verse among all Muslims is "Covet not that which God has bestowed on some of you in preference to others" (Qur'an 4:36). Beggars often quote phrases from the Qur'an and are particularly fond of the following verse: "Good deeds drive away evil deeds" (Qur'an 11:116).

Qur'an and the Bible

The Qur'an, like the Bible, affirms the existence of a supreme being/God who is a transcendent, omnipotent, omniscient, eternal creator and who controls all human actions and historical processes. Again, the Qur'an, like the Jewish and Christian scriptures, asserts that human life consists of a single existence (in contrast to rebirth or reincarnation) and that human beings are morally accountable to God.

In addition, the Qur'an indicates a familiarity with a number of biblical characters, including Adam, Abraham, Ishmael, Isaac, Jacob, Moses, King David, the biblical prophets, and Jesus. Several passages in the Qur'an mention specifically that God revealed his message to Jews and Christians through those biblical individuals (Qur'an 5:48–51, 74; 22:16; 61:5–6; 62:1).

However, some non-Muslim scholars have been quick to point to discrepancies between Qur'anic references and statements that predate the Qur'an in the scriptures of the Christians and Jews, if only because the Qur'an claims to correct the imperfections of previous scriptures.[12] The controversies that have raged through the long centuries are too complicated for even a brief summary.[13] The point is that Muslims will not accept the authority of Jewish and Christian scriptures. They are largely irrelevant to Muslims in identifying the authentic words of God, which is documented definitively only in the Qur'an. For instance, Muslims, confirmed in their convictions by Qur'anic authority, reject as unthinkable—even gross and offensive—many dogmas that are central to Christianity.[14] The following concepts, common to most Christians, are rejected by Muslims:

- God as father
- The crucifixion, death, descent into hell, and resurrection of Jesus
- The Trinity
- Humanity's relationship to God as children or sons of God
- Hereditary depravity or original sin
- Sin as an offense to God
- The divinity of Jesus
- The duty of expiation
- The communion of saints

In addition to refuting fundamental Christian doctrines, the Qur'an is explicit about the position and role of Jews and Christians. If both Jew and Christian regard themselves as "children of God, his beloved ones," why then does God punish them for their sins (Qur³an 5:21)? Jews received the Torah from God (Qur³an 5:47), but because "they perverted its meaning, followed falsehood and broke the Covenant, God cursed them both here in this world and in the world to come" (Qur³an 5:16, 45, 46).

Muslims dismiss Christians on the basis of similar Qur³anic judgments, since their claim is as heirs to the old Jewish covenant renewed through Christ. As the Qur³an puts it, God "sent Jesus, son of Mary, confirming the Torah before him, and gave him the Gospel" (Qur³an 5:50). But Christians too "have forgotten part of what they were admonished and, except for a few, act treacherously" (Qur³an 5:16). Both Jews and Christians are guilty of "concealing and effacing" God's message (Qur³an 5:18). In fact both "utter perversions and conform to unbelievers" (Qur³an 9:30); their "rabbis and monks lust and greed for gold and silver" (Qur³an 9:34–35).

These Qur³anic judgments on Jews and Christians represent only a few of the many references to them. Ultimately the basic message to both groups is the same. It enjoins them to stop their stubborn disbelief and to accept "the Messenger" (i.e., Muhammad) and "the Book" (i.e., the Qur³an) of God (Qur³an 5:18, 23). All true believers of God are admonished "not to betake Jews and Christians as friends since they are evildoers, and whoever associates with them is one of them" (Qur³an 5:56).

Besides the admonitions against Jewish and Christian "disbelievers," the Qur³an has a denunciatory message for "idolaters." Worshippers of idols are "worse than disbelievers" (Qur³an 5:65), "unclean, unfit to enter the Holy Mosque" (Qur³an 9:28), and deserve "God's chastisement" (Qur³an 16:86–90) and "eternal fire" (Qur³an 9:17). In fact, the "disbelievers of the People of the Book and the idolaters, who are the worst of creatures, shall be in the fire of Hell forever" (Qur³an 98:5).

It must be noted, however, that the Qur³an enjoins Muslims to proclaim the truth to disbelievers, be they Jews, Christians, or idolaters. At no time is coercion to be used. Rather, Muslims are to remind, warn, and exhort disbelievers. The following passages from the Qur³an clearly state this position:

No compulsion is there in religion. (Qur³an 2:257)

Had your Lord willed, whoever is on earth would have believed. . . . Would you then compel the people, until they are believers? (Qur³an 10:99)

Say: "The truth is from your Lord; so let whosoever will believe, and let whosoever will disbelieve." (Qur³an 18:29)

Dispute not with the People of the Book save in the fairer manner . . . and say: we believe in what has been sent down to us, and what has been sent down to you; our God and your God is One. (Qur³an 29:45–46)

Then remind them! You are only a reminder; you are not charged to oversee them. (Qur³an 88:21)

To summarize, then, Muslims maintain that the Qur'an contains God's words as delivered to Muhammad during the twenty years of his public ministry. These divine messages were revealed through the angel Gabriel transmitted by him from an original, heavenly source. The present official recension of the text, arranged by ʿUthman, the third caliph, in no way negates or diminishes its divine authority. On the contrary, the Qur'an is accepted as matchless and incomparable. Its relevance is seen as universal—a guide for meeting every eventuality with fortitude. Hence, it is customary for Muslims to say the following prayer after completing the recitation of the Qur'an:

> O God, make the Qur'an a mercy for me, and set it for me as a model, a light, a guidance and a mercy.[15]

Although both the Qur'an and the Bible closely parallel each other on divine principles of dogma (such as the oneness of God, revelation, prophecy, scripture, and eschatological events), they differ in their understanding of doctrinal matters.[16] The doctrines that provoke conflict between Islam and Christianity are relatively few, but they are fundamental to the faith each represents. They are associated with four Christian dogmas, emphatically rejected or denied by Islam, namely: fatherhood of God, divinity of Christ, doctrine of original sin, and Christian scriptures.

Fatherhood of God

The term "fatherhood" in reference to God is abhorrent to Muslims because it denotes a physical relationship. To consider God as "father" is, for Muslims, to imply that God has a wife and an issue—both of which are blasphemous concepts. Nor are Muslims prepared to rationalize the term "father" in a metaphorical sense as "father of all humankind" because in Islamic teaching, human beings are chattels—creatures and servants of God, not his children. Nor do Muslims recognize the idea of God the "father" as presented in the Christian concept of the Trinity. Trinitarianism is flatly condemned in Islam on the grounds that it denies the sole worship of God. The severity of Qur'anic judgment on those who hold the doctrine of the Trinity is affirmed by Muhammad's exhortation addressed to Christians, people of the Book:

> O people of the Book; come let us make an agreement, that we serve none but God, and that we associate none with Him. (Qur'an 3:57)

The Qur'an makes a fundamental distinction between God and all else, including human beings who are finite creatures. God alone is infinite as well as absolute. To point to an individual such as Jesus, with delimitations of birthplace and birthdate, and then to say simply that he is God, or the second person in the godhead, is, according to the Qur'an, impossible and unpardonable. The Qur'anic judgment against those who uphold the doctrine of the Trinity is similar to its judgment against idolaters.

Those who say: "the Messiah, son of Mary, is God," are infidels. . . . Those who say: "God is the third of three," are infidels, for there is no God but One. . . . Those who associate anything with God, God will prohibit them from entering Paradise, and their refuge shall be Hell. (Qur'an 5:76–77)

To Muslims, the doctrine of the Trinity is absolutely repellent since in the end it negates the oneness of God—the only absolute reality. To associate another entity, be it Christ or the Holy Spirit, with the worship of God is akin to worshipping a multiplicity of gods—a form of polytheism. So fundamental is the unity of God to Muslims that to discredit it or to introduce an ambiguity or a paradox is reckoned as an unforgivable sin.

Divinity of Christ

So far as Islam is concerned, Jesus is recognized as one of the prophets with a divine mission who preceded Muhammad. Like all other prophets, Jesus was neither free from human frailty nor from physical want. Muslims accept Jesus as one who prayed in the wilderness and on the hillside, who conversed with people of all walks of life, and who entered the homes of the rich as well as of the poor. What makes Jesus unique in the minds of Muslims is not his life but the divine message he brought to humanity.

To Muslims, Jesus was one of the greatest moral teachers of the world, entrusted by God with both a universal message and a particular message. His universal mission was to rescue humanity from idol worship and from following false gods. His particular message was directed to his own people, the Jews. In the eyes of Muslims, Jesus was committed to "redeeming" the Jews from the bondage of the law (Torah), with its accretion of irrelevant rites and practices. In that sense, according to Muslims, Jesus was the "Messiah" of the Jews, but in all else he preached a universal message advocating humility, love, charity, compassion, purity, justice, and truth.

In addition, Islam recognizes the virgin birth of Jesus as the sign of messengership or prophethood (Qur'an 19:22f). In fact, the veneration of Mary, the mother of Jesus, is profound in Islam (Qur'an 3:37f; 19:16f). She is regarded as one of the four respected women—the other three being Khadijah, 'A'ishah, and Fatimah, the prophet Muhammad's wives and daughter, respectively.

Also, according to Muslim tradition, Jesus was at the last moment saved by divine intervention from an ignominious death (Qur'an 4:156f). Orthodox Muslims believe that Jesus was translated to heaven. Rationalist Muslims explain the disappearance of Jesus in non-miraculous terms. One view is that Jesus was rescued by supporters (not necessarily his disciples) who revered him and kept him concealed until the threat to his life had subsided, after which they sent him to the regions of the East (India?), where he pursued his universal mission and eventually died there peacefully.[17]

Thus, Islam accepts Jesus as one of the great universal teachers and the Messiah of the Jews. He is sent in particular to regenerate and to reform the backsliding Jewish race. His mission is then at once universal and particular. Consequently he is regarded as essentially a link in the chain of prophets (Qurʾan 5:50), whose teachings remained incomplete until God sent another messenger, Muhammad the Prophet, with similar human limitations to convey to humanity God's message for the last time.

On the other hand, the Christian doctrine of the divinity of Christ, in particular the dogmas of sonship, intercessor, crucifixion, and resurrection, have no place in Islam and are categorically denied in the Qurʾan (Qurʾan 5:76, 116; 9:30f; 10:69; 19:36, 91). Moreover, the notion of "justification by faith in Christ" is, according to Islamic thinkers, preposterous and utterly disastrous to human morals.[18] All such teachings, Muslims insist, were once borrowed from foreign, mainly pagan, sources and interpolated with the teachings of Jesus. In fact, Muslims see the idea of vicarious offering and atonement in Christianity as a survival of the concept of the appeasement of an angry god through the offering of a sacrifice—a concept which prevailed among the nations of antiquity. Accordingly, Muslims believe that "Islam represents true Christianity."[19]

Doctrine of Original Sin

The Christian doctrine of original sin is absolutely repudiated in Islam. Hereditary depravity and natural sinfulness (i.e., a sinful nature), as affirmed in Christianity, are emphatically denied. The Muslim cannot conceive how God, the almighty creator of the universe, could create a world fated to contamination by inherent human sinfulness. At no time can the Muslim interpret the story of Adam and Eve as reflecting the "fall" of human generations from God's grace. Unlike Christianity, Islam makes no attempt to derive from the Garden of Eden allegory any lessons or rules about human nature (Qurʾan 7:17-24; 19:115-124). Not only do Muslims reject the concept of original sin, they find it incomprehensible that almighty God is incapable of rooting out original sin except by offering himself through his only begotten son as a sacrifice to save humanity from eternal perdition. Such teachings are not simply unintelligible, but irreverent and insulting since they challenge the credibility of God's power and omnipotence.

Sin is generally represented in Islam as disobedience to God's command, not as a transgression against some divine standard. According to Islamic teaching, God demands obedience from humans and is ready to punish or pardon them according to their actions. God is absolutely unaffected by human deeds. He ordains what is to be done and what is to be avoided. It follows, therefore, that there is no absolute standard of right or wrong, because this would imply another authority alongside God—an impossible concept. Islam's preoccupation, then, is not so much with sin as with acts of disobedience.

The Qurʾan refers to Adam and Eve's act in eating from the fruit of the tree as "disobedience to God," for which they sought God's pardon and received his forgiveness (Qurʾan 7:18-24; 20:118-123). Moreover, Islamic tradition records that, according to the prophet Muhammad, every human being is born pure and religiously constituted. Two impulses, or inclinations, exist within each individual, prompting him or her to do good or evil. To those who seek God's help in resisting evil, God is ready to show his mercy and guide them on the right path. Hence, each individual from Adam onward is personally responsible for acts of disobedience.

Christian Scriptures

Muslims possess an instinctive sense of "Holy Books," the highest and greatest of which is the Qur²an. The Holy Book of Islam is revered as the product of God's message delivered directly to one human intelligence operating over a period of twenty-three years. In contrast, Muslims find the Christian Holy Book to consist of a varied collection of documents (including the Jewish Holy Book), all of independent authorship, spanning more than a thousand years. For Muslims, the Qur²an is the speech of God communicated to Muhammad (as a verbal transmission from heaven) and immediately transcribed for all to see and hear. It does not represent what others may have reported Muhammad to have said. Such reports constitute Tradition (*Hadith*) and are of lesser value.

Not so the Christian scriptures, they state. The writings of the Old Testament, the Gospels and the Epistles, all represent vicarious experiences retold second-, third-, or fourth-hand by their authors, with an additional reworking by redactors and editors. Within the New Testament are four Gospels, utterly incomprehensible to Muslims, since the Gospel entrusted by God to Jesus was reputedly a single book. The conclusion derived by Muslims is that because there are four, none of them are valid or reliable. In fact, the popular Islamic explanation is that the early Christian community lost the original Gospel received from Jesus and set about to make good the deficiency by substituting for one sequential account an intricately woven fabric of writings and traditions of many periods and different generations. Thus, according to Muslims, the teachings of Jesus might now be irretrievably lost to posterity were it not that their substance is reserved in the Qur²an. The Qur²an is also cited as the appropriate authority when it makes reference to people and events also chronicled in either the Old or New Testaments. Where there are differences or discrepancies between the biblical and Qur²anic accounts, Muslims explain the biblical record as some form of corruption. There is no better evidence of this than the words of the eminent twentieth-century scholar Sayyid Amir Ali:

> It is an article of faith among Muslims of all shades of opinion that the Christian Gospels in their present shape give an imperfect and erroneous view of the life and preachings of Jesus, and that his sayings have been garbled and tampered with according to the idiosyncrasies of individual compilers or the environments of the times and the requirements of factions and sects.[20]

Thus, differences between biblical and Qur²anic accounts are explained in terms of distortions in the present canonical biblical versions of the originals.

Those differences are particularly apparent in a comparison between the Qur'anic and New Testament presentation of Jesus. Muslims argue that Christians (and Jews) were not fit custodians of their own Holy Books and that they tampered with them in various ways, particularly by suppressing or obscuring what otherwise would have confirmed Islam and the true nature and identity of the Qur'an.[21]

Stated differently, the Islamic view is that the content of Christian scriptures does not match the content of the Qur'an; in their original form they did match. The original form is irrecoverable and corruption has occurred in the present versions. But this does not matter, because the Qur'an preserves the essentials of the original form. In this sense, the Qur'an is infallible and is the "true" word of God. All other scriptures ought to conform to the Qur'an, but they do not. Therefore, they are distortions, representing human interpolations rather than the direct words of God, and their integrity is questionable. Here is how the Qur'an states it:

> People of the Book, now there has come to you our [i.e., God's] messenger, making clear to you many things you have been concealing from the Book, and effacing many things. (Qur'an 5:18)

In modern times, some Muslims have quoted recent Western biblical criticism in support of their arguments challenging the authenticity of Christian scriptures. Few if any have contributed to or participated in discussions of biblical criticism that have occupied Christian thinkers for a long time. Nevertheless, educated Muslims are familiar with the works of biblical scholars. The problem is that some Muslims do not properly understand or simply disregard the preoccupation of Western scholars with inquiry based on science alone. They accept any evidence (revealed or suggested by Western research) that throws doubt on the authenticity or accuracy of Christian scripture. Muslims are quick to assume that Christians themselves dispute the validity of their own scriptures. Despite such misunderstandings, the Muslim charge against Christians is quite clear: they have failed to preserve the original revealed words of God, substituting for it a spurious "word of God" reworked by redactors and editors.

5   Sunnah, Hadith, and Shariᶜah

Sunnah

From the very beginning up to the present day, the words and actions (*sunnah,* trodden path) of the prophet Muhammad have served as the ideal model for all Muslim believers to emulate. In other words, the actions, decisions, and practices that Muhammad approved, allowed, or condoned, as well as those he refrained from or disapproved of, are used by Muslims as examples for guidance in all aspects of life. As a result, the body of transmitted actions and sayings attributed to Muhammad and his immediate companions soon became a material source (*hadith,* report, narrative) of Islamic law (*shariᶜah,* path, way) alongside the Qurʾan. In fact, the most important literary material after the Qurʾan is the Hadith. It has had as much influence as the Qurʾan in shaping the Muslim communities throughout the world.

The literature of the Hadith includes the earliest biography of the prophet Muhammad, an account of the founding of the community, a portrait of Muhammad as founder and legislator of the community, and of Muhammad as the model and guide for Muslims. In addition, the collections in the Hadith deal with everyday problems related to social, political, economic, and domestic life, as well as with esoteric questions probing cosmology, metaphysics, and eschatology.

Numerous stories recorded in the Hadith depict in vivid detail the personal character of the prophet Muhammad as he dealt with the daily affairs of life. Everything he did and said was accepted as worthy of study and emulation. Here are some self-explanatory excerpts.

"What is the greatest sin?" asked a man to the Prophet Muhammad.
"To make an idol for God who created you."
"Then what?"
"To kill your own child for motives based on economic factors" [infanticide was common in Arabia].
"And then what?"
"To commit adultery with your neighbor's wife."[1]

A bedouin came to the Prophet and said: "Do you kiss children? We never do."
The Prophet replied: "What shall I do to give back to you the mercy God has taken from your heart?"[2]

The Prophet of God said: "When a man says to his brother, 'You infidel!' one of the two deserves the name."[3]

The father of Musab ibn Sa'd asked the Prophet: "Who are the people who have the most severe tribulation?"

The Prophet replied: "The prophets, and then the ones who exemplify the prophets." [4]

One of the most popular themes recorded in the Hadith regarding the prophet Muhammad is the story of his night journey to Jerusalem, his ascent to heaven, and his vision of the afterlife. The compiler first presents the chain of narrators that authenticates his story.

> The following account reached me from 'Abdallah ibn Masoud and Abu Sayed al-Khudri, and 'A'ishah the Prophet's wife, and Mu'awiyah ibn Abu Sufyan and al-Hassan al-Basri and ibn Shihab al-Zuhri and Qatada, and other traditionalists, and Umm Hani, daughter of Abu Talib. It is pieced together in the story that follows. . . . Al-Hassan said that the Prophet said: While I was sleeping in the Hegra, Gabriel came and stirred me . . . he brought me out of the door . . . and there was a white animal, half mule half donkey, with wings at its sides . . . that stood still so I could mount it. Al-Hassan said: the Prophet and Gabriel went their way until they arrived at the temple in Jerusalem. There he found Abraham, Moses and Jesus, among a company of prophets. . . . Then one heard the Prophet say: After the completion of my business in Jerusalem a ladder was brought to me. . . . My companion and I mounted it until we arrived at the gates of heaven. . . . When I entered the lowest heaven, all the angels except one smiled and welcomed me. . . . The reason, Gabriel told me when I asked, was that he was the angel of hell. . . . Then I saw a man. . . . Gabriel told me this was our father Adam. . . . Then I saw men with lips like camels. . . . I was told that these sinfully devoured the wealth of orphans. . . . Then I saw men with bellies I had never seen before. . . . These were the usurers. . . . Then I saw women hanging by their breasts. These were those who fathered bastards. . . . Then I was taken up to the second heaven, and there were the two maternal cousins, Jesus son of Mary and John son of Zachariah. . . . Then to the third heaven, and there was a man whose face was like the full moon. This was my brother Joseph, son of Jacob. Then to the seventh heaven, and there was a man sitting on a throne . . . never have I seen a man more like myself. This was my father Abraham. He took me into Paradise. [5]

The Qur'anic basis for this account is Qur'an 17:1, and Muslims commemorate annually "the night of ascension" (*laylat al-mi'raj*) on the 26th of Rajab—the seventh month of the Islamic calendar. It is assumed that the general plot as well as the many small details of Dante's *Divine Comedy* reflect a fanciful treatment of this Islamic theme. [6]

Thus, the *sunnah* of Muhammad as recorded in the Hadith is the vital integrating force directing the daily lives of millions of Muslims the world over. For more than thirteen hundred years Muslims have modeled their lives after their prophet Muhammad. They awaken every morning as he awakened; they eat as he ate; they wash as he washed; and they behave even in the minutest acts of daily life as he behaved. The presence of the Prophet is felt, as it were, in a tangible way, as much through the Hadith as through the Qur'an.

Hadith

The collection of narrative material included in the Hadith is massive.[7] Unlike the Qurʾan, some of it is considered spurious by Muslim scholars.[8] Even among selections accepted by earlier scholars, there are many which are nowadays rejected by modern Muslim critics. Sunni Muslims (the majority group) accept six authentic collections, namely, the compilations of al-Bukhari (d. 870), Muslim ibn al-Hajjaj (d. 875), Ibn Maja (d. 887), Abu Dawud (d. 889), al-Tirmidhi (d. 892), and al-Nasaʾi (d. 915). One should add the name of Ahmad ibn Hanbal (d. 855), whose great encyclopedia of traditions, called *musnad,* is the subject of pious reading among other Muslims. However, some Muslim groups accept items in the collection that are unacceptable to others. Hence, no absolute canon of Hadith has ever been established.

Nevertheless, no matter how dubious the authenticity of some of the material may be, the collection of narrative materials in the Hadith preserves precious information about the early history of Islam and the moral precepts taught by the prophet Muhammad. In addition to its historical significance and its catalog of moral values, the Hadith reflects the religious opinions or "consensus" of the first generation of pious Muslim scholars—values which these early generations of experts identified as Islamic and which became vital in the formulation of Islamic law and doctrine.

The distinguishing mark of an extract or item from the Hadith is the chain of narrators presumed to have transmitted the traditional narrative from the prophet Muhammad himself or from his companions. In other words, an authentic extract or item from the Hadith must include the name of each human link in the chain between the prophet Muhammad and the individual who finally transcribed or transmitted it. Here is a typical example:

> al-Bukhari writes: ʿAbdallah ibn al-Aswad told me: al-Fadl ibn al-ʿAta told us: Ismaʿil ibn Umayya told us on the authority of Yaha ibn ʿAbdallah ibn Sayfi that he heard abu Mabad, the freedman of ibn ʿAbbas, say: I heard ibn ʿAbbas say: When the Prophet, peace and blessings of God be upon him, sent Muʿadh to Yemen, he said to him. . . . [9]

A large number of Hadith materials are assumed to have come into circulation within two or three generations after the death of the prophet Muhammad. At first the narratives were transmitted orally. Later, they were written down, though exactly when is not known. These written narratives retained the distinctive characteristic of oral composition rather than the literary style of later transcribers. They recorded facts and events in the life of the prophet Muhammad, speeches and statements made by him on points of law and doctrine, events in the lives of those who questioned Muhammad or spoke to him, and statements by companions of the Prophet who referred to him as their authority.

In time, legal maxims, aphorisms from Greek philosophy, and even quotations from Jewish and Christian sources were attributed to the prophet Muhammad. There seems to have been no limit to the process of fabrication.

Soon, however, serious students of the Hadith recognized the urgent need to establish the authenticity of Hadith materials in order to sift what was genuine from the mass of forgeries. A "science of Hadith criticism" gradually developed, starting around the ninth and tenth centuries. The primary task of this new "science" was to gather reliable bibliographical data about the narrators, a task which soon created another vast compilation of literature in the form of bibliographical "dictionaries." The earliest authoritative work of this nature is Ibn Saʿd's *Great Book of Classes*, in eight volumes. Bibliographical dictionaries which include legalists, Qurʾan reciters, and Islamic scholars have proliferated in almost every century down to the present time.

This research into the sources of narrative materials resulted in a system of classification comprising three main categories: genuine (or sound), good, and weak—although the number of terms to identify intermediate degrees of authenticity gradually increased to fifty. A Hadith report, account, or tradition came to be accepted as genuine in terms of its source—a chain of narrators (each accredited or authenticated by appropriate documentation) dating back without a break to the Prophet or to a companion of the Prophet.

The second category of material from the Hadith collection is reserved for items with a chain of sources, which, although complete, includes one weak link. In the event such a deficiency can be offset by confirmation or affirmation in Hadith material classed as "good" or authentic, then the material can be accepted as good for inclusion in the second category.

The third category identifies items attributed to the collection that are weak: demonstrably false, spurious, or forged.

Two collections of Hadith materials judged to be genuine acquired almost canonical authority. Both these authenticated collections, one by Muhammad ibn Ismaʿil al-Bukhari (810–870) and the other by Muslim ibn al-Hajjaj (d. 875), were compiled in the ninth century. Of the two, al-Bukhari's collection acquired, and still maintains, a significance in Muslim literature second only to the Qurʾan.

Al-Bukhari's work is divided into ninety-seven volumes, subdivided into 3,450 chapters, containing a total of 7,300 separate items of Hadith material. It is believed that he made his selection from no less than 600,000 traditional accounts and commentaries. If this is true, then only one of every two hundred items (0.5 percent) circulated in his day passed his test of authenticity.

Each of al-Bukhari's volumes is devoted to a major subject such as faith, works, testimony, prayer, fasting, alms, marriage, surety, finance, and so on. His main objective, it seems, was to present, and to arrange for ready reference, the most carefully scrutinized and authenticated narrative materials on matters of faith and conduct. Viewed as a whole, his work is a monument to scrupulous scholarship.

The collections of the narrative materials of al-Bukhari and his contemporary al-Hajjaj in no way inhibited their imitators. On the contrary, the elabora-

tion of legal systems, the omission of some topics from the two first compilations, and factional discord encouraged later compilers to make collections that
reflected their own particular interpretation of Islamic orthodoxy, sometimes
at the expense of strict rules of scientific criticism. In spite of the inclusion of
many weak or unauthenticated items, four other works were accepted eventually as Hadith. These four compilations are attributed to Abu Dawud (d. 889),
Ibn Maja (d. 887), al-Tirmidhi (d. 892), and al-Nasaʾi (d. 915) respectively.

Other collections continued to accumulate for several centuries, even though
they ranked below the six collections completed within the first three hundred
years after the Prophet's death. Such distinctions did not seem to compromise
them in the eyes of early Muslim scholars.

However, modern Western scholars remain skeptical of the premises on which
Hadith materials were authenticated, including the "science of Hadith criticism" which governed the choice of materials in the first six collections. Some
European critics have even advocated a radical rejection of the entire system as
an artificial, pious invention of Muslim scholasticism.[10] Others, both Western
and Muslim scholars, argue that a sound discretion is preferable to outright
skepticism and is more likely to lead to satisfying and constructive conclusions.[11] A few would even go so far as to agree with the words of a modern Islamicist, Fazlur Rahman: "A candid and responsible investigation into the development of the Hadith by Muslims themselves is a desideratum of the first
order."[12]

No matter how scholars choose to judge the contents of the Hadith—as pious
inventions or as reliable sources—all the evidence points to the conclusion that
the Hadith has left a profound imprint upon all Muslims throughout the centuries, an imprint that distinguishes Islamic society from all others and a pattern in the image of which it has lived and modeled itself since its inception.
Moreover, the Hadith has been to Muslims as vital a source of spiritual guidance
as the Qurʾan. For Muslims, to reject the Hadith is to reject the Qurʾan. In a
sense, to excise the Hadith means to sever at one stroke a unique chain of human as opposed to supernal contact with the prophet Muhammad. The deep-
rooted associations linking the Hadith, the Qurʾan, and the prophet Muhammad
are inseparable concomitants, in the expectations of all Muslims, to divine intervention.

The genuine concern of modern scholars, however, cannot be totally ignored
and needs to be allayed if not disarmed. The danger is that uncompromising,
conservative attitudes to scholarly research may throw the baby out with the
bathwater. Dismissing the Hadith without taking into account the circumstances under which it was developed violates the spirit if not the letter of disciplined research. In this respect, the words of H. A. R. Gibb, the respected Western Islamicist, are particularly apposite. The Hadith "serves as a mirror in which
the growth and development of Islam as a way of life and of the larger Islamic
community are most truly reflected. From this historical angle, it is precisely the
non-authentic and invented elements in much early and all later tradition that
gives it special documentary value."[13]

Thus, it is possible to trace in the various recensions of the Hadith the tensions and struggles of the early Sunnis and Shiʿis, the two rival factions, successors to the Prophet's mantle; the growth and fragmentation of the Shiʿis into many sects; the rise of doctrinal and legal controversies; the beginnings of the mystical Sufi orders; and the efforts of the later ʿAbbasid dynasty to establish its right to the caliphate by inheritance. All these different movements within Islam led to the formulation of separate collections of Hadith. The Shiʿis, for instance, repudiated the six Hadith of the Sunnis and composed their own standard work: the Hadith derived from ʿAli (the fourth caliph, cousin and son-in-law of the prophet Muhammad) and his supporters. As a result, Hadith literature, in both Sunni and Shiʿi traditions, represents a monumental treasury of wisdom. It is at once a commentary on the Qurʾan and a complement to its teachings.

Shariʿah

Islamic law, known as Shariʿah, constitutes a divinely ordained path, or system of duties, that is incumbent upon all Muslims to follow as the expression of their religious conviction and as evidence of their submission. In fact, the study and interpretation of the law, rather than theology, is a primary concern and a basic characteristic of Islamic scholarship. This fundamental concept of the law follows naturally from the Qurʾan, in which God is seen to command, proscribe, reward, and punish.[14]

God commands and humans submit. Thus, the Qurʾan is acknowledged as the principal authority for Islamic law. Second only to the Qurʾan is the Sunnah, in which regulations governing behavior and prescribing ethical ideals are recorded as directives for action but in general terms. Both the Qurʾan and Sunnah require interpretation and analysis to be applied to specific situations, be they political, social, or religious. Analogical reasoning (*qiyas*) is a third source of Islamic law that is applied to situations not explicitly covered by the Qurʾan or the Sunnah. The fourth and final application of the law is the outcome of a general consensus (*ijmaʿ*) completed and documented in legal manuals compiled over the centuries. The highest value in life, then, is to live in joyful conformity to Islamic law.

Islamic law differs from Western legal systems in at least two major respects: scope and value. Western systems of law govern one's relationship to the state and to fellow beings. The scope of Islamic law is much wider. It regulates one's relationship with God and conscience in addition to the state and to fellow beings. In this sense, Islamic law is a comprehensive code of behavior that embraces both private and public acts.

The second major distinction poses some fundamental problems for Islamic social progress. Western legal systems adapt to the changing circumstances of contemporary society. Islamic law, however, is conceived as the immutable embodiment of divine will, imposed by God upon Islamic society. The process of interpretation and adaptation of Islamic law is held to have been completed in the past with the crystallization of the legal manuals. In a sense, then, Islamic law governs and controls society. Islamic society merely reflects the law. It does not mold or fashion it.

So total and inclusive is Islamic law with regard to legal matters and ethical standards that all acts are classified according to five categories:

- obligatory
- preferred or laudable, but not obligatory
- neutral
- discouraged as objectionable but not forbidden
- prohibited

Conformity to Islamic law—that is, acceptance of interpretations hallowed by convention and responses appropriate to them—is accorded divine favor. In the world of Islam, any statement on conformity is no more than a generalization because, from very early times, the Islamic community registered a protest against the activities and enactments of the legists. Some felt that the Islamic spirit was in danger of being lost in the legalistic debates of jurisprudence. The Sufis, for instance, argued that the individual must submit to God, not to Islamic law. Others rejected the interpretation of the Qur'an and the Sunnah developed by the process of Islamic consensus (*ijma*ᶜ). The Shiᶜis, for instance, developed their own legal provisions. In many countries, Islamic rulers overruled the verdicts of the legal courts. Modern Islamic governments such as the governments of Turkey, Egypt, and Tunisia have abandoned certain provisions of Islamic law in favor of Western secular legal systems.[15] Others have introduced "customary law" (ᶜ*ada*) to complement Islamic law.

Still, the practical embodiment of the principles of Islamic law constitute in the eyes of Muslims a divinely ordained path. Thus, five important Islamic schools or codes of law survive today: Maliki, Hanafi, Shafiᶜi, Hanbali, and Imami.[16] These schools developed gradually according to the needs of time and place. From the outset, the differences between them represented geographical rather than ideological differences, and each society—from simple nomadic to complex urban—developed its own set of rules and principles.

Consequently, there is no unified system of basic legal principles. Every Sunni follows the precepts established by one of the first four schools, Maliki, Hanafi, Shafiᶜi, or Hanbali. The majority of Shiᶜis, on the other hand, follow Imami law.[17] A brief description of each of these five Islamic law schools will indicate the diversity of Islamic jurisprudence.

The Maliki School

Malik ibn Anas al-Asbahi (713–795), of Yemenite descent but born in Medina, was the founder of the Islamic law school known by his name and the first individual to codify Islamic law.[18] According to all accounts, he had a well-developed sense of his own importance. When Caliph Harun ar-Rashid wrote inviting Malik to teach at the court in Baghdad, Malik answered, "Knowledge does not travel but is traveled to." His student al-Qasim (d. 806) was responsible for expounding the doctrines of the Maliki school which survive today in the Islamic community of Egypt, the Sudan, and north and west Africa. Islamic Spain knew no other school of law during its seven centuries of history; neither did central and west Arabia until 1925 when the Wahhabis appropriated the territory and imposed the Hanbali law. The Maliki school tends toward simplistic principles of law, possibly because of the social environment of central and west Arabia at the time of its origin.

The Hanafi School

The founder of the Hanafi school was Nuʿman ibn Thabit (699–767) of Kufah, Iraq, better known by his title Abu Hanifah. He studied under great jurists, who accepted him into their company because of his superior intelligence. Though he spoke with an authority which commanded respect, advocating new prescriptive legislation that would apply to all Muslims at all times and places, he declined an appointment as supreme justice, even though the consequence of his refusal was imprisonment. He wrote no books, but a number of his best students did. They documented their mentor's interpretations and codified them as law. Today, adherents of the Hanafi school constitute the majority of Muslims in Iraq, Syria, Jordan, Egypt, Libya, Albania, Turkey, Afghanistan, India, and Pakistan.

The Shafiʿi School

Muhammad ibn Idris ash-Shafiʿi (767–820) was a descendant of the tribe of Quraysh, to which the prophet Muhammad belonged.[19] Shafiʿi was brought up in Mecca, but he studied in Medina under Malik ibn Anas. For a while he taught in Baghdad, but he spent most of his life in Egypt, where he died and is venerated to this day at his tomb, which has become the site of pilgrimage. The value of his work lies in his search for a systematic treatment of the principles of Islamic jurisprudence as a means for guiding the Muslim community. His view was widely accepted and is still applied in Egypt, the Sudan, south Arabia, east Africa, and central and southeast Asia, including Malaysia and Indonesia.

The Hanbali School

Ahmad ibn Hanbal (780–855) was born in Baghdad, the capital of the ruling ʿAbbasid dynasty.[20] Unlike his three predecessors, Hanbal's convictions were associated with theological and political movements that ran counter to the conventional wisdom of the day. The authorities hounded him, constantly subjecting him to beating and imprisonment, the effect of which was to make him a symbol of opposition for the masses, whose admiration and devotion he had won. He did not write much, but his followers elaborated and transmitted his teachings by providing a legal system—a canon law—based primarily on the Qur'an and the Hadith. The Wahhabis follow Hanbali law in modern Arabia.

The Imami School

Muhammad ibn al-Hasan al-Qummi (d. 903) is the founder of the Imami school, endorsed by the majority of modern Iranian, Iraqi, and Pakistani Shi'i Muslims. Because Shi'is maintain that the imam himself is a living source of law (a source almost as inviolate and authoritative as the prophet Muhammad was), they ascribe to the imam unlimited authority in political as well as jurisprudential matters.[21] They have their own canonical collections of Hadith recognized as a source for developing certain legal provisions. The basic difference between the other four schools and the Imami school is the rejection by the Imami school of the application of the analogical deduction process (*qiyas*)—a process which the four schools have applied to issues unresolved by divine revelation in the Qur'an or Hadith.

It is worth noting, however, that Muslims generally recognize that justice and equity have prior claims over loyalty to any one school. For instance, courses on Imami law, the legal code of most Shi'is, is offered with courses on other laws in non-Shi'i Muslim colleges with a view to placing all possible options for justice at the disposal of potential jurists. However, age-old Islamic legal distinctions are losing their significance and their authority. Islamic law is being challenged by the stress of political, social, and economic change.

The substance of traditional Islamic law places political and social rules on an equal footing with ordinances regarding worship and ritual, details of personal hygiene, greeting formulas, customs, and manners.[22] All these legal duties, therefore, can be broadly divided into two categories: duties to God on the one hand and duties to fellow human beings on the other. The first category is the subject of the next chapter. Here, four areas of the second category are briefly elaborated because they constitute law in the Western sense: family laws, inheritance laws, transactional laws, and penal laws.

Family Laws

Islamic law prescribes a patriarchal system for all family matters.[23] The status of children within the family group depends upon their legitimacy. The legal relationship of an illegitimate child is to the mother, not to the father. Guardianship of children conceived during legal wedlock belongs to the father, or a close paternal relative if the father dies. The right of custody of children whose parents are separated or divorced belongs to the mother, or to a female maternal relative. The guardianship of children involves maintenance, control of education, the right to contract daughters in marriage (whether as minors or as adults), and rights of succession and inheritance.

Inheritance Laws

Sunni and Shiʿi schemes of inheritance differ radically in several respects.[24] Sunni inheritance laws are based strictly on a system of agnate ties (descent from a common male antecedent) with a limited number of females and non-agnates inheriting a fixed fractional portion. The priority of agnates is determined by three principles: class, degree, and blood tie. Females receive only half the share of males, while a surviving wife inherits a nominal portion of the estate. In contrast to the Sunni legal system of strict agnate ties, Shiʿi laws include both paternal and maternal connections under the following three categories in descending order: lineal descent of parents; grandparents, brothers, sisters, and their issue; and uncles, aunts, and their issue. Thus, within each category, the closer the relationship, the stronger the claim of a potential heir and the more remote the relationship, the weaker the claim. By the same token, a full-blood tie takes precedence over a half-blood tie. In both Sunni and Shiʿi inheritance rules, a male inherits double the share of a female and an individual's power to dispose of or bequeath his estate is restricted to one-third of his assets. The remaining two-thirds must be distributed among the legal heirs to an estate in accordance with regulations governing inheritance. Sunni law goes further by disallowing any bequest that is not prescribed by law in favor of even a legal heir.

Transactional Laws

The Islamic law of transactions is determined generally by the prohibition of usury (*riba*).[25] Furthermore, any person who lacks "prudent judgment" (*rashid*) on account of immaturity, prodigality, or mental deficiency is considered unfit to transact affairs effectively. Consequently, such individuals are prohibited from managing their affairs without the consent of a guardian.

Specific business and land tenancy transactions may be grouped under four basic principles of Islamic law: sale, hire, gratuitous loans or transfers, and gifts. A fifth unique Islamic transaction is the *waqf* ("charitable endowment"), whereby an individual endows, as it were, the ownership of real estate to God, the income of which is dedicated in perpetuity to some pious or charitable cause. A settlement portion may be included in the income in favor of the owner's family.[26]

Penal Laws

Punishments for offenses and crimes are specifically fixed in Islamic law. Apostasy, theft, assault, fornication, adultery, drinking intoxicants, and other forbidden acts against society are crimes, for which the Qurʾan mentions different degrees of punishment, from mild to severe (e.g., Qurʾan 2:219; 5:42, 92; 24:2–5). Conviction of such crimes requires either confession or the testimony of a number of witnesses (two or four, depending on the nature of the crime), who themselves can be liable for equal punishment for false accusation. In practice, punishments found in the Islamic law more often than not play a role of deterrent. The discretion of court officials is more often applied than is the letter of the law.[27]

Traditionally, the system of procedure and evidence was administered by a single judge (*qadi*), whose initial task was to assess the guilt of the accused and then to preside over the appropriate process of Islamic law. On difficult legal issues the judge sought the advice of a professional jurist (*mufti*). There was no appeal for either plaintiff or defendant, because no hierarchy of courts or organized system of appeal existed.

The impact of Western civilization upon Islamic societies has brought about a radical change in all matters of Islamic law, be it civil, criminal, business, or family. Some Muslim countries (e.g., Egypt, Tunisia, and Turkey) have substituted a unified system of national courts in place of traditional Islamic laws.[28] Other Muslim countries (e.g., Syria and Pakistan) have retained traditional Islamic laws with some major modifications.[29] A few countries (notably those in the Arabian peninsula) still formally apply traditional Islamic law in its entirety, and a group of hard-core traditionalists adamantly proclaim the validity of divinely ordained Islamic law. Far from being ignored, their orthodoxy is steadily gaining in strength because the whole process of legal reform runs counter to the way the majority of Muslims think and live. Islamic practice developed from Islamic principle. They were in harmony. Legal reform has created discord because, according to Muslims, God, not humans, disposes.

Such problems are, naturally, inevitable during a transitional stage in Islamic evolution. In many Muslim countries the gulf between reformers and traditionalists is probably too wide to bridge, but the point is that the reformers are a group of leaders in the minority whose aims do not satisfy the standards of the conservative masses. Legislation authorizing new codes has little if any significance for the members of traditional Islamic communities, who consider all "progressive" social reforms to be contrary to fundamental Islamic ideologies. The question that now exercises the critical faculties of many Muslim thinkers is how Islamic law can relate the dictates of the divine will to the problems of contemporary society. The answer they provide will determine whether or not Islamic law survives the inroads of modern technology.

Women's Rights and Status

Patriarchal readings of the Qur᾿an and the Hadith, both of which are the source of Shariᶜah, are directly responsible for the role and status of Muslim women at all times throughout the world. Taken together, they address the social and religious regulations pertaining to Muslim women. Issues such as marriage, divorce, polygamy, inheritance, legal rights, dress codes, gender roles, and religious duties are among the subjects proscribed for women. Unquestionably, the Qur᾿an and the Hadith markedly improved the role and status of women relative to the pre-Islamic period, but on social and economic issues the Qur᾿an seemingly favored men (Qur'an 4:38). The conditions prevailing at the time the Qur'an was produced justified gender inequalities. Later, legal matters adduced by Muslim jurists provided the mechanisms for interpreting certain passages in the Qur'an as categorically favoring men over women. This provision remained in effect until modern times.

Debates over Muslim women's legal rights and status emerged in the mid-nineteenth century and continue to this day.[30] Millions of Muslim women around the world have formed various groups, leagues, associations, and organizations to modify the existing gender inequities.[31] The pace of change has increased since the 1980s, but the struggles and achievements (or failures) of Muslim women have not been uniform. There are wide variations between and within countries, across social classes, and within political movements.[32] Rulers, governments, state officials, religious leaders, and the masses all have rallied for or against the emancipation of Muslim women. Those who support reform are called "modernists," "reformists," "liberals," or "secularists"; opposers are known as "conservatives," "fundamentalists," "scripturalists," or "Islamists."[33]

Today, a large number of Muslim women insist on gender equality in national, secular, and religious spheres. They challenge various patriarchal systems, reject the constraints placed upon them, defy domination by men, and try to redefine their identity as women. Some even go as far as contesting repressive regimes and hostile societal environments. The traditional patriarchal Qur'anic injunction is largely determined by cultural factors and differs from society to society. Some Islamic cultures, notably those in parts of Africa and regions of southeast Asia, are matriarchal. For instance, among the Berbers or the Kirghiz, women have much liberty, but in neighboring Muslim societies, women may be restricted. This is not surprising at all. Because Islam embraces peoples of diverse cultures such as Chinese, Indian, Arab, African, and European, its range of social relationships is equally vast. Consequently, different forms of "feminist" thinking have emerged in Muslim societies.[34]

Most feminist movements and discourses are led by Muslim women of the upper and middle classes. Their ideas and activities are diverse and vary from community to community at different moments in history.[35] In some areas, necessity compels Muslim women to combine political and religious goals, such as among the Shi'is of Lebanon. In the absence of their men, who were imprisoned or fighting, Muslim women resisted Israeli occupation. To assert communal identity and to prevent harassment by the Israelis, they started wearing the *hijab* (Arabic word used for head, face, or body covering; "veil"). The same course of action was taken by the Muslim women of the Palestine Liberation Organization (PLO) in the occupied West Bank and the Gaza Strip.[36] But it must be realized that wearing the *hijab* (also known as *purdah* or *chador*) does not simply imply a political act; it is recognized as a sign of modesty and is commonplace in Islamic countries.

Basically, three major modes of feminist expression are employed: literary writings, daily activities, and organized movements. The first includes scholarly works, articles, essays, novels, short stories, poems, and autobiographies.[37] The second focuses on individuals who attempt to reform women's deplorable conditions,[38] and the third is the active engagement of a group of women who form regional and/or international alliances to advance the causes of Muslim women living under Islamic laws and customs.[39] These three methods are not mutually exclusive. On the contrary, they share many similar concerns and aims: to counter patriarchal hegemony; to strive for egalitarian arrangements in families, communities, and nations; to expose women's oppression; to confront issues related to women's dress, bodies, and mobility; and to create feminist consciousness and thought.[40]

Another area Muslim women strive to reform are the age-old barriers to formal training for religious scholars or jurists. Only recently have Muslim women begun systematic investigation of the Qurʾan and Hadith, entering an interpretive arena previously monopolized by Muslim men.[41] Using a Muslim "liberation theology" method, such women demonstrate the Qurʾanic pronouncements of gender equality and the influence of cultural practices that have resulted in androcentric readings of the Qurʾan.

Thus, the Qurʾan, Hadith, and certain legal principles, or Shariʿah, adduced by earlier jurists are being challenged in the modern age by millions of Muslims throughout the world. Although some reform in personal status and gender equality has been achieved, the resurgence of militant Muslims has caused some regression. What the future holds is difficult to predict. However, the conflict between modernists and traditionalists regarding the rights and status of women will more than likely continue for years to come.

6 Faith and Action

Articles of Faith

The elaboration of Islamic faith (*iman*) was greatly accelerated by Islamic political and social history. For instance, Muslims became acquainted with Greek thought, particularly with Greek philosophy, through early Christians and through the conversion to Islam of people who had once lived under Greco-Roman rule. Soon, Muslim philosophers made a name for themselves, and their insights in matters of knowledge (*ʿilm*) were applied to theology (*kalam*) and dogma.

This need for clear formulations of Islamic faith became apparent after the death of the prophet Muhammad. The Qurʾan prescribed certain specific directives regarding religious rites and practices, but it provided neither a systematic exposition of beliefs nor a consistent body of doctrine. At best, it presented a number of brief and variant statements on faith, piety, and practice. The spread of Islam, the large number of converts to Islam, and the rise of dissident groups within the Islamic community sharpened the urgency of formulating Islamic doctrines. Consequently, Islamic theology did not originate or develop questions of pure philosophical speculation; instead it dealt with practical problems arising within the Islamic community.[1]

Two important passages in the Qurʾan illustrate what constitutes Islamic piety, belief, and disbelief:

> True piety is this: to believe in God, the Last Day, the Angels, the Book, and the Prophets. (Qurʾan 2:171)

> O believers, believe in God, and in His Messenger, and in the Book which He has sent down to His Messenger, and the Book which He sent down previously. For whosoever disbelieves in God, and His Angels, and His Books, and His Messengers, and the Last Day, has indeed strayed far in error. (Qurʾan 4:135–136)

Five important doctrines, commonly known as the Articles of Faith, are immediately apparent in these scriptural declarations: God, angels, books, prophets, and the Last Day.[2]

God

The first and most essential element in Islamic theology is the doctrine of God (*Allah*). True belief demands an uncompromising monotheism. The prophet Muhammad denounced all forms of theism that detracted from the oneness and unity of God. He accused Christians of polytheism because of their belief in the Trinity. "Praise belongs to God," said he, "who has not taken to Him a son, and who has not any associate in the Kingdom" (Qur'an 17:110). God is one, and there is no other god except him.

Thus it follows that the greatest of all sins, in fact the one unforgivable sin in Islam, is *shirk* ("association"); that is, attributing to any one or any thing God's unique sovereignty. Those who associate a creature with God, or worship any creature other than God, violate the unity of God and commit the most heinous offense against God. *Shirk* is the only sin that God cannot forgive, because it denies God and prevents forgiveness. This is clearly stated in the Qur'an: "God forgives not the association of anything with Him; other than that, He forgives whomsoever He pleases. But whosoever associates anything with God has conceived indeed a monstrous sin" (Qur'an 4:51 cf. 4:116).

Islam's literal and specific interpretation of monotheism illustrates one fundamental and irreconcilable difference between Muslims and Christians. Another difference is in the Christian doctrine of "original sin." Islamic theology, like Judaic theology, developed (from the story of Adam's act of disobedience) the concept that humans are finite creatures and therefore bound to be imperfect. According to Islamic as well as Judaic theology, sin is neither communal nor transferable; nor is it hereditary. As a consequence, both Muslims and Jews reject the Christian assertion that all human beings are born with Adam's original sin. And since sin is not innate, Islamic theology concludes that mature individuals (and not children) are personally responsible for their own actions, good or bad, right or wrong. Thus, in Muslim thought, though humans are imperfect and vulnerable to sinful influences, they do not carry the inevitable blemish of an inherent original sin through Adam. Offenders can choose to seek God's forgiveness by submitting to his guidance. This is precisely what Adam did, and therefore God forgave his act of disobedience.

Islamic theology later elaborated the concept of sin, particularly as it related to faith (*iman*). It held that apostasy—abandonment of Islam for another religion—was equivalent to the denial of God and of his unity. To deny God in this way was to forfeit one's status as a member of the Islamic community.

The dogma encouraged sectarian groups who had motives for distinguishing themselves from the majority. For instance, the Khawarij were committed to a caliphate descended in a direct line from ʿAli, whom they saw as the true inheritor of the Prophet's mantle. When ʿAli's claim was submitted to arbitration, the Khawarij disowned the participants and anyone who accepted the judgment, which went against ʿAli. Anyone, in their sectarian view, who had abrogated the right of direct succession of the caliphate had committed a "mortal" or "grave" sin analogous to the denial of God and of his unity. Since a "mortal" or "grave" sin was never officially or theologically defined, it became a catch-all justification that anyone could use to ostracize others.

Another group, known as the Muʿtazili, insisted that all those who believed that God possessed human attributes such as anger or love denied God's unity and ascribed multiplicity to him. In accordance with their literal and narrow interpretation of God's unity, the Muʿtazili argued that God's attributes were not in his essence, but were his essence. For a while, their theological position received official favor until the distinctions they debated gradually became academic.

Besides its uncompromising monotheism, Islamic theology promulgates three additional doctrines related to God: (1) the essence or being of God; (2) the attributes of God; and (3) the activities of God.

(1) The essence of God is defined in terms of nine characteristics: necessary existence, being from all eternity, being to all eternity, essentiality, uniqueness, unsubstantiality, unembodiedness, formlessness, omnipresence.
(2) God is said to embody seven attributes: life, knowledge, power, will, speech, sensibility, activity.
(3) The activities of God comprise four divine prerogatives: creation, preservation, revelation, predestination.

The theological paradox of a doctrine that accepts the concept of free will operating within the limitations imposed by predestined factors or elements of life occupied the minds of Muslim thinkers from the early period of Islamic history.[3] The Muʿtazili, for instance, felt keenly the moral difficulty presented by orthodox Muslim thinkers who asserted that God predestined or determined everything. The ultimate logical conclusion of such a view, the Muʿtazili argued, would mean that God is responsible for misleading sinners in the first place, for judging them in the second place, and finally for punishing them. The orthodox rebuttal was that the principle of determinism meant that an individual whom God had decreed to be a Muslim would remain a Muslim always.

Qurʾanic references do little to resolve the debate. They are inconsistent. Certain passages clearly assert that humans are responsible for their own actions. But on the whole it seems that God's predestination is absolute, because "He guides whomsoever He wills and leads astray whomsoever He wills" (Qurʾan 70:34). Thus human fate, like everything else, is fixed by God even before birth. Because of these inconsistent passages, the theological debate was bound, almost predestined, to follow a tortuous path. The Muʿtazili maintained that they did not deny the all-embracing power of God, but that they recognized a difference between what God willed and what he commanded.

Abu al-Hasan al-Ashʿari (873–935) was for a time a prominent Muʿtazili thinker. At about the age of forty, he abandoned the Muʿtazili school and established his own orthodox school. Despite his repudiation, he went on to apply the Muʿtazili use of dialectic methods to the dogmas of orthodox Islam. In fact, he legitimized some of the Muʿtazilite methods, and, through his followers, his influence became considerable. He argued that God is one, that he is the sole creator and sustainer of all creation, and that everything that happens is determined by his will and eternal decree.

In the end, the orthodox view prevailed. Islamic theology teaches, then, the absolute predestination of good and evil. All human thoughts, words, and deeds, whether evil or good, are predetermined and decreed to all eternity by God.

How then do Muslims explain God's justice and mercy, particularly as they relate to human acts that are termed sinful and that require repentance and God's forgiveness? The justification most commonly offered by orthodox Islamic theologians is the doctrine of "acquired action" (*iktisab*). This doctrine proposes that God foreordains human actions, but that humans act voluntarily on the basis of attributes, values, or circumstances acquired from God, thus identifying themselves with God's decreed actions. To put it differently, individuals are responsible for all their actions, but their actions are performed in accordance with God's decree. After all, a Muslim is one who has completely and absolutely resigned himself to the will of God.

Submission to the will of God is, by its very nature, an acknowledgment of the mystery that surrounds God. Humans are finite beings and therefore cannot describe or characterize God in an absolute sense. However, indefinability does not preclude, especially in addressing God, the use of devotional forms of address expressed in human terms. Islamic theology provides one of the most comprehensive lists of devotional expressions about God. It consists of ninety-nine "most beautiful names" (*asma* *al-husna*) of God (see appendix 3). Pious male Muslims recite these ninety-nine names of God by running their fingers three times through a rosary consisting of thirty-three beads with a tassel. They also invoke God when making a supplication by choosing a name from the list that is most appropriate to the content of their petition.

The purpose of reciting the whole sequence of names is to make Muslims constantly aware of God's sovereignty over all affairs. It is not intended as an intellectual exercise or test. It reminds them that God is the "Lord of the worlds" (*rabb al-ʿalamin*). He exists from all eternity to all eternity. Everything comes into existence by his command. He alone grants life and death. Although he is regarded as the majestic, the terrible, and the stern who punishes all offenders, yet he is also the merciful, the compassionate, and the forgiving toward penitents.

Thus God, in Islamic theology, is "nearer to man than his neck-vein," yet at no time revealed within the circumscribed orbit of human knowledge and understanding. He is unknowable, except insofar as he chooses to reveal himself. Humans are called only to believe and to submit.

Angels

Angels are frequently mentioned in the Qurʾan. Like humans, they are created by God; but unlike humans, they are sexless, immortal, and resplendent, created of light to inhabit the invisible world. They are God's messengers who exercise a potent influence on both the life of humans and the life of the universe.

According to the Qurʾan, angels perform their missions by virtue of two, three, or four pairs of wings and worship God:

Praise be to God, Creator of the heavens and the earth, who appointed the angels as messengers, having wings, two, three and four. (Qur'an 35:1)

Everything in the heavens and every creature crawling on earth and the angels, bow to God. (Qur'an 14:51)

In addition, angels are said to act as intermediaries asking God to forgive the offenses of believers (Qur'an 40:7). At the time of death, the souls of humans are received by angels (Qur'an 6:93; 8:52; 16:30; 47:29), who have kept a record of their actions (Qur'an 6:61; 43:80; 82:10) and will witness for or against them on the day of judgment (Qur'an 21:103; 13:24; 33:43).

Angels support God's throne and guard the gates of hell. According to Islamic theology, they rank above humanity but below the prophets. For instance, in the Qur'anic story of creation, angels are represented as losers in a test of wits against Adam. With one exception they all prostrate themselves before Adam at God's command. One angel arrogantly refuses on the grounds that he is made of light, an element he considers to be superior to clay, out of which Adam was made. This act of disobedience and pride in refusing to honor Adam results in his fall from the state of an angel to that of a *jinn*, a being made of fire inhabiting the subtle world. He is cursed and his role is reduced to leading humans astray to commit errors and offenses (Qur'an 15:28–43). Jinn are discussed in further detail below.

Islamic theology later systematized Qur'anic teachings on angels and classified them under three categories: archangels, ministering angels, and fallen angels.

ARCHANGELS

Four angels seem to rank as archangels in Islamic belief: Gabriel, the angel of revelation; Michael, the angel of providence; Israfil, the angel who will blow the last trumpet; and 'Izra'il, the angel of death.

MINISTERING ANGELS

There are an unspecified number of huge and powerful angels in this category. Some angels bear or surround God's throne; others record the words, thoughts, and actions of each individual on earth; still others receive souls at the time of death. The angels Munkar and Nakir question the dead. The angel Malik is in charge of hell, while Ridwan is in charge of paradise.

FALLEN ANGELS

The leader of all rebellious angels is Iblis (from Greek *diabolos*, "the slanderer" and hence "the devil"). Originally, he was one of the angels, the only one who refused to bow down to Adam when so commanded by God. Then there are Harut and Marut, two angels who teach sorcery, sow division, mislead victims, and cause mischief (Qur'an 2:96).

Associated with the doctrine of angels, but quite distinct from them, is the

Islamic belief in beings called *jinn*. These jinn (sing. *jinni*) are created of fire and are frequently mentioned in the Qur'an:

> We [i.e., God] created man from clay of molded mud; but We created the jinn earlier from the *samum* [i.e., fire of the scorching wind].(Qur'an 15:26–77)

> I [i.e., God] have not created jinn and mankind except to serve Me. I do not desire any provision from them, nor do I desire that they should feed Me. (Qur'an: 51:56–57)

Jinn are mortal beings who exist mainly in communal groups, marrying and living an existence comparable to the rest of humanity. They are normally invisible but may appear in human or other forms, or may live in trees, waste places, ruins, and sometimes in inhabited homes.

A person may be jinn-possessed (a condition identified as *majnun*), that is to say a "mad person." Astrologers, diviners, soothsayers, and poets, among others, are to some degree subject to possession by jinn. The prophet Muhammad indignantly denied being a poet, the implication being that he was jinn-possessed.

In popular Islamic belief, jinn are considered hostile beings who exert harmful influences on people. Tales of mixed marriages between humans and jinn have led Muslims to believe that the famous Queen of Sheba was the daughter of such a liaison (Qur'an 27:20–45). Some modern Muslims explain references to jinn in the Qur'an as allusions to natural forces or causes of disease, but the majority of Muslims hold to the belief that jinn are creatures whom God created before he created humanity. They assume subtle forms or take various shapes, and they wander at will on earth. And just as humans ultimately return to dust, the material from which they were created, so also do jinn return to fire (Qur'an 55:1–75).

Prophets (Messengers)

The importance of the doctrine of the prophets is as crucial as the doctrine that proclaims the oneness of God.[4] To all peoples and in all ages, God sent prophets or messengers to proclaim the oneness of God and to warn humanity of the future judgment (Qur'an 10:47; 16:36). According to Islamic theology a messenger (*rasul*, pl. *rusul*) is considered to rank a grade higher than a prophet (*nabi*, pl. *anbiya'*). A messenger is one who is sent by God to a special community with a book (scripture) containing rules and laws for human conduct. A prophet merely preaches a message sent by a messenger. Prophets are not necessarily messengers, but all messengers are also prophets. An Islamic tradition states that there have been 124,000 prophets, 315 of whom were messengers.[5]

Muslim theology later made a distinction between the more general messengers and the special prophetic succession of twenty-eight messengers stretching from Adam to Muhammad, who represents the last and the seal of the prophetic order. The Qur'an identifies the series of twenty-eight prophets by name: Adam, Enoch, Noah, Lot, Abraham, Ishmael, Isaac, Jacob, Joseph, Moses, Aaron, Elijah,

Elisha, David, Solomon, Job, Jonah, Zachariah, Ezra, Luqman, Dhuʾl-Qarnain, Hud, Salih, Shuʿayb, Dhuʾl-Kifl, John, Jesus, Muhammad (Qurʾan 6:83–90).

Eighteen prophets are Old Testament figures; three are from the New Testament; four are associated with Arab traditions; and three are difficult to identify. Muslims are required to believe in all these twenty-eight prophets just as they are required to believe in the oneness of God.

The Qurʾan further records that most of these prophets, if not all, were persecuted and rejected by their fellow citizens. Some were endowed by God with special powers to perform miracles. Of such were Moses and Jesus, who seem to hold a special place among the prophets of Islam. Muslim thinkers developed later the view of the sinlessness of the prophets, even though this doctrine has no place in the Qurʾan or the classical traditions.

Just as Adam is regarded by Muslims as the first prophet sent by God, so Muhammad is the "seal of the prophets" through whom God reveals his eternal message in its definitive form (Qurʾan 33:40). Muhammad's life and death marked the end of prophecy since his prophetic mission satisfied for all time any need or demand for another prophet. Pious reformers there may be, but no more prophets.

Books (Scriptures)

Orthodox Muslims hold to the belief that there is a celestial archetype of scripture, often called the Preserved Tablet (Qurʾan 85:21, 22; 80:13, 14; 56:78) or the Mother of the Book (Qurʾan 13:39; 43:4), from which God revealed his message, as necessity arose, through the angel Gabriel to various prophets in succession. Whenever chaos, confusion, or evil suffused human society, God sent a fresh message to urge people to repent and to renew their submission to him. God's messages, then, are really one and the role of each successive messenger is simply to confirm the messages that have gone before.

One of the central doctrines of Islamic faith is belief in all of God's revealed messages, which now consist of four books: Torah, Psalms, Gospels, and Qurʾan. These four books are to be regarded as holy scriptures, even though the three books preceding the Qurʾan include certain human imperfections. With the appearance of the Qurʾan, the noblest of the books, these earlier books, it is believed, were abrogated. The basis for this conclusion is that the Qurʾan, according to Muslims, contains God's final revelation and as such is the perfection and culmination of all the divine messages contained in earlier books. As a matter of fact, it is an article of faith that the purpose of the Qurʾan is to preserve original divine revelations by restoring the eternal truth of God. This doctrine is clearly declared in the Qurʾan:

> Truly We [i.e., God] sent down the Torah in which is guidance and a light. . . .
> And we made Jesus, son of Mary, follow in their traces [i.e., Jews], confirming the
> Torah that was before him; and We gave him the Gospel, in which is guidance and
> a light. . . . (Qurʾan 5:44–48)

Since the Qurʾan abrogates all earlier books, its ordinances continue to remain in force until the day of judgment, when faithful Muslims are to be arbiters of the fate of those communities who also received holy books. The following selection vividly anticipates the drama of the event.

> Then there will come a call from God Most High: "Where is the Preserved Tablet?" It will be brought to Him in great distress. Then God Most High will ask [i.e., of the Preserved Tablet]: "Where is what I wrote about you in the Torah, the Gospels, the Psalms and the Qurʾan?" And it [i.e., the Preserved Tablet] will answer: "O Lord, the faithful Spirit [i.e., angel Gabriel] transmitted it from me." Then Gabriel will be brought in terror-stricken and knees shaking, and God will say to him: "O Gabriel, this Tablet claims that you transmitted from It My word and My revelation; is that true?" Gabriel will answer: "Yes, O Lord." Then He will say: "And what did you do with It?" He [Gabriel] will answer: "I passed on the Torah to Moses, the Psalms to David, the Gospels to Jesus, and the Qurʾan to Muhammad. . . ." Then a herald will summon each prophet with his community . . . while Muhammad and his community will give witness for or against them [on the basis of the Qurʾan].[6]

In addition to these four books, Muslims are required to accept a fifth book—a collection of scrolls (*suhuf*) revealed to Abraham that unfortunately has since been lost. Consequently, Muslims acknowledge and respect the four books that were delivered to various prophets at different times for the guidance of humanity.

Last Day

The Last Day, or the final day of judgment, occupies a very important place in the Qurʾan and in the Hadith. The vivid description of the events leading up to the Last Day and the elaborate portrayal of the final judgment are similar to the book of Revelation in the New Testament, yet more powerful. The cataclysmic events of the Last Day are to occur suddenly, with great cosmic changes and at a time known only to God. On that day, "when the trumpet sounds, the sun shall darken, the stars shall fall, the heavens shall split asunder, the mountains shall turn to dust, the earth shall be crushed, the beasts shall be scattered all over, the seas shall boil, angels shall appear and terror shall strike everywhere" (Qurʾan 81:1–14; cf. also 82:1–19; 69:13–37).

Besides these various visible signs that announce the approaching hour of the Last Day, Islamic doctrine associates the coming of "the Guided One" (*Mahdi*) with signs that foreshadow the Last Day.[7] In other words, the end of the world will be heralded by the coming of the Guided One—a messianic figure who will appear in the last days. Some Sunni Muslims believe that an individual from the family of the prophet Muhammad will appear and reign for seven years to make the religion of Islam triumphant throughout the world before the end comes. Most Sunni scholars, however, identify this messianic figure with the prophet Jesus. Among Ismaʿili Muslims, the belief is that Ismaʿil, son of the sixth imam, will return as the Guided One. Imami Muslims, however, hold to the view that Muhammad al-Muntazar, the twelfth imam, who disappeared in 878, is in occlusion until he returns as the Guided One to revive Islam and conquer the world.

The doctrine is viewed with skepticism by some Muslims. Several impostors, for instance, have over the course of Islamic history succeeded in persuading a substantial following in various Muslim countries to accept them, in turn, as the Guided One. Such fraudulence gave a number of famous Muslims, such as Ibn Khaldun, ample justification for scorning and rejecting any messianic expectation. These critics justified their skepticism with the argument that there is no reference to any such person either in the Qur'an or in early editions of the Traditions. Nevertheless, Muslims generally associate the approach of the Last Day with the appearance of the Guided One.

In addition, Muslims believe that on the Last Day, the graves will open, the dead will be resurrected, and a judgment will be pronounced on every individual according to his or her deeds. Two terrible angels will question the dead, an inquisition that is anticipated with so much dread by the living that they recite the profession of faith to the dying. (Only the souls of martyrs pass straight into heaven where they join a sainted host in heavenly bliss.) The actions of every individual in life are then weighed in the divine balance and judgment served by the presentation of a book. If the book is placed in the right hand, that individual is counted among the blessed; but if the book is placed in the left hand, that individual is counted among the damned (Qur'an 69:13–37).

These eschatological accounts of the consummation of all things as described in the Qur'an have been elaborated by generations of Islamic commentators. The two recording angels, the scales on which deeds are weighed, and the dreadful angels of hell, including the horrors of that place, are as thoroughly documented by Islamic theologians as are the pleasures of paradise, with beautiful gardens and pretty virgins. Islamic tradition promises space and bliss in heavenly mansions to pious Muslims who fulfill penitential obligations such as the repetition of certain prayers for a stipulated number of times.

No description can evoke or convey the significance of the heavenly bliss awaiting pious Muslims. All the humble and charitable, all those who suffered persecution for God's sake, all those, especially those who fought in the name of and for God, shall qualify to an exalted estate with all its appurtenances: beautiful clothes, music, feasting, lovely maidens, and divine bliss in the garden of paradise. On the other hand, all idolaters, all criminals, and all the proud are doomed to the fires of hell, where they shall suffer forever, with no release from their torments.

Heaven and hell, according to Islamic doctrine, are both spiritual and physical. Besides suffering physically in hell, the damned will also experience fire "in their hearts." Similarly, the blessed will experience the greatest spiritual happiness in addition to physical pleasures.

After the judgment of the dead, death will be summoned and slain by God.

The announcement that there is no more death will add grief to those in hell and joy to those in paradise. Strictly speaking, there is no doctrine of intercession in Islam, except that God himself, in his mercy, may forgive certain offenders.

Two characteristics of the eschatology (doctrine related to death, judgment, heaven, and hell) of Islam are of unusual interest. One is the extent to which material of varied provenance (e.g., ancient Egyptian, Iranian, Christian) has been incorporated, partly by the prophet Muhammad, but to a large extent by Muslim theologians of later times. A second is that Islamic eschatology began to exercise, in its turn, an extraordinary influence on Chinese and Christian thought. Among numerous popular eschatological works written by Christians, Dante's *Divine Comedy* is an example of Islamic influence.

The Five Pillars

Soon after the death of the prophet Muhammad, five basic religious duties were singled out as necessary acts of worship or obedience demanded of a Muslim.[8] These religious duties are usually known as the "five pillars" of Islam and consist of: profession of faith (*shahadah*), prayer (*salat*), almsgiving (*zakat*), fasting (*sawm*), and pilgrimage (*hajj*). To these five, some Muslim groups add a sixth pillar, the holy war (*jihad*), though this was never accorded the same significance by the general Islamic community.

Profession of Faith

No religion in the world professes a shorter or more incisive creed than the Islamic profession of faith: "There is no other god but God; and Muhammad is the Messenger of God" (*la ilaha ill'Allah, Muhammad rasul Allah*). This brief, simple, and yet explicit sentence is the only articulated creed.[9] It is whispered in the ear of a newborn baby; it is one of the first sentences a child is taught to utter; it is repeated several times daily by pious Muslims; and it is the last utterance of the dying.

It is commonly asserted that merely professing this creed is sufficient to make one a convert to Islam. Orthodox Muslims, however, insist that six conditions connected with the profession of faith must be observed before one can effectively be a Muslim. These conditions are: repeat it aloud; understand it perfectly; believe it in the heart; profess it until death; recite it correctly; declare it without hesitation.

Five times during the day, a similar, though longer, formula is proclaimed by a summoner to prayer (*muezzin*) from the tower (*minaret*) of the Islamic mosque. The loud voice of the *muezzin* (now more often than not amplified) rather than pealing bells summons Muslims to prayer:

> God is great! God is great!
> I bear witness that there is no god but God!

I bear witness that Muhammad is the Prophet of God!
Come to prayer! Come to prayer!

The five doctrines of the Islamic faith—God, angels, prophets, books, the day of judgment—are commonly associated with the profession of faith. Anyone who abandons Islam, either voluntarily or under compulsion, is regarded as having committed a most heinous act. Apostasy is neither accepted, condoned, nor permitted. Those who are brought up Muslims and those who convert to Islam are committed to the Islamic religion. According to Islamic law, the punishment for apostasy is, for male adults, death, and for females, confinement until they recant or die. Dissenting minors are kept under surveillance until they reach adulthood, when they are dealt with.

At present, Islamic law as it relates to apostates remains in effect, and in 1903 and 1924 some Ahmadiyyah Muslims were stoned to death in Afghanistan on the ground of apostasy. Normally, however, the law is never invoked, since it is difficult if not impossible for a Muslim living within the community of Islam to change religion. This is because even though many Muslim countries have adopted a policy of religious freedom, any attempt to convert a Muslim to another religion is forbidden by law.

Prayer

The next most important religious duty after the profession of faith is prayer.[10] Qurʾanic texts prescribe only three prayers a day, but Islamic tradition requires five, at dawn, noon, mid-afternoon, evening, and night. Strictly speaking, Muslims may not waive the obligation to pray five times daily even if they are sick or on a journey. The sick are to pray in bed and, if necessary, lying down. Travelers are enjoined to pray at dawn, to combine noon with mid-afternoon prayer and evening prayer with prayers that follow nightfall, thus praying three times daily. In practice, however, action may fall short of disciplined compliance.

Prayers may be said either in private or in public worship. Many Muslims pray at home or wherever they happen to be. Others attend public worship in a mosque, where a prayer leader (*imam*) directs the ritual. Customarily, prayers performed in public are said in Arabic, though Turkey has adopted the Turkish language. The use of Arabic is not compulsory in private prayer (*duʿa*)—that is, in petitions for the fulfillment of special needs, such as help or solace in time of trouble, or success in an undertaking. In such circumstances, the linguistic and cultural background of the worshipper is permitted to govern the choice of words.

All public or ritual prayers must be preceded by ritual purification both of the individual and the place. Ablutions (*wuduʾ* or *ghusl*) secure bodily purity. Hence, Muslims wash their foreheads, hands, and feet before they pray, and the courtyards of mosques are equipped with washing facilities. If no water is available, then hands and feet may be wiped with fine, clean sand. Muslims pray on a mat or rug as a token of purity secured for the spot or place. Shoes or sandals are removed before devotees step on their prayer rugs. In this state of purity, a worshipper prays facing in the direction of Mecca (*qiblah*), a direction which is indicated in mosques by a niche in the wall (*mihrab*).

One day a week is set aside as a day of public prayer. What sunset on Friday to sunset on Saturday is for Judaism, and Sunday is for Christianity, Friday is for Islam—though it is not necessarily regarded as "a day of rest." Rather, the day is thought of as a day on which all business activities are temporarily suspended for an interval of communal prayer in the mosque. Hence, large numbers of pious Muslims assemble every Friday noon in the mosque and surrounding area to solemnize the observance of community prayer.

By tradition, prayers are offered with heads covered, but nowadays some pray bareheaded. No images of any kind, neither paintings nor pictorial windows, are allowed in mosques. Instead, Qur'anic texts are written on the walls in Arabic. There are no seats or pews in the mosques, since everyone spreads his prayer rug.

Since there is a fixed order of worship and prayer, worshippers follow a standard sequence consisting of praise to God, recitation of Qur'anic passages, prayer formulas, obeisance, and prostration. When prayer starts, the leader of the prayer (*imam*) takes his place at the front facing in the direction of Mecca, while worshippers stand behind him in rows, following him in various postures. At every change in posture they recite "God is great." Tradition determines the exact posture to be assumed and the precise words to be used at each stage.

There are seven stages or steps, accompanied by appropriate postures and recitations:[11]

- standing with hands at sides to express an intent to begin devotions acknowledging divine lordship;
- standing with thumbs on lobes of ears and fingers spread out when reciting the initial profession of faith, "God is great";
- standing with the palm of the right hand resting on the back of the left hand with arms loosely extended in front of the body when expressing God's praise and reciting Qur'anic verses;
- bowing with hands on knees while expressing God's greatness;
- standing with hands at sides when expressing assurance that God hears the praises addressed to him;
- kneeling prostrate with the forehead touching the ground when extolling God's holiness;
- sitting on heels while declaring God's greatness.

After this sequence of prayer comes the invocation of blessings on the prophet Muhammad. The index finger of the right hand is raised during a declaration of the profession of faith: "There is no other god but God; and Muhammad is the Messenger of God." Then a prayer of blessing for Muhammad and his family (just as God blessed Abraham and his family) is followed by a prayer asking God to bless the worshipper in this world as well as in the next, and to deliver him from the horrors of hell. The worshipper then turns his head to the

Ritual of Ablution

The ceremonial washing of parts of the body (hands, face/head, and feet) are part of the preparation for prayer, and the courtyards of mosques are equipped with facilities for such washing. *Courtesy of Robert Monroe.*

Communal Prayer on Friday

Muslim communal gathering for prayer takes place weekly on Friday at noon in a mosque. Every Muslim unrolls his or her prayer mat and stands barefoot facing Mecca. Normal activities and usual duties are resumed as on any other day after the communal prayer. *From the private collection of the author.*

right, then to the left, while declaring, "Peace be upon you." This is addressed to those who are on either side as well as to angels and departed spirits. Finally, special petitions are made to God with hands held open in front with palms upward.

Following the formal prayer is the sermon (*khutba*) given by the leader. This sermon or address may be of a moral or social or political content, usually delivered in the form of admonitions to piety. God's blessing is then invoked on the leaders of the Muslim states, and the formal Friday prayer period ends.

Women attended these formal Friday prayers in mosques during the Prophet's time, though they stood either behind the men or to one side. But a traditional saying ascribed to the Prophet states that it is far better for women to pray at home than to attend a mosque. Consequently, Muslim women do not attend public prayers, although some mosques have a room or section set aside for them.

Besides these prescribed prayers, pious Muslims perform extra prayers, not as an obligatory duty but as a sign of sincere piety. These special prayers are offered at times of special danger (such as drought), at funeral services, at annual festivals, and at an eclipse of the moon. Additional or supererogatory prayers are frequently recommended, especially during the night.

Prayer is the heart and essence of Islam. Any Muslim who willfully avoids prayer is considered to have forsaken Islam. This is clearly stated in the Hadith where the Prophet is reported to have said, "He who abandons prayer, demolishes the very pillar of religion." Again, one learns from the Tradition that "if one's prayer is marked perfect, all his other deeds win the satisfaction of the merciful Lord." So important is prayer to Muslims that it is considered the first duty imposed by God upon humanity, after the belief in his oneness. Indeed, prayer is submission to God; it strengthens the foundation of one's faith and helps an individual gain inner peace and stability. Patience, courage, sincerity, and hope all result from the discipline of prayer. The obligation to pray is a command enjoined as the duty of all Muslims; it is also primarily an act of homage to God.

Almsgiving

The third duty of a Muslim is to give alms to the poor as an outward sign of true piety. There are two kinds of almsgiving: legal (*zakat*) and voluntary (*sadaqa*). In Muslim canon law, legal alms are assessed at one-fortieth of an individual's income in kind or money, and they are collected by civil servants. This legal contribution was once exacted from all members of the Islamic community.

Regulations for payment, as prescribed in Islamic tradition and canon law, suggest a tax levy designed mainly for an agricultural or pastoral society. Payments varied according to the value placed on different kinds of products or properties. Regulations, for instance, specify a heavier assessment on animals

Appointed Times of Prayer
Muslims are enjoined to pray at five appointed times each day wherever they happen to be: at home, in an office, in the market, at a railway station, by the roadside, or in a mosque. *Courtesy of Turkish Tourism and Information Office.*

Duty of Women to Pray

Muslim women as well as Muslim men must pray and worship God. Although Muslim women tend to pray at home, today in many parts of the world Muslim women are seen in great numbers praying in mosques. Here, two Muslim women descend the steps of the Dome of the Rock in Jerusalem after performing their prayer. *Courtesy of Israel Government Tourist Office, Ministry of Tourism.*

pastured at large than on those fed at home, the reason being that the latter incurred greater expense. On the same principle, crops watered by rain were taxed more heavily than those artificially irrigated. Cash and precious metals were taxed less than crops and animals. Various types of tools or articles essential to a particular trade or occupation such as military service in a holy war, or service as a theologian, cleric, or scribe, were tax exempt. All payments were collectable by the state and were to be used primarily for the poor, for redeeming bad debts, for ransoming Muslim war captives, for those employed in its collection, for holy wars, for travelers, and for any other worthwhile cause.

Legal almsgiving is now more or less defunct because many Muslim states have adopted Western systems of taxation. Several Middle Eastern countries still officially collect payments defined in Islamic regulations as legal alms (*zakat*), but they are collected only on a voluntary basis. This legal contribution, as it were, is regarded now as a free-will offering, not as a levied tax.

Fasting

The fourth duty of a Muslim is to fast during the entire twenty-nine days of the ninth month of the Islamic lunar calendar (*Ramadan*).[12] What distinguishes this observance from other fasts is that during the day Muslims abstain from food, drink, and sexual intercourse; but these proscriptions are lifted between sunset and sunrise. Tradition states that it was in this month that the prophet Muhammad received his first revelations. Consequently, fasting during this month is considered thirty times more efficacious than in any other period. Those who observe the fast faithfully and in a spirit of sincere repentance are assured of a remission of sins.

Because the Islamic calendar is lunar (rather than solar such as the Zoroastrian calendar, or luni-solar such as the Gregorian-Christian calendar), the month of Ramadan advances through the seasons. When Ramadan falls in the winter months, a religious fast does not seem too demanding; but during the summer months, especially in hot countries, the obligation to fast becomes particularly rigorous.

During the entire twenty-nine days of Ramadan, all adult male and female Muslims fast from sunrise to sunset. Only children, the sick, nursing or pregnant mothers, the aged, and travelers are exempt, though anyone exempted by reason of temporary disability or circumstances is expected to make up an equivalent period of fasting. The end of each daytime abstention is celebrated joyfully after sunset.

In addition, most pious Muslims observe the "withdrawal to a mosque" (*i'tikaf*), especially during the last ten days of the fast. This retreat commemorates the first revelation received by the prophet Muhammad and is identified as the "night of power" (*laylat al-qadr*). A three-day festival (*'id al-fitr*) follows immediately at the end of the fast period, when everyone joins in a celebration marked by feasting and merriment.

Voluntary fasts at various times during the year other than the month of Ramadan are also considered as meritorious acts undertaken to expiate various breaches in the observance of Islamic law. None, however, other than Ramadan, may last any more than three consecutive days. The observance of a period of fasting, then, especially during the month of Ramadan, is considered one of the most prominent external characteristics of the religious life of Islam.

Pilgrimage

The fifth prescribed religious duty of every Muslim is to make a pilgrimage to the holy shrine of Ka'bah in Mecca. It is an obligation to be fulfilled at least once in a lifetime by every adult who is sane, healthy, financially capable of supporting his family during his absence, and able to underwrite the expenses of the journey.[13] The pilgrimage rite to the holy city of Mecca can be performed only on specified days (the seventh to the tenth) in the last month (*Dhu'l-Hijjah,* the twelfth month) of the Islamic calendar. Needless to say, the importance of this annual gathering of Muslims from many countries can hardly be overstated. A cross-section of Muslims from all walks of life and of varying color, race, and nationality realize their equality before God as they meet on common ground at least once a year.

The black stone in the Ka'bah and the adjacent well of Zamzam are not the only factors that make Mecca a holy city. Eight years after the prophet Muhammad fled Mecca, he returned triumphantly to the city of his birth with some ten thousand followers. Walking first seven times around the outside of the Ka'bah, Muhammad entered the shrine and destroyed all 360 of the idols and images that had been accumulated there over the years. Then he dedicated the Ka'bah to God and proclaimed Mecca to be the holiest city of Islam.[14]

Each year following this incident, Muhammad and his followers came to Mecca on a pilgrimage to the holy shrine. His last pilgrimage in 632 attracted a hundred thousand faithful followers, who performed various solemn rites. Since then, no religious ritual has done more to unite Muslims than the rite of pilgrimage. Each year, hundreds of thousands of Muslims—Arabs, Turks, Iranians, Indians, Chinese, blacks, and whites—all meet at the holy site in Mecca as equals before God. But simply visiting Mecca is not enough. Before entering the holy precincts, all pilgrims are obliged to conform to a set of appropriate observances. Three main stages with various duties are prescribed.

The first stage starts with the arrival of pilgrims. When pilgrims are about ten kilometers (six miles) from the holy city, they enter upon the state of sanctity (*ihram*). This consists of discarding their own clothing; wearing two white seamless garments, one wrapped around the waist and reaching below the knees and the other over the left shoulder and tied at the right side, with head and face uncovered; removing shoes or sandals; performing ablution rites; praying and declaring the intention of performing the pilgrimage rite; abstaining from shaving any part of the body, cutting nails, using oil or perfumes, entering into sexual relations, plucking grass, or cutting trees.

Then, like their prophet Muhammad, pilgrims approach the Ka'bah and walk around it counterclockwise seven times, three times quickly and four times slowly. On each circuit they pause to kiss or, if the crowd is too great, to touch with the hand or a stick the southeast corner of the Ka'bah, where the black stone is located. Next, pilgrims go to certain spots for prayers, after which they walk quickly seven times across the valley between two mounds (Safa and Marwa), some 457 meters (500 yards) apart, in commemoration of Hagar's frantic search for water.

For the second stage, pilgrims proceed from Mecca to Mount Mercy, in the plain of 'Arafat, about twenty-four kilometers (fifteen miles) from Mecca. This ceremony is a day's journey on foot, but many stop to rest at the sanctuary of Mina, about halfway. All pilgrims must, however, arrive at Mount Mercy on the following morning. Once there, they "stand before God" (*wuquf*) from noon to sunset, absorbed in pious meditation. This "standing before God" is one of the most significant acts of the pilgrimage.

The third stage starts after sunset when pilgrims return to Muzdalifa, a site

Annual Pilgrimage to Mecca

The Kaʿbah at Mecca in Saudi Arabia has been the focal point of the annual pilgrimage by Muslims since the days of the prophet Muhammad. Pilgrims in white robes, including women with covered heads, some in black, gather around the cubic stone structure covered with a black silk cloth. They circumambulate the Kaʿbah seven times and kiss or touch it. *Courtesy of Royal Embassy of Saudi Arabia.*

between Mina and ʿArafat, to spend the night in the open. The following morning they return to Mina and throw seven stones at each of the three pillars said to represent Satan, who is reputed to have tempted Ishmael three times to run away when Abraham intended to sacrifice him (Qurʾan 37:99–113). Then animals are offered as sacrifices, and three days of festivities known as the Feast of Sacrifice (ʿid-al-Adha) follow. A final circuit of the Kaʿbah back in Mecca, the discarding of the seamless garment, and a haircut (the ceremonial clipping of a few hairs for women) completes the pilgrimage. The pilgrim is now permitted to assume the special title of *hajj* or *hajji*—one who has made the pilgrimage to the holy city.

Naturally, the pilgrimage is impossible for millions of Muslims because they cannot meet the fourth requirement: covering expenses. The custom now is for pilgrims who cannot go in person to contribute as much as they can afford to send a substitute. The substitute brings merit upon all those who make his pilgrimage possible.

In modern times, Muslim countries send official delegates to represent them in pilgrimage, though the occasion is increasingly being used for socio-political congresses. Certain Muslim countries impose restrictions on the number of outgoing pilgrims from time to time to control imbalances in foreign exchange.

Jihad *(Holy War)*

The Qur'an calls upon true believers to undertake holy war (*jihad*) to eradicate or neutralize infidels, disbelievers, and idolaters, in the interest of the spread of the true religion, Islam (Qur'an 2:187–189, 212; 4:86, 90–93; 8:40, 65; 9:36, 125). Believers who are killed or defeated in holy war are amply rewarded by God (Qur'an 4:75–79; 9:112; 47:4–8).[15] Devout Muslims put the interest of Islam before anything else in this world and are never content to surrender the principles of Islam to expediency.

In early days, one of the prime methods of gaining merit was to "fight" or "strive" in the cause of God. To die on the battlefield fighting against infidels made one a martyr, a status that guaranteed a highly favored position in the hereafter as attested by innumerable passages in the Qur'an.

> God has bought from believers their souls and possessions in return for the gift of Paradise; they fight in the way of God; they kill and are killed; that is a promise binding upon God. . . . (Qur'an 9:112)

> When you meet unbelievers, smite their necks; after you have made a large-scale slaughter of them, tie fast the bonds. . . . Those who are slain in the way of God, He will guide them and He will admit them to Paradise. . . . (Qur'an 47:4–8)

When the prophet Muhammad left Mecca for Medina, the Meccans offered a ransom for his capture and return, dead or alive. Muhammad reacted in keeping with a message received from God commanding him to resist and fight his enemies with his small groups of Muslims.

> O Prophet! God is sufficient for you; so also the steadfast believers who follow you. O Prophet! Urge the believers to fight. If there be twenty of you, they will overcome two hundred; if there be a hundred of you, they will overcome a thousand unbelievers. . . . (Qur'an 8:65)

Fighting against Jews and Christians (people of the book) was also required until they paid the poll tax levied against them.

> Fight such men who do not practice the true religion—as those who have been given the book—until they pay their proper tribute and are humbled. (Qur'an 2:29)

The command in the Qurʾan is to "fight in God's way," a recourse that Muslims apply against aggressors as a last resort if all other methods have failed.

> Fight in the way of God against those who fight with you. . . . Fight them, till there is no persecution and the religion is God's. . . . Whoever commits an aggression against you, you likewise commit an aggression against him. . . . (Qurʾan 2:187–190)

> Fight the unbelievers totally even as they fight you totally. . . . (Qurʾan 9:36)

Fighting in defense of Islam is a duty that is to be carried out at all costs. The Qurʾanic statement is clear on this issue. God grants security to those Muslims who fight in order to halt or repel aggression.

> Permission to fight is granted to those who are wronged; surely God has the power to help them. . . . If God does not repel aggression by means of fighting, then monasteries, churches, synagogues and mosques would be destroyed. . . . (Qurʾan 22:40–42)

Thus, the duty to halt aggression or to strive for the preservation of Islamic principles may involve fighting. Muslim states unable to settle a dispute by the implementation of just and peaceful means are obliged to fight courageously and steadfastly against recalcitrant states, be they Muslim or non-Muslim.

> A large number of devoted men fought beside many prophets; they did not slacken for what befell them in God's way, nor did they weaken, nor did they humiliate themselves. God loves the steadfast. The only words they said were: "Lord, forgive us our errors; let us exceed in our conduct; make our foothold sure, and help us against the unbelievers." God gave them the reward of this world as well as the fairest reward of the world to come. (Qurʾan 3:140–141)

> God loves those who fight in His way in ranks, as though they were a strong cemented structure. (Qurʾan 61:4)

Fear, hesitation, or irresolution among the ranks of forces committed to battle on behalf of God invite his anger and damnation.

> O believers, when you encounter unbelievers in war, do not withdraw from them. Whoever withdraws, except for changing ranks or maneuvering in battle, will incur God's wrath, and his refuge is Hell. (Qurʾan 8:15–17)

The obligation to fight in no way absolves a Muslim from performing the prescribed ritual of daily prayers. Even on the battlefield during the course of an engagement, a Muslim is required to keep in constant touch with God through the required rite of prayer.

> When you stand among them, and lead the prayer for them, let a group of them stand in prayer with you, with their weapons beside them. After they perform their prostrations, let them go to the rear, and let another group who has not prayed come forward and pray with you, with every means of precaution and with weapons beside them. . . . When you have performed the prayer, remember God, while

standing, as well as sitting and lying down. When you are secure from danger, then observe prayer in the prescribed form. Surely, prayer is enjoined on believers to be offered at appointed times. (Qur³an 4:102–105)

Thus, fighting in the cause of God is yet one more expression of an inner conviction: total submission to God. A Muslim is one who has committed his complete life and total property to God in return for gaining God's approval and pleasure.

If fighting is seen as inevitable, then it should be waged courageously and swiftly so as to cause the least damage to life and property. Should the enemy propose a truce or indicate a willingness to stop hostilities, Muslims are to be ready to avail themselves of the offer. Muslims are to seek at all times the opportunity of putting an end to fighting and resolving differences through peaceful methods. Prisoners or captives taken during the course of fighting are to be securely guarded, but not ill-treated. Once fighting is over, prisoners are to be released, humanely with some prospect of survival, or returned for ransom (Qur³an 47:5). In fact, the ransoming of prisoners by Muslims themselves is highly recommended as a charitable act (Qur³an 2:178).

The idea of war as holy is not new and does not appeal to a generation growing up under the shadow of nuclear holocaust. In earlier times the apparent contradiction in the concept of fighting to achieve harmony was less difficult to reconcile. In Qur³anic terms, to be actively engaged in holy war, inwardly and outwardly, against everything that negates truth or God is to bring peace and harmony—to establish an equilibrium between the destructive forces unleashed when good clashes with evil. Islam, to a greater degree than any other religion, has always advocated aggression as a positive and appropriate means of securing peace. However, it is necessary to point out that Qur³anic advocacy of holy warfare is interpreted differently by different Islamic groups. The command to wage war is spiritualized by the mystics as a "struggle" against the evil forces within. It is interpreted literally by militants as a "struggle" to bring unsubdued geographical regions of the world under the dominion of the Islamic faith, politically, legally, and spiritually.

In modern times, the evidence suggests that Muslims are no more addicted to war than anyone else, and that they are prepared to make concessions to accommodate neighboring non-Muslim people. The concept of *jihad* survives but in less uncompromising forms than it used to take. Some Muslims, like the Sufis, promote the conquest of one's self as "the greater holy war," while they disparage conflict with unbelievers or infidels as "the lesser holy war." Others put forward the argument that fighting, or holy war, is justified only in self-defense. And to support this argument they quote Qur³an 2:186, which exhorts Muslim believers "to fight in God's way those who fight them." Still others, like the Zaydi and the Ahmadiyyah, reject the idea of fighting or holy war and advocate peaceful negotiation as the most effective means for upholding the principles of Islam. Any pursuit or activity that tends to disturb the preservation of peace is severely condemned. In their estimation, the message of Islam is best communicated to all humanity if Muslims themselves are able to live exemplary lives.

Moral and Social Behavior

Tradition states that proper conduct and good works improve the status even of individuals destined to enter paradise, in spite of the doctrine of predestination. In consequence, many Muslims exceed the minimal standards outlined in the five pillars of obligations. They recite more prayers than the normal five daily prayers prescribed by Tradition, they fast beyond Ramadan and throughout the year, they give more to charity than they are obliged to, spend more time at devotional reading, and even go on additional pilgrimages to other sacred sites (e.g., Medina), or to tombs of famous saints, in the pious expectation that they are accumulating a rich repository of incontrovertible merit.[16]

Within this general pattern, the Qur'an lays down detailed instructions for proper moral conduct and social behavior.[17] Monasticism and asceticism are inimical to Islam (Qur'an 57:28), because righteous living can be applied only to the full acceptance of life. It cannot be applied in a vacuum created by withdrawal from or rejection of life. Islam teaches that all human attributes, be they inner faculties or external possessions, since they represent a God-given endowment, must be put to appropriate use (Qur'an 2:4). Consequently, all natural instincts and tendencies are to be channeled through the discipline imposed by proper regulation to produce moral acts. In Islam, the value of human conduct is determined by the motive and intent that inspires it (Qur'an 2:285; 6:152).

Furthermore, Islam makes a distinction between voluntary and involuntary thoughts and acts (Qur'an 2:226; 11:115). The former possess a moral quality and involve accountability and responsibility. The latter arise from an impulse, or a reaction that needs to be properly exercised before it acquires a moral quality. A Muslim who consistently fosters good morals is in a position to subdue all evil tendencies. Regulating moral behavior affects the individual as well as others. Every Muslim has an obligation to safeguard and promote his or her own welfare as well as the welfare of others (Qur'an 3:111, 115). To impose a penalty on an offender is morally permissible to establish a moral balance; but to forgive is to tip the balance in favor of moral excellence. To go further and to exercise benevolence toward an offender is morally the highest standard (Qur'an 3:135; 42:40–44). Again, slander, abuse, spite, falsehood, revenge, and immodesty are not compatible with moral thinking and righteous conduct. A person of high moral character endures wrong patiently, forgives offenders, and suppresses all natural instincts for redress or retribution (Qur'an 3:187; 15:48; 31:18; 42:44; 49:12).

What a Muslim understands by moral conduct and proper social behavior may best be illustrated by the Islamic concept of love. According to Islam, love is a natural quality instilled in every human nature. When unregulated and selfish, love is a vice—a liability. But when it is properly regulated, love is transforming and transcendent, raising all it touches to new heights of moral purity. Hence, the love of God and the love of the messenger of God take precedence over the love of parents, children, kinsfolk, nation, or business. Next in the order of precedence is the love of parents, which, according to the Qur'an, stands in close juxtaposition with the duty owed God (Qur'an 17:24–25; 31:15; 46:16). "Paradise is at the feet of your mothers," a saying attributed to Muhammad, is the way the idea is expressed in the Tradition. Then comes the love of children, which involves their proper upbringing and their security in the future, both here and in the hereafter (Qur'an 66:7). This hierarchy of precedence determines how moral character is judged or assessed. The more closely an individual applies this hierarchy of love and responsibility, the greater his merit. In all matters, the Qur'an and Tradition set the standard of values.

Social values are not separable from moral values in the world of Islam. Every aspect of human relationship is governed by social behavior based on moral qualities. A lengthy passage in the Qur'an represents the fullest statement of the code of behavior every Muslim must follow:

> Do not set up another god with God, lest you find yourself condemned or forsaken. . . . Show kindness to your parents, whether one or both of them attain old age with you. . . . Give to the kinsfolk, the needy and the wayfarer his due. . . . Do not squander your substance, for spendthrifts are brothers of Satan. . . . Do not chain your hand to your neck [i.e., be niggardly], nor be open-handed to extreme excess. . . . Slay not your children for fear of poverty, for We [i.e., God] will provide both for you and for them. . . . Do not commit adultery, for it is an indecent and evil path. . . . Do not kill anyone unjustly, for God forbids it. . . . Do not treat the orphans except in the fairest manner until he comes of age. . . . Give full measure when you measure and weigh with just scales. . . . Do not pursue that which you have no knowledge of. . . . Do not walk exultantly [i.e., proudly] on earth, for you can neither split the earth open nor match the mountains in stature. . . . (Qur'an 17:22–39)

In some ways these ethical injunctions and prohibitions resemble the biblical Ten Commandments. Integrity, humility, and kindliness are interspersed with the positive and negative commands appropriate to idolatry, parents, infanticide, murder, adultery, property, wealth, trade, and orphans. Extravagance and niggardliness are condemned as undesirable characteristics (see also, Qur'an 2:262–269, 272–275). Due provisions and hospitality are to be extended to the poor and the traveler as to kinsfolk. Orphans are to be treated with particular care. Young people are admonished to show filial piety and due respect to older generations. Thus, the obligation is laid upon every Muslim to refrain from evil and to seek what is right and proper.

Women's Religious Duties

The Qur'an assigns the same religious duties and promises, and offers the same spiritual rewards, to both men and women. Thus, Muslim women, like men, are obliged to fulfill the five pillars of the faith: profession of faith, prayer, almsgiving, fasting, and pilgrimage. But unlike men, they enjoy certain exemptions.

To disavow God's oneness amounts to apostasy, and Islamic law prescribes death as the penalty. The punishment for female apostates, however, is usually less severe.

Again, ritual prayer at five specified periods is incumbent upon every male Muslim. Women are totally exempt from these prayers during menstruation for a maximum of ten days, and after childbirth for a maximum of forty days. They are, moreover, under no obligation to compensate for this dispensation. As for the public Friday noon prayers at a mosque, women are free either to pray in public by attending and retaining their proper place in a mosque, or to perform their prayer at home.

The annual payment of legal alms for the needy is a voluntary religious duty accepted by many Muslims. Women enjoy the special privilege of being able to exempt the cost of their personal ornaments from any assessment made for legal alms.

To keep a total fast from dawn to sunset during the month of Ramadan is a requirement observed by all Muslims. Women who are either menstruating, or pregnant, or ill, or in confinement, are exempt from fasting, but they must make up for it later at a more convenient time.

To make a pilgrimage to the holy city of Mecca at least once in a lifetime is incumbent upon every adult Muslim who is physically, mentally, and financially capable of doing so. Women who wish to perform the pilgrimage are required to be accompanied by their husband or male relative. To enter the state of sanctity (*ihram*), men are required to don a special garment consisting of two large pieces of white seamless cloth. Women, however, are permitted to wear any clothing that covers the entire body except the face and the hands, though some women prefer to veil their faces too. If menstruation occurs during the period of sanctity, women are then relieved from performing some rites, while other rites are postponed until they are restored to a state of purity.

According to Islamic theology and law, men and women are equal before God, but this ideal is seldom realized in practice. In ancient times, the status of women in society probably did not vary appreciably from culture to culture, with some isolated exceptions. In the past, discrimination against women paled into insignificance beside the savage and focused brutality directed against minorities and dissenters everywhere.

It is only by modern, largely Western standards that women in Islamic communities seem to suffer discrimination today. The status of women in Islam is only one of many Islamic characteristics that distinguish the world of Islam from the world, say, of Europe or the Americas. Arabs, Iranians, and Pakistanis, for instance, are not like Britons or North Americans, and by and large they do not want to be like them. Their concern is to reconcile their culture with the disruptive influences of Western cultural imperialism. They see the issue of the status of women in Islamic nations as their problem, not the problem of Western nations.

Disenchantment about the status of women in Islamic communities is likely to be resolved in terms of how Muslim women can take their rightful place in Islamic society and carry out their obligations so that they contribute fully to the development of their communities. Islamic tradition and Western liberalism offer radically opposing solutions to an issue that continues to create tension and disruption even in Western societies. Obviously, whatever changes are to be made must be introduced carefully within the framework of the Islamic tradition, not as models cut from Western patterns.

7 Observances and Festivals

Milestones in Life

In addition to the rules of conduct, there are a number of social customs that are as binding upon Muslims as religious duties are. Four of the most important ones are associated with birth, circumcision, marriage, and death.

Birth

Seven days after birth, parents name the child, cut its hair, and sacrifice an animal as an offering to God in thanks, with the meat distributed among the poor. A monetary offering corresponding to the weight of the child's hair is also distributed in alms. This occasion is usually marked by family gatherings and festivities.

Circumcision

The justification offered in modern times for removing the foreskin or prepuce of a male genital organ is hygiene. It was not always so. Though the practice has always been widespread and dates back to antiquity, its origin and purpose are matters of conjecture. Generally it appears that circumcision was originally an initiatory rite that involved the offering of part of the genital organ to a deity.

The custom in pre-Islamic Arabia was to circumcise both males and females (clitoral excision).[1] There is no reference to circumcision in the Qur'an, but the practice is mentioned in both the Tradition and in Islamic law books. Advocates of the Shafi'i school consider circumcision of males and females an obligatory rite; others treat it as a traditional custom. Whether obligatory or traditional, circumcision of males is universally practiced among Muslims. This rite is performed sometime between the ages of seven to thirteen, though there have been some instances as early as four. Family gatherings and festivities usually follow the circumcision rite.

Converts to Islam are expected to accept the rite of circumcision, if they are not already circumcised, in keeping with advice to a prospective convert attributed in the Tradition to the prophet Muhammad: "Get rid of the long hair of paganism and be circumcised."[2] Circumcision, then, is a religious duty to be observed by those who profess Islam.

Marriage

In Islam, the basic unit of society is the family, and the foundation of the family is marriage.[3] Hence, neither celibacy nor monasticism are encouraged in Islam as a way of life, except under unusual or extenuating circumstances. Many Sufis prefer celibacy because they regard women as evil distractions from piety, but their abstention is not considered normal in Islam. On the contrary, marriage in Islam provides a legitimate channel for physical, emotional, social, and spiritual enjoyment.[4]

Chastity outside marriage is regarded as a prime virtue, and the Qur'an recommends early marriage as a way to ensure abstinence from all unlawful sexual activity. Those who reach marriageable age without finding a suitable mate are exhorted to observe complete abstinence from sexual activity until the right opportunity presents itself (Qur'an 24:34). Extramarital relations are altogether forbidden (Qur'an 17:33). Polygamy is permitted provided the number of wives does not exceed four and provided that all of them are treated justly and equitably. However, polyandry (marrying more than one husband) is not allowed under any circumstances. In general, Muslims tend to live monogamous lives.

Customs associated with Muslim weddings are as varied as the cultures represented by the participants. Essential to the marriage ceremony, however, are the presence of witnesses and a contract specifying the bridal gift (*mahr*). The bridal gift varies according to the social standing of the parties and national customs, but its significance is the same throughout Islam. Money or goods are given by the groom (or by his father) to the bride (or the bride's father) in return for marital rights (Qur'an 4:3; 5:7; 24:33). As a rule, the bride keeps all of the bridal gift in the case of divorce, and part of it if the marriage is dissolved before consummation. Today, in certain Islamic countries, a bride can stipulate some of the terms of her marriage contract. Such terms may entitle her to retain full control of her dowry and all other personal property. Or she may demand monogamy from her husband as well as the right to obtain a divorce from him whenever she desires, without stating the grounds. Two competent witnesses are required to seal this civil contract.

It was not uncommon at one time for children to be married even before they reached puberty, though they were not permitted to cohabit until they were at least sexually mature. Today, some Islamic states have introduced laws regulating the ages at which young people may marry: no earlier than fourteen or sixteen for girls, and sixteen or eighteen for boys. Muslim males are allowed to marry non-Muslims, such as Christians or Jews, but not polytheists. Muslim females, however, are restricted to Muslim marriage partners.

The Qur'anic ethic is that the marital bond rests on mutual love, concern, and loyalty. The relationship between husband and wife is described as being as close as "each other's garment" (Qur'an 2:183). Just as clothing is in close, enveloping contact with one's skin, so husband and wife are bound together in close union one with the other. Both are, therefore, required to cooperate, to sacrifice, and to look to each other for comfort and advice. In addition, both are responsible for running the home and rearing the children.

The role of the husband is to provide the necessary finances, to protect and guard members of the household, and to formulate policies and priorities, if necessary, without being inconsiderate or tyrannical. He must at all times remember the words of the Prophet: "The best among you is he who treats best the members of his family." This means that he ought to treat all members of his family, including his wife, with kindness, generosity, understanding, and respect. The role of the wife is to see to the comfort and well-being of her husband and her family, to be honest and faithful to him, to obey him and be careful with his possessions, and to bring joy, warmth, and peace to her home.

Since marriage is a civil contract involving mutual duties and responsibilities, Islam permits divorce, the dissolution of the contract. But it is not advocated or encouraged by Tradition, which attributes these cautionary words to the Prophet: "Among all things permitted, the most obnoxious act in the sight of God is divorce." On another occasion he is reported to have said: "Divorce causes the shaking of God's throne." To exercise the right of divorce without a legitimate and compelling reason is frowned upon by Muslims. Every effort must be made, be it through counsel or mediators, to smooth out differences and to find means of reconciliation. If, however, in spite of every effort, irreconcilable differences remain and divorce is finally decided upon, then certain obligations must be met.

If the wife is divorced by the husband, she is entitled to support for a specified waiting period (ʿidda), at the end of which the divorce is final and the woman is free to remarry. This waiting period is measured by three menstrual cycles to confirm or disprove the onset of pregnancy; in the event of pregnancy the waiting period is extended until the child is born (Qurʾan 2:236). If husband and wife are reconciled to each other during this period, the divorce proceedings are dropped (Qurʾan 2:229–230).

In Islamic law (Sunni law), a husband can divorce his wife by either oral or written repudiation. The approved form of repudiation is declaring "I divorce you" in the presence of two or more witnesses. Stated only once, the repudiation is revocable until the end of the waiting period. Repeated twice on other occasions, particularly after the end of the waiting period, the divorce is legally binding and irrevocable.

Normally, the right to divorce belongs to the husband. But nowadays, the wife may obtain a civil divorce on specific grounds: impotence, insanity, any debilitating disease, failure to pay the dowry, failure to support her, desertion or lengthy absence, physical or emotional cruelty, false accusation of adultery, and apostasy.

Some Islamic countries have introduced rules of divorce granted only through the courts and based on the equality of the sexes. In addition, certain countries entitle the wife to special compensation for damage from divorce. Custody of children up to a certain age (seven for boys, nine for girls) devolves automatically to the mother, unless she disqualifies herself on moral grounds. After reaching the appropriate age, children are free to choose to live with whichever parent they prefer.

Thus, the traditional status and role of the Muslim male is different from the status and role of the female by virtue of his gender. But in no way does this imply that the female is inferior to the male. Rather, the differences between them arise out of differences in gender, which determine a complementary relationship of roles, not a competitive one. To submit to the authority of a male means to be provided and cared for—protected and respected by him. Domestic, social, and moral responsibilities are shared equally between them. As a mother, the female enjoys a rank higher than the male because of her involvement in the child's conception, birth, and care. Hence, both males and females have their proper place of honor and therefore complement each other.

In matters of sexual morality, both males and females are forbidden to behave in ways that lead to immorality, and severe penalties are prescribed for both parties (Qurʾan 24:2). The Qurʾan enjoins both to be chaste and modest in their behavior.

> Tell male believers to lower their gaze and cover their private parts. . . . Tell female believers to lower their gaze and cover their private parts. . . . (Qurʾan 24:30–31)

Modesty among females is further emphasized by regulations governing their appearance and conduct in society (Qurʾan 24:30–31). A woman may not compromise her morality or stir the passions of males by her immodest clothing or conduct (Qurʾan 24:31). Such admonition is offered in order to protect the reputation of females from unjustified accusations of immorality (Qurʾan 24:4). Thus, all practices of immorality are soundly condemned in Islam. Men and women are enjoined to fulfill the respective roles which they have assumed as members of their society.

Death

When a Muslim dies, the body is washed with water, usually by a member of the same gender, and clothed in its shroud.[5] Women wail loudly with disconcerting sounds from the moment of death up to the disposal of the corpse. Burial follows promptly with the corpse being carried on a bier, sometimes to the mosque, but more often directly to the cemetery. Men take turns carrying the bier, while the entire procession chants the familiar profession of faith: "There is no god but God, and Muhammad is God's Messenger." An imam leads the mourners in appropriate prayers, including praise to God and the invocation of blessings on Muhammad. Then mourners spend some time seated in silent meditation and prayer.[6]

The corpse is then laid in the grave resting on its right side and facing Mecca. Males and females are never buried in the same grave unless joint interment is unavoidable, in which case a partition is raised to separate the corpses. After the grave is filled in, the attending mourners recite on behalf of the dead the following Qur²anic prayer (known as *fatihah*):

> In the name of God, the most merciful! Praise belongs to God, Lord of all the worlds; the all-merciful, the all-compassionate, master of the day of judgment. We serve You only, we beseech Your help only. Guide us in the right path, in the path of those whom You have blessed; not of those against whom You are angered, nor of those who go astray. (Qur²an 1)

Following the recitation of this prayer, mourners return home. In general, the official period of mourning is short. Friends and relatives visit the bereaved, offer prayers, and for a few nights recite the same invocation they raised at the graveside. On the first Friday after the funeral, some members of the bereaved family visit the grave to place on it a palm branch, a symbol of peace. They also distribute food to the poor. This procedure is repeated for two more Fridays and on the Friday following the fortieth day after the funeral.

According to strict Muslim teaching, no structure or monument may be erected over a grave, but this rule is not generally observed. In most Islamic countries, elaborate tombs to commemorate important Muslims are common. The Taj Mahal at Agra, India, for instance, is a fine example of architecture erected by a Mahal. However, many Muslims, particularly the Wahhabis, express strong disapproval of sepulchral monuments. Some have gone so far as to destroy tombs, even those of their own Sufi saints.

Islamic tradition details exactly what happens to the dead after their burial. Two angels, Munkar and Nakir, come to question them on their religion. Pious believers who identify themselves by responding appropriately reap immediate benefits. Their graves are expanded, their darkness is dispelled and they are surrounded by light, and they are shown the place they are to occupy in paradise after their resurrection. Faithless sinners and unbelievers betray themselves with unsatisfactory answers. The immediate result is a severe beating. Then they are made to feel the grave pressing in on them and are shown their place of punishment in hell.

The torments of the wicked and the rewards of the righteous after death are fully documented in the Qur²an and are carefully described in later tradition. Several illustrations of these conditions have already appeared in an earlier chapter. The Qur²an makes it clear that no promise nor threat about the life hereafter can compare in importance with the responsibility of doing God's will here and now. In Islamic doctrine, right conduct in the present takes precedence over the realization in the future of the deepest aspirations of the human soul. Belief in life after death follows from this central doctrine and is a corollary;[7] it reinforces the requirement to live life fully according to God's law now and provides a reward for doing so. To deny the existence of life after death is to deny the existence of God.

To the majority of Muslims, life after death means the reconstitution of corpses, the resurrection of the bodies from the graves and their reuniting with

Islamic Calendar	Month	Days
Muharram	First	29
Safar	Second	30
Rabiᶜ al-Awwal	Third	30
Rabiᶜ ath-Thani	Fourth	29
Jumada-l-Ula	Fifth	30
Jumada-th-Thaniyyah	Sixth	30
Rajab	Seventh	29
Shaᶜban	Eighth	30
Ramadan	Ninth	29
Shawwal	Tenth	29
Dhu-l-Qaᶜdah	Eleventh	30
Dhu-l-Hijjah	Twelfth	29

souls to face the final judgment (Qurʾan 17:51–54; 75:3–4). For a few, however, it is a purely spiritual condition, undefinable and inexpressible in human terms, words, and analogies, which are limited to this life. Humans, with their limited faculties, are incapable of grasping or realizing the true nature and condition of life after death. The best they are capable of is understanding it intuitively and expressing it in approximation.

Memorial Days and Festivals

Muslims calculate the dates of their ceremonies and festivals according to the Islamic religious calendar.[8] The Islamic year is lunar and therefore shorter than the solar year by eleven days (354 days instead of 365 days). Though the Islamic year consists of twelve months, they vary from thirty to twenty-nine days each. Consequently, Islamic festivals, including the New Year, move back through the seasons. There is no Western Gregorian equivalent that consistently matches Islamic dates.[9] Islamic feasts and holy days are observed in almost every Islamic country, though they differ from country to country and even in different regions of the same country. There are, however, several feasts, which are observed as occasions of communal rejoicing throughout the Islamic world.[10]

Feast of Sacrifice (ᶜid al-Adha)

This feast, also known as the Great Feast (ᶜid al-Kabir; in Turkish, Qurban Bairam), commemorates the story of Abraham's sacrifice of a sheep instead of his son—held by Muslims to have been Ishmael, not Isaac. The feast extends in some countries to four days and is associated with the annual pilgrimage to Mecca. Pilgrims celebrate it from the tenth to the thirteenth of Dhu-l-Hijjah (the Islamic twelfth month) in the valley of Mina, the site where it is believed Abraham offered the sacrifice. Non-pilgrims observe the feast at home.

Every Muslim is expected to sacrifice an animal according to his means, though this rite is not a legal duty except in fulfillment of a vow. Observance of the festival follows a short period of fasting and a public prayer at the mosque according to a sequence hallowed by tradition. The sacrificial animal (a lamb, goat, cow, or camel) is placed with its head facing Mecca and is killed with one stroke of the knife at its throat. If these conditions cannot be met, as may be the case for Muslims living in non-Muslim countries, then worshippers make the sacrifice at home after appropriate prayers. The animal is cooked and divided into three parts: one for the family, one for relatives or neighbors, and one for the poor. An exchange of gifts has also become common practice on these occasions.

After the feast is over, most families visit the graves of their relatives to mark them with palm fronds. The more affluent carry food to distribute to the poor gathered at the cemetery gates. Some Muslims hire professional reciters to pray at the graveside; others, mainly women, maintain a vigil throughout the day and spend the night in a tent at the cemetery.

Feast of Ending the Fast (ʿid al-Fitr)

The feast that marks the end of the fast of Ramadan lasts for three or more days in Shawwal (the Islamic tenth month). This feast, which is also known as the Little Feast (ʿid al-Saghir; in Turkish, Kuchuk Bairam), is celebrated with great joy and with the offering of alms or food to the less fortunate. Muslim men assemble in the mosques for prayer, families and friends visit each other, everyone dresses in new or clean clothes, and gifts are exchanged, especially cakes and candies. Young Indonesian Muslims ask parents and grandparents to forgive their offenses, often kneeling before them and asking their blessings for the coming year.

New Year Festival (Muharram)

The Muslim New Year's festival is celebrated on the first and succeeding days of Muharram (the Islamic first month). Among Shiʿis it has become traditionally connected with ten days' mourning for the martyrdom of ʿAli (son-in-law of the prophet Muhammad) and his two sons, Hasan and Husayn (Hussein). The incident that sets the mood for this commemorative day is the tragic death of Husayn at Karbala, Iraq, rather than the assassination of ʿAli. The commemoration of Husayn's passion and martyrdom (known as ʿAshura) is charged with unusual emotions among the Shiʿis throughout the world.[11] Thus, for the entire ten-day period, Shiʿi Muslims wear mourning clothes, refrain from shaving and bathing, and adopt a simple diet. In the mosques, the story of Husayn's death is narrated and chanted while faithful mourners sit on the floor beating their chests and crying loudly, "Husayn, Husayn."

The climax of this mourning period is the celebration of a passion play, cul-minating on the tenth day of Muharram with a re-enactment of the suffer-ing and death of Husayn. A solemn procession, designed as a funeral parade, dramatizes Husayn's burial. If this is not possible, then a number of scenes are staged to portray the events that led to the martyrdom of Husayn. Dramatic in-terpretations of Husayn's life highlight the events leading up to his death. Forty days later another passion play called "the return of the head" is re-enacted, with the emphasis on Husayn's role as intercessor between God and his crea-tures. To this day many Shiʿis choose to die, or at least to be buried, at Karbala, the site of Husayn's death, because tradition asserts that those who are buried by the shrine of Husayn will certainly enter paradise.

Sunni Muslims observe the tenth of Muharram with a different emphasis: the celebration of creation. Man and woman, paradise and hell, life and death, are said to have been created on this day.

Prophet's Birthday/Birthplace (Mawlid an-Nabi)

The celebration of the birthday of the prophet Muhammad is tradition-ally observed on the twelfth day of Rabiʿ al-Awwal (the Islamic third month). The custom is a relatively late development that was opposed by legists and theologians. Gradually, however, it was adopted in many countries by force of public sentiment. The occasion is marked by special prayers, the reading or reci-tation of Qurʾanic passages and literary and poetic compositions, and proces-sions.

The Prophet's birthplace in Mecca was once identified by a building with a dome and a minaret. The site was first honored by Khayzuran, mother of Caliph Harun ar-Rashid, and was recognized as a holy site until the Wahhabis took Mecca in 1925. Since then, the dome and the minaret have been destroyed and all ornaments within the building removed. This was in keeping with a Wahhabi proscription against all representations and honors remotely resem-bling idolatry. For the same reason, they oppose on principle the observance of the birthday of the prophet Muhammad.

Nocturnal Journey (Laylat al-Miʿraj)

This feast is celebrated on the night of the twenty-seventh of Rajab (the Islamic seventh month).[12] Mosques and minarets are lit, and popular devotional accounts of the prophet Muhammad's ascent, or journey, to heaven by night are read. Tradition states that while Muhammad was asleep, the angel Gabriel awak-ened him and led him on a night journey from the Kaʿbah in Mecca to the temple in Jerusalem on a white winged beast, resembling a donkey (buraq).[13] (Some traditional accounts interpret events less literally, claiming that Muham-mad's spirit traveled to Jerusalem while his body remained in Mecca.) There he met with Abraham, Moses, and Jesus, after which he led them in prayer and then ascended to the various levels of paradise, accompanied by the angel Gabriel.

Once in paradise, he met prophets and messengers of earlier times at different levels, ranked according to their status. At the highest level of paradise, God commanded Muhammad to extract from his people a commitment to pray fifty times daily. But Moses overheard the divine command from a level or two below, and he made a point of meeting Muhammad during his descent to suggest that Muhammad return to God to plead for a reduction in the number of prayers. Eventually Muhammad succeeded in having God agree to reduce the commitment from fifty to five times daily.

Some Muslims treat this incident as a dream. Others interpret it in terms of the journey a soul might make to the divine throne of judgment after death. The Sufis explain the incident in terms of the ascent of a soul from the veils of the sensual (the world of the flesh) to the heights of mystical knowledge, culminating in the unveiled presence of God (i.e., a mystical union with God).

The account of this nocturnal journey is based on a single Qur'anic passage that reads:

> Glory be to Him who carried His servant by night from the holy temple to the farthest temple—whose precincts We have blessed—that We may show him some of Our signs. (Qur'an 17:1)

This single Qur'anic verse is the source of a whole literature of tradition. Two separate traditional stories are then combined to account for the Prophet's nocturnal journey.

The first story is the Prophet's night journey (*isra'*) to Jerusalem on the strange *buraq*, half-mule and half-donkey. The angel Gabriel accompanies Muhammad to Jerusalem, where he meets Abraham, Moses, Jesus, and a number of other prophets. When he relates his experiences on his return to Mecca, his followers give no credibility to the story and treat it as a visionary experience.

The second story follows the first account. After Muhammad arrives in Jerusalem, a ladder is brought to him on which both he and his companion, the angel Gabriel, ascend to the door of paradise, which is guarded by another angel. On the first level of paradise, Muhammad is shown the site of hell, where he gets a glimpse of the torments of different categories of sinners before the flames drive him back and the lid clangs inexorably on the pit. On the second level, he meets Jesus and John the Baptist. On the third level, he meets the patriarch Joseph. On the fourth, Enoch (Idris); on the fifth, Aaron; on the sixth, Moses; and on the seventh, Abraham. Here, Muhammad also receives the divine command to order his followers to pray five times daily.

These two accounts, based on one cryptic Qur'anic passage, represent a host of accretions now collected in the canonical Tradition. The literary importance of the stories of the Prophet's nocturnal journey is that it served as the model for Dante's *Inferno*.

Other Celebrations

There are various other Islamic observances and festivals, but the dates and the events commemorated depend largely on the history and racial background of Muslims. For instance, Indian Muslims observe the anniversary of the death of Hasan (the brother of Husayn and son of ᶜAli), on the twenty-eighth day of Safar (the Islamic second month). Other Muslims observe the birthday of Husayn on the third of Shaᶜban (the Islamic eighth month). Still others, mainly Indian and Indonesian Muslims, celebrate the Night of Privilege (*Laylat al-Baraᶜa*) on the fifteenth of Shaᶜban, in commemoration of their dead. Egyptian Muslims, however, observe this same ceremony with the belief that after sunset the "heavenly tree" will be shaken and the leaves that fall from the tree will identify the human beings who will die in the following year.

Again, Shiᶜi Muslims commemorate the birthday and martyrdom of ᶜAli on the eighth and fifteenth of Jumada-l-Ula (the Islamic fifth month) respectively. Indian Muslims, however, commemorate the death of ᶜAli on the twenty-first of Ramadan. Another purely Shiᶜi observance is the *ᶜid al-ghadir,* celebrated on the eighteenth of Dhu-l-Hijjah (the Islamic twelfth month), in memory of the Prophet's nomination of ᶜAli as his successor. Many Muslims also observe the feast of the night of Fulfilled Desires (*Laylat ar-Raghaʾib*) on the twelfth of Rajab (the Islamic seventh month), because it is said that the prophet Muhammad was conceived on that night.

Appendix 1
Key Dates

CE

c. 570	Birth of Muhammad (d. 632)
610	Muhammad's first revelation
620	Death of Khadijah, Muhammad's wife
622	Migration of Muhammad (*hijrah* or *hegira*) from Mecca to Medina
630	Mecca controlled by Muhammad
632	Muhammad succeeded by Abu Bakr
634	Abu Bakr succeeded by ʿUmar
644	ʿUmar succeeded by ʿUthman
c. 650	Canonization of the Qurʾan
661	Assassination of ʿAli by a Khariji rebel; establishment of Umayyad dynasty (661–750)
680	Husayn, son of ʿAli assassinated at Karbala
691	The Dome of the Rock is completed in Jerusalem
750	Establishment of the ʿAbbasid dynasty (750–1258)
801	Death of Rabiʿah al-ʿAdawiyyah, the first great woman mystic
874	"Disappearance" of Abu al-Qasim Muhammad, the twelfth imam
922	Execution of the Persian mystic al-Hallaj
1058	Birth of al-Ghazali (d. 1111)
1095	Pope Urban II preaches the First Crusade
1099	The Crusaders conquer Jerusalem
1205	Beginning of Muslim domination of India, establishment of sultanate of Delhi
1273	Death of Jalal al-Din Rumi, founder of the Whirling Dervishes, in Turkey
1288	ʿUthman, a *ghazi* on the Byzantine frontier, founds the Ottoman dynasty in Turkey
1453	Memed II "the Conqueror" conquers Constantinople (Istanbul) and makes it the capital of the Ottoman Empire
1492	The Muslim kingdom of Granada is conquered by the Catholic monarchs Ferdinand and Isabella
1526	Founding of Mughal Empire by Babar (1526–1707)
1529	The Ottomans besiege Vienna
1653	Completion of Taj Mahal in India
c. 1760	Establishment of Wahhabi reform movement
1763	The British expand their control over India
1830	France occupies Algeria
1857	Indian mutiny against British rule
1881	France occupies Tunisia

1889	Britain occupies the Sudan
1917	The Balfour Declaration formally gives British support to the creation of a Jewish homeland in Palestine
1924	Abolishment of the Islamic caliphate by the Turkish government
1932	Kingdom of Saudi Arabia founded
1945	Formation of the Arab League
1947	Establishment of Pakistan as separate Muslim state
1948	Creation of the Jewish state of Israel
1963	Ayatollah Ruhollah Khomeini attacks the Pahlavi regime in Iran, is imprisoned and eventually exiled to Iraq
1964	Palestine Liberation Organization (PLO) established in Jerusalem
1967	The Six-Day War between Israel and its Arab neighbors
1970s	Militant Islamic groups like AMAL, Hizbꞌuꞌllah, and al-Jihad arise in Lebanon
1973	Egypt and Syria attack Israel on Yom Kippur
1978	Egypt and Israel sign the Camp David Accord
1979	Shah of Iran overthrown; revolutionary Islamic regime in Iran headed by Khomeini
1981	Muslim extremists assassinate President Anwar Sadat of Egypt
1987	Uprising of the *intifadah* against the Israeli occupation of the West Bank and the Gaza Strip
1989	Ayatollah Khomeini issues a *fatwah* against Salman Rushdie for his novel *The Satanic Verses*
1989	Death of Ayatollah Khomeini
1990	Iraqi president Saddam Hussein invades Kuwait
1991	The United States and its allies launch Operation Desert Storm against Iraq
1992	Members of the Bharatiya Janarta Party (BJP) dismantle the Mosque of Babur at Ayodhya, India
1992–1999	Serbian and Croatian nationalists kill and force Muslim inhabitants of Bosnia and Kosovo to leave their homes
1993	Israel and the Palestinians sign the Oslo Accord
1994	Israeli president Yitzak Rabin assassinated by a Jewish extremist
1994	A Jewish extremist assassinates 29 Muslims in the Hebron mosque in Israel; in retaliation Hamas suicide bombers attack Jewish civilians in Israel
1994	Taliban "fundamentalists" rise to power in Afghanistan
1995	Islamic militants bomb the American military at the National Guard Headquarters in Riyadh, Saudi Arabia
1996	Yasser Arafat elected president of the executive council of the Palestinian legislative assembly
1996	Islamic militants bomb the United States military housing compound in Dhahran, Saudi Arabia
2001	On September 11, Muslim terrorists destroy the towers of the World Trade Center in New York and damage the Pentagon in Washington; American president Bush declares "war on terrorism"
2002	Israeli president Ariel Sharon declares war on terrorists (suicide bombers), destroys Palestinian compounds and infrastructure; isolates Palestinian president Yasser Arafat
2003	U.S. and British troops dismantle President Saddam Hussein and occupy Iraq

Appendix 2
Muslim Dynasties

The chronology of Islamic dynasties is adopted from C. E. Bosworth, The Islamic Dynasties *(Edinburgh: Edinburgh University Press, 1972), pp. 5, 7–8, 11, 136–137, 172, 179, 210.*

The First Four Caliphs

Abu Bakr	632–34
ʿUmar I	634–44
ʿUthman	644–56
ʿAli	656–61

The Umayyads in Syria

Muʿawiya I	661–80
Yazid I	680–83
Muʿawiya II	683–84
Marwan I	684–85
ʿAbd al-Malik	685–705
al-Walid I	705–15
Sulaiman	715–17
ʿUmar II	717–20
Yazid II	720–24
Hisham	724–43
al-Walid II	743–44
Yazid III	744
Ibrahim	744
Marwan II	744–50
continued in Spain	

The Ummayads in Spain

ʿAbd ar-Rahman I	756–88
Hisham I	788–96
al-Hakam I	796–822
ʿAbd ar-Rahman II	822–52
Muhammad I	852–86
al-Mundhir	886–88

ʿAbd Allah	888–912
ʿAbd ar-Rahman III	912–61
al-Hakam II	961–76
Hisham II	976–1009
Civil War	1009–27
Hisham III	1027–31

The ʿAbbasids in Iraq

Abu al-ʿAbbas	749–54
al-Mansur	754–75
al-Mahdi	775–85
al-Hadi	785–86
Harun ar-Rashid	786–809
al-Amin	809–13
al-Maʾmun	813–33
al-Muʿtasim	833–42
al-Wathiq	842–47
al-Mutawakkil	847–61
al-Muntasir	861–62
al-Mustaʿin	862–66
al-Muʿtazz	866–69
al-Muhtadi	869–70
al-Muʿtamid	870–92
al-Muʿtadid	892–902
al-Muktafi	902–908
al-Muqtadir	908–32
al-Qahir	932–34
ar-Radi	934–40
al-Muttaqi	940–44
al-Mustakfi	944–46
al-Mutiʿ	946–74
at-Taʾiʿ	974–91
al-Qadir	991–1031
al-Qaʾim	1031–75
al-Muqtadi	1075–94
al-Mustazhir	1094–1118
al-Mustarshid	1118–35
ar-Rashid	1135–36
al-Muqtafi	1136–40
al-Mustanjid	1160–70
al-Mustadi	1170–80
al-Nasir	1180–1225
az-Zahir	1225–26
al-Mustansir	1226–42
al-Mustaʿsim	1242–58
Caliphate continued in Cairo	1261–1517

The Mughals in India

Babar	1526–30
Humayun	1530–56
Akbar I	1556–1605
Jahangir	1605–27
Bakhsh	1627–28
Jihan I	1628–58
Aurangzeb I	1658–1707
Bahadur I	1707–12
Jihandar	1712
Farrukh-siyar	1712–19
Muhammad	1719–48
Ahmed	1748–54
ᶜAlamgir II	1754–59
ᶜAlam II	1759–1806
Akbar II	1806–37
Bahadur II	1837–58

The Safavids in Persia

Ismaᶜil I	1501–24
Tahmasp I	1524–76
Ismaᶜil II	1576–78
Muhammad Khudabanda	1578–88
ᶜAbbas I	1588–1629
Safi I	1629–42
ᶜAbbas II	1642–66
Sulayman	1666–94
Husayn I	1694–1722
Tahmasp II	1722–32

nominal rulers in certain parts of Persia only:

ᶜAbbas III	1732
Nadir	1736
Adil	1747
Rukh	1748
Sulayman II	1749
Ismaᶜil III	1750
Husayn II	1753
Muhammad	1786

The Qajars in Persia

Agha Muhammad	1779–97
Fath ᶜAli	1797–1834
Muhammad	1834–48
Nasir-ad-Din	1848–96

Muzaffar-ad-Din	1896–1907
Muhammad ʿAli	1907–1909
Ahmad	1909–25

The Ottomans in Turkey

Osman I (ʿUthman I)	1281–1324
Orkhan I	1324–60
Murad I	1360–89
Bayazid I	1389–1402
Muhammad I	1403–21
Sulayman I	1403–10 [contestant]
Murad II	1421–51
Muhammad II	1451–81
Bayazid II	1481–1512
Selim I	1512–20
Sulayman II	1520–66
Selim II	1566–74
Murad III	1574–95
Muhammad III	1595–1603
Ahmed I	1603–17
Mustafa I	1617–18; 1622–23
Osman II	1618–22
Murad IV	1623–40
Ibrahim I	1640–48
Muhammad IV	1648–87
Sulayman III	1687–91
Ahmed II	1691–95
Mustafa II	1695–1703
Ahmed III	1703–30
Mahmud I	1730–54
Osman III	1754–57
Mustafa III	1757–74
ʿAbdul Hamid I	1774–89
Selim III	1789–1807
Mustafa IV	1807–1808
Mahmud II	1808–39
ʿAbdul Majid I	1839–61
ʿAbdul ʿAziz	1861–76
Murad V	1876
ʿAbdul Hamid II	1876–1909
Muhammad V	1909–18
Muhammad VI	1918–22
ʿAbdul Majid II	1922–24

Appendix 3
The Ninety-Nine Names of God

1.	al-Rahman	The Compassionate
2.	al-Rahim	The Merciful
3.	al-Malik	The King
4.	al-Quddus	The Holy
5.	al-Salam	The Source of Peace
6.	al-Muʾmin	The Preserver of Security
7.	al-Muhaymin	The Protector
8.	al-ʿAziz	The Mighty
9.	al-Jabbār	The Overpowering
10.	al-Mutakabbir	The Great in Majesty
11.	al-Khaliq	The Creator
12.	al-Bāriʾ	The Maker
13.	al-Musawwir	The Fashioner
14.	al-Ghaffār	The Forgiver
15.	al-Qahhār	The Dominant
16.	al-Wahhāb	The Bestower
17.	al-Razzāq	The Provider
18.	al-Fattah	The Decider
19.	al-ʿAlim	The Knower
20.	al-Qābid	The Withholder
21.	al-Bāsit	The Plentiful Giver
22.	al-Khāfid	The Abaser
23.	al-Rafiʿ	The Exalter
24.	al-Muʿizz	The Honourer
25.	al-Mudhill	The Humiliator
26.	al-Samīʿ	The Hearer
27.	al-Basīr	The Seer
28.	al-Hakam	The Judge
29.	al-ʿAdl	The Just
30.	al-Latīf	The Gracious
31.	al-Khabīr	The Informed
32.	al-Halīm	The Clement
33.	al-ʿAzīm	The Incomparably Great
34.	al-Ghafūr	The Forgiving
35.	al-Shakūr	The Rewarder
36.	al-ʿAlī	The Most High
37.	al-Kabīr	The Most Great
38.	al-Hafīz	The Preserver
39.	al-Muqīt	The Sustainer

40. al-Hasīb	The Reckoner
41. al-Jalīl	The Majestic
42. al-Karīm	The Generous
43. al-Raqīb	The Watcher
44. al-Mujīb	The Answerer
45. al-Wāsiʾ	The Liberal
46. al-Hakīm	The Wise
47. al-Wadūd	The Loving
48. al-Majīd	The Glorious
49. al-Bāʾith	The Raiser
50. al-Shahid	The Witness
51. al-Haqq	The Real
52. al-Wakīl	The Trustee
53. al-Qawī	The Strong
54. al-Matīn	The Firm
55. al-Walī	The Patron
56. al-Hamīd	The Praiseworthy
57. al-Muhsī	The All-Knowing
58. al-Mubdiʾ	The Originator
59. al-Muʿīd	The Restorer to life
60. al-Muhyī	The Giver of life
61. al-Mumīt	The Giver of death
62. al-Hayy	The Living
63. al-Qayyūm	The Eternal
64. al-Wājid	The Self-sufficient
65. al-Mājid	The Grand
66. al-Wāhid	The One
67. al-Ahad	The Single
68. al-Samad	He to whom men repair
69. al-Qādir	The Powerful
70. al-Muqtadir	The Prevailing
71. al-Muqaddim	The Advancer
72. al-Muʾakhkhir	The Delayer
73. al-Awwal	The First
74. al-Ākhir	The Last
75. al-Zāhir	The Outward
76. al-Bātin	The Inward
77. al-Wālī	The Governor
78. al-Mutaʿālī	The Sublime
79. al-Barr	The Amply Beneficient
80. al-Tawwāb	The Acceptor of repentance
81. al-Muntaqim	The Avenger
82. al-ʿAfūw	The Pardoner
83. al-Raʾūf	The Kindly
84. Mālik al-Mulk	The Ruler of The Kingdom
85. Dhul Jalāl wal Ikrām	The Lord of Majesty and Splendour
86. al-Muqsit	The Equitable
87. al-Jāmiʿ	The Gatherer
88. al-Ghanī	The Independent

89.	al-Mughnī	The Enricher
90.	al-Māniᶜ	The Depriver
91.	al-Dārr	The Harmer
92.	al-Nāfiᶜ	The Benefiter
93.	al-Nūr	The Light
94.	al-Hādi	The Guide
95.	al-Badīᶜ	The First Cause (or, The Incomparable)
96.	al-Bāqī	The Enduring
97.	al-Wārith	The Inheritor
98.	al-Rashīd	The Director
99.	al-Sabūr	The Patient

Reproduced from Abu Hurayra, given by Tirmidhi, as listed in *Dictionary of Comparative Religion*, ed. by S. G. F. Brandon (New York: Charles Scribner's Sons, 1970), pp. 306–307.

Glossary

ʿabd	slave, servant
abu	father of
ʿada	custom, customary law
ahl al-kitab	people of the book
ʿalamin	spheres, realms
Allah	God
amir	military commander
amrʾ	order, command
azha	sacrifice
bab	door, forerunner
baqa	arrive
baraʿa	privilege
bayt	house, temple, shrine
buraq	winged beast
dar al-harb	territory of war
dar al-Islam	territory of Islam
dar as-sulh	territory of peace
dhikr	remembrance, mention
dhimmi	protected people
din	religion
duʿa	supplication, invocation
fana	pass
fatihah	opening, beginning, first chapter of the Qurʾan
fidaʿis	suicide squad
fiqh	jurisprudence, understanding, insight
ghulat	extremists
ghusal	ablution, bathing
Hadith	Tradition
hajj	pilgrimage
haqq	truth
hashashin	pot-smokers, assassins
hashish	hash, pot
hijrah	flight (Hegira)
hikmah	knowledge

Iblis	Satan, Devil
ibn	son of
ʿId	Feast
ʿidda	waiting period
Idris	Enoch
ihram	sanctity
ijmaʿ	consensus
iktisab	acquired action
ʿilm	knowledge
Imam	leader
imam	spiritual leader
iman	faith, belief
Injil	Gospel
iʿtikaf	withdrawal to a mosque
jihad	holy war
jinn	genie, spirits
jizya	poll-tax
Kaʿbah	(cube) shrine in Mecca
kabir	great, big
kafir	unbeliever, infidel
kalam	speech, theology
Khalifa	Caliph, successor
khatam	seal
khutba	sermon, address
laylat	night
laylat al-baraʿa	night of privileges
laylat al-miʿraj	night of journey, ascension
madrasa	center of learning, school
Mahdi	Guided One
majnun	insane, mad, jinn-possessed
mawali	non-Arabs, freed slaves
mawlid an-Nabi	Prophet's birthday/birthplace
mihrab	niche in wall of mosque
minaret	tower of mosque
muezzin	one who calls to prayer
mufti	jurist
muhajiran	emigrants
mullah	religious master, leader
mutʿa	temporary marriage
nabi	prophet
natiq	utterer, speaker
qadi	judge
qadr	power

qiblah	direction of prayer (toward Mecca)
qiyas	deduction process, analogical reasoning
rab	lord
ragha'ib	desire
rasul	messenger (apostle)
riba	usury
sadaqa	voluntary or charitable alms
saghir	small
salat	prayer
sawm	fasting
shahadah	profession, confession, witness
Shaitan	Satan
shari'ah	law, regulations
shaykh	leader, title of respect
shirk	association
silsilah	mystical succession
siyam	fasting
suf	wool
suhuf	scrolls, sheets
sunnah	custom, practice, tradition
surah	chapter, section
taqiyya	concealment of belief, dissimulation
taqlid	authority
tariq	path, order
Taurat	Torah
'ulama	divines, theologians, teachers of religion
ummah	community (Islamic)
waqf	charitable endowment
wasi	silent, mute
wudu	ablution
wuquf	standing (before God)
Zabur	Psalms
zakat	almsgiving

Notes

Introduction

1. On the *dhimmi*, see Bat, *Islam and Dhimmitude: Where Civilizations Collide;* idem, *The Dhimmi: Jews and Christians under Islam.*

2. For Islam in the modern world, see Voll, *Islam, Continuity and Change in the Modern World;* Haddad, *Contemporary Islam and the Challenge of History;* Rahman, *Islam and Modernity: The Transformation of an Intellectual Tradition.*

3. For instance, see Ibn Warraq, *Why I Am Not a Muslim.*

4. For an understanding of the forces behind the dramatic events in the Islamic world today, see Pullapilly, ed., *Islam;* Lewis, *What Went Wrong?: Western Impact and Middle Eastern Response.*

5. For acts of hostilities between Israelis and Palestinians, see Smith, *Palestine and the Arab-Israeli Conflict;* for differences between European Zionists and Middle Eastern Arabs, see Friedman, *From Beirut to Jerusalem.*

6. Mishal, *The PLO Under ʿArafat: Between Gun and Olive Branch;* Sahliyeh, *The PLO after the Lebanon War;* Gresh, *The PLO: The Struggle Within—Towards an Independent Palestinian State;* Brynen, *Sanctuary and Survival: The PLO in Lebanon.*

7. Some Muslims consider the present Israeli government to be pursuing an "ethnic cleansing" policy; see, for instance, Ahmed, *Islam Today: A Short Introduction to the Muslim World,* 136.

8. For the revolution in Iran, see Fischer, *Iran: From Religious Dispute to Revolution.*

9. For a Muslim view of the Gulf War, see Heikal, *Illusions of Triumph: An Arab View of the Gulf War.*

10. Norton, *Amal and the Shiʿa: Struggle for the Soul of Lebanon.*

11. Kramer, *Hezbollah's Vision of the West.*

12. Deeb, *Militant Islamic Movements in Lebanon: Origins, Social Basis, and Ideology.*

13. For the conflict between Islam and the West over the course of centuries, see Esposito, *The Islamic Threat: Myth or Reality?;* Hourani, *Islam in European Thought;* idem, *Western Attitudes towards Islam;* Rodinson, "The Western Image and Western Studies of Islam," 9–62; Daniel, *Islam and the West: The Making of an Image;* Southern, *Western Views of Islam in the Middle Ages.*

14. On Afghanistan and the rise of the Taliban, see Goodson, *Afghanistan's Endless War: State Failure, Regional Politics, and the Rise of the Taliban;* Gohari, *The Taliban: Ascent to Power;* Rashid, *Taliban: Militant Islam, Oil, and Funda-*

mentalism in Central Asia; Marsden, *The Taliban: War, Religion and the New Order in Afghanistan;* Ahmed, *Pukhtun Economy and Society: Traditional Structure and Economic Development in a Tribal Society.*

1. Muhammad, Messenger of God

1. For a one-volume survey of the region and its peoples from prehistory to the rise of Islam, see Hoyland, *Arabia and the Arabs: From the Bronze Age to the Coming of Islam.*

2. Pritchard, ed., *Ancient Near Eastern Texts Relating to the Old Testament,* 2nd ed., 279.

3. Ibid., 283–86, 291, 292, 297–301, 316, 430.

4. On the history of the Arabs, see, among others, Hourani, *A History of the Arab Peoples;* Weiss and Green, *A Survey of Arab History;* Mansfield, *The Arabs,* 3rd ed.; Rodinson, *The Arabs;* Lewis, *The Arabs in History;* Hitti, *History of the Arabs,* 9th ed.

5. On pre-Islamic and Islamic legend concerning Abraham and Mecca, see Firestone, *Journeys in Holy Lands: The Evolution of the Abraham-Ishmael Legends in Islamic Exegesis.*

6. Motzki, ed., *The Biography of Muhammad: The Issue of the Sources,* xiv; all of the ten articles collected in this volume attempt to tackle the problem of the sources on Muhammad.

7. A survey of the sources is found in Cook, *Muhammad,* 61–76.

8. For an appraisal of the earliest non-Muslim references to Muhammad, see Hoyland, "The Earliest Christian Writings on Muhammad: An Appraisal," 276–97.

9. For a critical analysis, see Donner, *Narratives of Islamic Origins: The Beginnings of Islamic Historical Writing,* 1–31; Cameron et al., eds., *The Byzantine and Early Islamic Near East: Problems in the Literary Source Material,* vol. 1, 1–24 (see particularly p. 4 n. 4, and p. 15 nn. 15–23).

10. For instance, Wansbrough, *Qurʾanic Studies: Sources and Methods of Scriptural Interpretation;* Cook, *Muhammad.*

11. For instance, see Gibb, *Islam: A Historical Survey;* Watt, *Muhammad: Prophet and Statesman.*

12. On the prophet Muhammad, see Forward, *Muhammad: A Short Biography;* Peters, *Muhammad and the Origins of Islam;* Armstrong, *Muhammad: A Biography of the Prophet;* Cook, *Muhammad;* Lings, *Muhammad: His Life Based on the Earliest Sources;* Rodinson, *Mohammed.*

13. From al-Tabari's *Taʾrikh ar-rusul waʾl-muluk,* I, 1147–52.

14. Cited in Guillaume, *The Life of Muhammad: A Translation of Ibn Ishaq's Sirat Rasul Allah,* 107.

15. For a short history of the Muslim people, see Armstrong, *Islam: A Short History;* for the origins of the institution of the caliphate, see Kennedy, *The Prophet and the Age of the Caliphates: The Islamic Near East from the Sixth to the Eleventh Century.*

16. For an account of both the religious and political career of Muhammad, see Watt, *Muhammad: Prophet and Statesman.*

17. For a discussion of the role of Muhammad in popular Muslim piety, see Schimmel, *And Muhammad Is His Messenger: The Veneration of the Prophet in Islamic Piety.*

18. Mawdudi, *Towards Understanding Islam,* 65, 73.

19. Nasr, *Ideals and Realities of Islam,* 86.

2. Islam in History

1. The chronology of Islamic dynasties is adopted from Bosworth, *The Islamic Dynasties.* See Appendix 2.

2. On the early conquests, see Donner, *The Early Islamic Conquests.*

3. On the Umayyad period, see Donner, *The Early Islamic Conquests;* Wellhausen, *The Arab Kingdom and Its Fall.*

4. Sharon, *Black Banners from the East.*

5. Bosworth, *The Ghaznavids: Their Empire in Afghanistan and Eastern Iran, 994–1040;* idem, *The Later Ghaznavids: Splendour and Decay—The Dynasty in Afghanistan and Northern India.*

6. For one of the rare monographs, though dated, see O'Leary, *A Short History of the Fatimid Khaliphate.*

7. See Lev, *State and Society in Fatimid Egypt;* al-Imad, *The Fatimid Vizierate 969–1172.*

8. For instance, see Cardini, *Europe and Islam;* Housley, *Crusading and Warfare in Medieval and Renaissance Europe;* Richard, *The Crusades c.1071– c.1291.*

9. In the area of the arts, for instance, the famous ʿUmar Khayyam (Omar Khayyam) succeeded in solving the cubic equations, algebraically and geometrically. His fame as a mathematician caused the sultan Malikshah Jalal ad-Din to charge him with a reform of the calendar. ʿUmar Khayyam's popularity in European circles rests primarily on the witty Persian quatrains under his name, paraphrased into English by Fitzgerald and into German by Rosen. Modern scholarship has questioned ʿUmar Khayyam's authorship of the quatrains.

10. For the history of the Mongols, see Allsen, *Culture and Conquest in Mongol Eurasia;* Amitai-Preiss and Morgan, eds., *The Mongol Empire and Its Legacy.*

11. Onon, *The Secret History of the Mongols: The Life and Times of Chinggis Khan.*

12. Athar, *The Mughal Nobility under Aurangzeb.*

13. Savory, *Iran under the Safavids.*

14. For names of Qajar leaders in Persia, see Appendix 2.

15. Bosworth and Hillenbrand, eds., *Qajar Iran: Political, Social, and Cultural Change, 1800–1925;* Bayat, *Mysticism and Dissent: Socioreligious Thought in Qajar Iran;* Bakhash, *Iran: Monarchy, Bureaucracy, and Reform under the Qajars, 1858–1896.*

16. On the origin of the Ottoman Empire, see Inalçik, *The Ottoman Empire: The Classical Age, 1300–1600*; Wittek, *The Rise of the Ottoman Empire*.

17. On the rise and expansion of the Ottoman Empire, see Shaw, *The History of the Ottoman Empire and Modern Turkey*.

18. For example, see Shaw, *Between Old and New: The Ottoman Empire under Sultan Selim III, 1789–1807*.

19. Trimingham, *The Influence of Islam upon Africa*; Lewis, ed., *Islam in Tropical Africa*.

20. Blyden, *Christianity, Islam, and the Negro Race*.

21. Marsh, *From Black Muslims to Muslims: The Transition from Separatism to Islam, 1930–1980*; Lee, *The Nation of Islam: An American Millenarian Movement*.

22. Haddad and Smith, *Mission to America: Five Islamic Sectarian Communities in North America*.

23. Nielsen, *Muslims in Western Europe*; Haddad and Smith, eds., *Muslim Communities in North America*; Lewis, *Islamic Britain: Religion, Politics, and Identity among British Muslims*.

24. On various ideologies in the modern Islamic world, see Sahliyeh, ed., *Religious Resurgence and Politics in the Contemporary World*; Binder, *Islamic Liberalism: A Critique of Development Ideologies*.

25. The modern Muslim world is divided on issues such as politics, society, religion, authority, interpretation, and so on. Numerous books, written by both Muslim and non-Muslim scholars, deal extensively with such issues. For an overview, see Ahmed, *Islam Today: A Short Introduction to the Muslim World*, 96–237; Esposito, *Islam: The Straight Path*, 3rd ed., 115–252; idem, *Islam and Politics*; Fischer and Abedi, *Debating Muslims: Cultural Dialogues in Postmodernity and Tradition*.

3. Muslim Groups

1. For an English translation of al-Ghazali's *Tahafut al-falasifah*, see Kamali, *Incoherence of the Philosophers*.

2. Al-Yassini, *Religion and State in the Kingdom of Saudi Arabia*.

3. Still the most comprehensive description is that of Ahmad, *Invitation to Ahmadiyyat*.

4. Ahmad, *Jesus in India: Being an Account of Jesus' Escape from Death on the Cross and of His Journey to India*.

5. For the history of the Ahmadiyyah and its expansion, see Friedmann, *Prophecy Continuous: Aspects of Ahmadi Religious Thought and Its Medieval Background*.

6. On the Shiʿis, see Arjomand, ed., *Authority and Political Culture in Shiʿism*; Cole and Keddie, eds., *Shiʿism and Social Protest*; Momen, *An Introduction to Shiʿi Islam*; Tabatabaʾi, *An Introduction to Shiʿi Law*.

7. For a study of Islamic sects, as opposed to prevailing authority, see Khuri, *Imams and Emirs: State, Religion, and Sects in Islam.*

8. Sachedina, *Islamic Messianism: The Idea of the Mahdi in Twelver Shiʿism.*

9. Hussain, *The Occultation of the Twelfth Imam.*

10. For an overview of Yemeni history with discussions on Zaydi, see Dresch, *Tribes, Government, and History in Yemen.*

11. For a detailed survey up to modern times, see Daftary, *The Ismaʿilis: Their History and Doctrines;* idem, *A Short History of the Ismailis.*

12. According to other Imamis, Ismaʿil is said to have died before his father.

13. Hodgson, *The Order of Assassins: The Struggle of the Early Nizari Ismaʿilis against the Islamic World.*

14. Nanji, *The Nizari Ismaili Tradition in the Indo-Pakistan Subcontinent.*

15. For general studies on Sufism, see Baldick, *Mystical Islam: An Introduction to Sufism;* Andrae, *In the Garden of Myrtles: Studies in Early Islamic Mysticism;* Schimmel, *Mystical Dimensions of Islam.*

16. For Sufi views on God, the cosmos, the human soul, and gender issues, see Murata, *The Tao of Islam: A Sourcebook on Gender Relationships in Islamic Thought;* Nasr, ed., *Islamic Spirituality.*

17. Al-Isfahani, *Hilyat al-Awliyaʾ wa-tabaqat al-asfiyaʾ,* vol. II, 132f.

18. See Nurbakhsh, *Sufi Women;* Arberry, *Muslim Saints and Mystics.*

19. Arabic text in Massignon, *Recueil de textes inedits concernant l'histoire de la mystique en pays d'Islam,* 6; English translation in Nicholson, *Literary History of the Arabs,* 234.

20. Massignon, *The Passion of al-Hallaj: Mystic and Martyr of Islam.*

21. al-Ghazali, *Freedom and Fulfillment: An Annotated Translation of al-Ghazali's al-Munqidh min al-Dalal and Other Relevant Works of al-Ghazali.*

22. Chodkiewicz, *An Ocean without Shore: Ibn ʿArabi, the Book, and the Law.*

23. Chittick, *The Sufi Path of Love: The Spiritual Teachings of Rumi.*

24. Friedlander, *The Whirling Dervishes.*

25. Chabbi, "ʿAbd al-Kadir al-Djilani, personnage historique," 75–106.

26. Trimingham, *The Sufi Orders in Islam;* Rizvi, *A History of Sufism in India.*

27. Reeves, *The Hidden Government: Ritual, Clientelism, and Legitimation in Northern Egypt.*

28. See Dussaud, *Histoire et religion des Nosairis.*

29. Firro, *A History of the Druzes;* Betts, *The Druze;* Abu Izzeddin, *The Druzes: A New Study of Their History, Faith, and Society.*

30. On the Yezidis, see Allison, *The Yezidi Oral Tradition in Iraqi Kurdistan;* Kreyenbroek and Sperl, eds., *The Kurds: A Contemporary Overview.*

31. Smith, *The Babi and Bahaʾi Religions: From Messianic Shiʿism to a World Religion;* Hatcher, *The Bahaʾi Faith: The Emerging Global Religion;* Momen, *Islam and the Bahaʾi Faith.*

32. On the Black Muslims in America, see Lincoln, *The Black Muslims in America.*

33. See Muhammad, *Message to the Blackman in America*.

34. For criticisms of his father Elijah Muhammad, see Muhammad, *As the Light Shineth from the East*.

35. For dietary regulations, see Muhammad, *How to Eat to Live*.

36. For the collection of speeches by Malcolm X, see Malcolm X, *Malcolm X Speaks*.

37. For Malcolm X's biography and his views, see Perry, *Malcolm: The Life of a Man Who Changed Black America;* Malcolm X and Haley, *The Autobiography of Malcolm X*.

4. Qurʾan

1. So stated explicitly in Kateregga and Shenk, *Islam and Christianity: A Muslim and a Christian in Dialogue,* 25–26.

2. See Rahman, *Islam,* 30–33.

3. For a list of translations of the Qurʾan, see Jomier, *The Bible and the Koran,* 7–9.

4. Guillaume, *Islam,* 56.

5. On recitation of the Qurʾan as a religious practice, see Surty, *A Course in the Science of Reciting the Qurʾan;* Nelson, *The Art of Reciting the Qurʾan.*

6. Guillaume, *The Life of Muhammad: A Translation of Ibn Ishaq's Sirat Rasul Allah.*

7. Ibn Maja, *Sunan,* I. 92–95; al-Qasimi, *Maw ͨizat al-Mu ͨminin min Ihya ͨUlam ad-Din,* I. 99–102.

8. For an understanding of the Qurʾan from a Muslim point of view in response to polemical Western scholarship, see Rahman, *Major Themes of the Qurʾan;* for an analysis of the text, see Izutsu, *God and Man in the Koran: Semantics of the Koranic Weltanschauung.*

9. There are many commentaries on the Qurʾan. Among others, see Mahmoud Ayoub, *The Qurʾan and Its Interpreters;* Bell, *A Commentary on the Qurʾan.*

10. For a response to the feminist critique of Islam, see Wadud-Muhsin, *Qurʾan and Woman.*

11. On the duty of commanding right and forbidding wrong, see Cook, *Commanding Right and Forbidding Wrong in Islamic Thought.*

12. See, for instance, Jomier, *The Bible and the Koran;* Guillaume, *Islam,* 194–99.

13. For Christian, Jewish, and Zoroastrian perceptions on early Islam, see Hoyland, *Seeing Islam as Others Saw It: A Survey and Evaluation of Christian, Jewish, and Zoroastrian Writings on Early Islam.*

14. For a study of the portrayal of Christians and Christianity in the Qurʾan, see McAuliffe, *Qurʾanic Christians: An Analysis of Classical and Modern Exegesis.*

15. From al-Kurdi, *Tarikh al-Qurʾan,* 207.

16. Among other literature, see Gaudeul, *Encounters and Clashes: Islam and Christianity in History;* Haddad and Haddad, eds., *Christian-Muslim Encounters;*

Watt, *Muslim-Christian Encounters: Perceptions and Misperceptions;* Ellis, ed., *The Vatican, Islam, and the Middle East;* Kateregga and Shenk, *Islam and Christianity.*

17. Ali, "Islam and Christianity," 472.

18. Ibid.; also al-Faruqi and Sopher, eds., *Historical Atlas of the Religions of the World,* 246f; Dawe and Carman, eds., *Christian Faith in a Religiously Plural World,* 69–79.

19. Ali, "Christianity from the Islamic Standpoint."

20. Ibid.

21. Khan, *Islam,* 84–85.

5. Sunnah, Hadith, and Shariʿah

1. From al-Bukhari as cited by Krehl and Juynboll, eds., *al-Jamiʿ al-Sahih,* vol. 4, 115.

2. Ibid., 114.

3. Ibid., 139.

4. Al-Tirmidhi, *Al-Jamiʿal-Sahih,* zuhd, 45.

5. Guillaume, *The Traditions of Islam,* 263–70.

6. See Asin Palacios, *La Escatologia Musulmana En Ia Divina Comedia.*

7. For studies on the Hadith, see Goldziher, *Muslim Studies,* vol. 2; Siddiqi, *Hadith Literature: Its Origin, Development, Special Features, and Criticism;* Guillaume, *The Traditions of Islam.*

8. Rahman, *Islam,* 64; Nasr, *Ideals and Realities of Islam,* 80.

9. From al-Bukhari as cited by Krehl and Juynboll, eds., *al-Jamiʿ al-Sahih,* 445.

10. The argument is presented by Gibb, *Mohammedanism,* 2nd rev. ed., 56; and Rahman, *Islam,* 44–49.

11. So stated by Gibb, *Mohammedanism,* 56; and Rahman, *Islam,* 49.

12. Rahman, *Islam,* 67.

13. Gibb, *Mohammedanism,* 58f.

14. For a concise treatment on Islamic law, see Schacht, *An Introduction to Islamic Law.*

15. Dalrymple, *Law Reform in the Muslim World.*

16. For a discussion of the medieval legal schools and their modern derivations, see Cook, *Commanding Right and Forbidding Wrong in Islamic Thought;* Coulson, *A History of Islamic Law.*

17. Tabatabaʾi, *An Introduction to Shiʿi Law: A Bibliographical Study.*

18. al-Khuli, *Malik ibn Anas: Tarjamah Muharrarah.*

19. Abu Zahrah, *Al-Shafiʿi.*

20. Abu Zahrah, *Ibn Hanbal.*

21. Sachedina, *The Just Ruler (al-sultan al-ʿadil) in Shiʿite Islam: The Comprehensive Authority of the Jurist in Imamite Jurisprudence.*

22. For an analysis of traditional legal theory, see Mahmassani, *The Philosophy of Jurisprudence in Islam.*

23. Pearl, *Muslim Family Law;* Mahmood, *Personal Law in Islamic Countries: History, Texts, and Analysis;* Nasir, *The Islamic Law of Personal Status;* Esposito, *Women in Muslim Family Law.*

24. Coulson, *Succession in the Muslim Family.*

25. Mannan, *The Making of an Islamic Economic Society: Islamic Dimensions in Economic Analysis;* Ahmad, *Studies in Islamic Economics.*

26. Qureshi, *Waqfs in India: A Study of Administrative and Legislative Control;* Basar, ed., *Management and Development of Awqaf Properties.*

27. Bassiouni, ed., *The Islamic Criminal Justice System.*

28. Ziadeh, *Lawyers, the Rule of Law, and Liberalism in Modern Egypt.*

29. Marty and Appleby, eds., *Fundamentalisms and the State: Remaking Polities, Economies, and Militance;* Hooker, *Islamic Law in South-East Asia;* Ahmad, *Islamic Modernism in India and Pakistan, 1857–1964.*

30. Nasir, *The Status of Women under Islamic Law and under Modern Islamic Legislation.*

31. On social movements and gender issues, see Moghadam, *Modernizing Women: Gender and Social Change in the Middle East;* Ahmed, *Women and Gender in Islam: Historical Roots of a Modern Debate;* Karim, *Women and Culture: Between Mayal Adat and Islam;* Kandiyoti, ed., *Women, Islam, and the State;* Lateef, *Muslim Women in India: Political and Private Realities, 1890s–1980s;* Mernissi, *Beyond the Veil: Male-Female Dynamics in Modern Muslim Society;* Mumtaz and Shaheed, eds., *Women of Pakistan: Two Steps Forward, One Step Back?*

32. The literature on social reform in various principal areas of the Islamic world is extensive. For up-to-date sources, see Esposito, *The Oxford Encyclopedia of the Modern Islamic World,* vol. 4, 332–51.

33. Riesebrodt, *Pious Passion: The Emergence of Modern Fundamentalism in the United States and Iran.*

34. Badran, *Feminists, Islam, and Nation: Gender and the Making of Modern Egypt.*

35. For a collection of articles on this issue, see Moghadam, ed., *Identity Politics and Women: Cultural Reassertions and Feminisms in International Perspectives.*

36. Peteet, *Gender in Crisis: Women and the Palestine Resistance Movement.*

37. Al-Saʿdawi, *The Hidden Face of Eve: Women in the Arab World;* Malti-Douglas, *Woman's Body, Woman's Word: Gender and Discourse in Arabo- Islamic Writing;* Badran and Cooke, eds., *Opening the Gates: A Century of Arab Feminist Writing;* Shaʿrawi, *Harem Years: The Memoirs of an Egyptian Feminist.*

38. al-Hibri, ed., *Women and Islam.*

39. Ariffin, *Women and Development in Malaysia.*

40. Schuler, ed., *Freedom from Violence: Women's Strategies from around the World.*

41. On the examination of the Qurʾan and Hadith by Muslim women, see Wadud-Muhsin, *Qurʾan and Woman;* Mernissi, *Women and Islam: An His-*

torical and Theological Inquiry; Cooey, Eakin, and MacDaniel, eds., *After Patriarchy: Feminist Transformations of the World Religions.*

6. Faith and Action

1. Excellent summaries on the subject are found in Esposito, *Islam: The Straight Path*; Anawati, "Kalam," 231–42; Fakhry, *A History of Islamic Philosophy.*

2. Doctrinal interpretations regarding the Articles of Faith differ among Sunni and Shiʿi; see Ibn Babawayh, *A Shiʿite Creed*; ʿAbduh, *The Theology of Unity*; al-Ghazali, *The Foundations of the Articles of Faith.*

3. Watt, *Free Will and Predestination in Early Islam.*

4. On the nature of prophecy, see Rahman, *Prophecy in Islam: Philosophy and Orthodoxy.*

5. Brandon, ed., *Dictionary of Comparative Religion*, 512.

6. From Shaʿrani, *Mukhtasar al-Tadhkirah*, 51.

7. On the subject of Mahdi, see Smith and Haddad, *The Islamic Understanding of Death and Resurrection*; on Shiʿi ideas, see Sachedina, *Islamic Messianism: The Idea of Mahdi in Twelver Shiʿism*; on Sufi ideas, see Schimmel, *Mystical Dimensions of Islam.*

8. Padwick, *Muslim Devotions: A Study of Prayer-Manuals in Common Use.*

9. Wensinck, *The Muslim Creed: Its Genesis and Historical Development.*

10. Ghafuri, *The Ritual Prayer of Islam*; Muhammad, *Virtues of Salaat: An English Translation of Fazail-i-Namaz.*

11. Description adopted from Brandon, ed., *Dictionary of Comparative Religion*, 508.

12. Wagtendonk, *Fasting in the Koran.*

13. For a useful guide, see Kamal, *The Sacred Journey.*

14. On the Saudi administration of the pilgrimage (*hajj*), see Long, *The Hajj Today: A Survey of the Contemporary Makkah Pilgrimage.*

15. For the idea of "martyrdom" (Arabic *shahid*, meaning "witness") in Islam, see Abedi and Legenhausen, eds., *Jihad and Shahadat: Struggle and Martyrdom in Islam*; Ayoub, *Redemptive Suffering in Islam: A Study of the Devotional Aspects of "Ashura" in Twelver Shiʿism.*

16. On Mecca and Medina as shrine complexes, see Esin, *Mecca the Blessed, Madinah the Radiant*; Eickelman and Piscatori, eds., *Muslim Travellers: Pilgrimage, Migration, and the Religious Imagination.*

17. A brief but precise discussion on moral values is found in Khan, *Islam*, chapters 14–15.

7. Observances and Festivals

1. On clitoridectomy, see Shell-Duncan and Hernlund, eds., *Female "Circumcision" in Africa: Culture, Controversy, and Change*; al-Saʿdawi, *The Hidden Face of Eve: Women in the Arab World*; Giorgis, *Female Circumcision in Africa.*

2. Ibn al-Ukhuwa, *Ma'alim al-Qurba*, 164.

3. On Islamic family law, see Fluehr-Lobban, *Islamic Law and Society in the Sudan;* Esposito, *Women in Muslim Family Law.*

4. Salih, *The Wedding of Zein and Other Stories.*

5. Abdul-Rauf, *Islam: Creed and Worship.*

6. On Islamic funerary rites in North America, see Kutty, *Islamic Funeral Rites and Practices.*

7. Smith and Haddad, *The Islamic Understanding of Death and Resurrection.*

8. For a good discussion on the Islamic calendar, see Hodgson, *The Venture of Islam,* vol. 1.

9. For a comparison, see Freeman-Grenville, *The Muslim and Christian Calendars.*

10. On Islamic festivals, see Denny, *An Introduction to Islam,* 105–24; Von Grunebaum, *Muhammadan Festivals.*

11. The most important study of 'Ashura is that of Ayoub, *Redemptive Suffering in Islam;* also see Schubel, *Religious Performance in Contemporary Islam.*

12. Schimmel, *And Muhammad Is His Messenger,* chapter 9.

13. The account is found in al-Suyuti, *al-La'ali' al-masnu'ah fi al-ahadith al-mawdu'ah,* vol. 1, p. 39.

Bibliography

Translations of the Qurʾan

Ali, A. Yusuf, trans. *The Holy Quran: Text, Translation and Commentary.* New rev. ed. Brentwood, Md.: Amana Corp., 1989.

Arberry, Arthur John. *The Koran Interpreted.* London: Allen & Unwin, 1955; New York: Macmillan, 1964.

Ayoub, Mahmoud. *The Qurʾan and Its Interpreters,* 2 vols. Albany: SUNY Press, 1984.

Bell, Richard. *Bell's Introduction to the Qurʾan.* Revised and edited by W. Montgomery Watt. Edinburgh: Edinburgh University Press, 1970.

———. *A Commentary on the Qurʾan.* 2 vols., revised and edited by Clifford Edmund Bosworth and Mervyn Edwin John Richardson. *Journal of Semitic Studies, Monograph No. 16.* Manchester: University of Manchester, 1991.

Dawood, Nessim Joseph. *The Koran.* 5th rev. ed. Baltimore: Penguin Books, 1990.

Hodgson, Marshall G. S. *The Venture of Islam.* 3 vols. Chicago: University of Chicago Press, 1974.

Pickthall, Mohammed Marmaduke. *The Meaning of the Glorious Koran.* New York: New American Library and Mentor Books, 1963.

Reference Works

Adamec, Ludwig W. *Historical Dictionary of Islam.* Lanham, Md.: Scarecrow, 2001.

Ali, Muhammad. *A Manual of Hadith.* 2nd ed. London and New York: Curzon, 1978.

Anees, Munawar Ahmad, and Alia N. Athar. *Guide to Sira and Hadith Literature in Western Languages.* London: Mansell, 1986.

Azizullah, Muhammad. *Glimpses of the Hadith.* Takoma Park, Md.: The Crescent Publications, 1973.

Brandon, Samuel George Frederick, ed. *Dictionary of Comparative Religion.* New York: Charles Scribner's Sons, 1970.

Cameron, Averil, et al., eds. *The Byzantine and Early Islamic Near East.* 3 vols. *Studies in Late Antiquity and Early Islam 1.* Princeton, N.J.: Darwin, 1992–1995.

Eliade, Mircea, ed. *The Encyclopedia of Religion.* 16 vols. New York: Macmillan, 1987.

Esposito, John L., ed.-in-chief. *Oxford Encyclopedia of the Modern Islamic World.* 4 vols. New York: Oxford University Press, 1995.

al-Faruqi, Ismaʾil Rasi, and David E. Sopher, eds. *Historical Atlas of the Religions of the World.* New York: Macmillan, 1974.

Geddes, Charles L. *Guide to Reference Books for Islamic Studies.* Denver: American Institute of Islamic Studies, 1985.

Gibb, Hamilton A. R., et al., eds. *The Encyclopedia of Islam.* 4 vols. Leiden: E. J. Brill, 1960.

Glasse, Cyril. *The New Encyclopedia of Islam.* Rev. ed. Walnut Creek, Calif.: AltaMira, 2001.

Holt, Peter Malcolm, Ann Katherine S. Lambton, and Bernard Lewis, eds. *Cambridge History of Islam*. Cambridge: Cambridge University Press, 1970.

Krehl, Ludolf, and Theodorus G. I. Juynboll, eds. *Kitab al-Jamiᶜ al-Sahih*. Leiden: E. J. Brill, 1868–1908.

Rippin, Andrew, and Jan Knappert. *Textual Sources for the Study of Islam*. Totowa, N.J.: Barnes & Noble, 1987.

Siddiqi, Muhammad Zubayr. *Hadith Literature: Its Origin, Development, Special Features, and Criticism*. Edited and revised by Abdal Hakim Murad. Cambridge: Islamic Texts Society, 1993.

Weekes, Richard V., ed. *Muslim Peoples: A World Ethnographic Survey*. Westport, Conn.: Greenwood, 1978.

Secondary Sources

Abbott, Nabia. *Aishah, the Beloved of Mohammed*. Chicago: University of Chicago Press, 1942; New York: Arno, 1973.

ᶜAbduh, Muhammad. *The Theology of Unity*. Translated by Ishaq Musaᶜad and Kenneth Cragg. London: Allen and Unwin, 1966.

Abdul-Rauf, Muhammad. *Islam: Creed and Worship*. Washington, D.C.: Islamic Center, 1974.

———. *The Islamic View of Women and the Family*. New York: Robert Speller & Sons, 1977.

Abedi, Mehdi, and Gary Legenhausen, eds. *Jihad and Shahadat: Struggle and Martyrdom in Islam*. Houston: Institute for Research and Islamic Studies, 1986.

Abu Izzeddin, Nejla M. *The Druzes: A New Study of Their History, Faith, and Society*. Leiden: E. J. Brill, 1984.

Abu Zahrah, Muhammad. *Al-Shafiᶜi*. Cairo: Al-Qahirah Dar al-Fikr al-ᶜArabi, 1948.

———. *Ibn Hanbal*. Cairo: Al-Qahirah Dar al-Fikr al-ᶜArabi, 1947.

Ahmad, Aziz. *Islamic Modernism in India and Pakistan, 1857–1964*. London: Oxford University Press, 1967.

Ahmad, Bashiruddin Mahmud. *Invitation to Ahmadiyyat*. Rabwah, Pakistan: Ahmadiyya Muslim Foreign Missions, 1961.

Ahmad, Ghulam. *Jesus in India: Being an Account of Jesus' Escape from Death on the Cross and of His Journey to India*. Tilford, Surrey: Islam International Publications, 1989.

Ahmad, Khurshid. *Studies in Islamic Economics*. Leicester: The Islamic Foundation, 1980.

Ahmed, Akbar S. *Islam Today: A Short Introduction to the Muslim World*. London and New York: I. B. Tauris & Co., 1999.

———. *Postmodernism and Islam: Predicament and Promise*. London: Routledge, 1992.

———. *Pukhtun Economy and Society: Traditional Structure and Economic Development in a Tribal Society*. London: Routledge, 1980.

Ahmed, Leila. *Women and Gender in Islam: Historical Roots of a Modern Debate*. New Haven, Conn.: Yale University Press, 1992.

Ali, A. "Christianity from the Islamic Standpoint." *Hibbert Journal* IV, no. 2 (1906).

———. "Islam and Christianity." In *The Ways of Religion*. Edited by Roger Eastman. San Francisco: Canfield, 1975.

Allison, Christine. *The Yezidi Oral Tradition in Iraqi Kurdistan*. Richmond, UK: Curzon, 2001.

Allsen, Thomas T. *Culture and Conquest in Mongol Eurasia*. Cambridge and New York: Cambridge University Press, 2001.

Amitai-Preiss, Reuven, and David O. Morgan, eds. *The Mongol Empire and Its Legacy.* Leiden and Boston: Brill, 1999.

Anawati, Georges C. "Kalam." In *The Encyclopedia of Religion,* 16 vols. Edited by Mircea Eliade, vol. 8, pp. 231–42. New York: Macmillan, 1987.

Anderson, James Norman Dalrymple. *Law Reform in the Muslim World.* London: Athlone, 1976.

Andrae, Tor. *In the Garden of Myrtles: Studies in Early Islamic Mysticism.* Albany: SUNY Press, 1987.

———. *Mohammed: The Man and His Faith.* Translated by Theophil Menzel. New York: Harper, 1971.

Arberry, Arthur John. *Sufism: An Account of the Mystics of Islam.* New York: Harper Torchbooks, 1970.

———, ed. *Religion in the Middle East: Three Religions in Concord and Conflict.* 2 vols. Cambridge: Cambridge University Press, 1969.

———, trans. *Muslim Saints and Mystics.* London: Routledge and Kegan Paul, 1966.

Ariffin, Jamilah. *Women and Development in Malaysia.* Kuala Lumpur: Pelanduk Publications, 1992.

Arjomand, Said Amir, ed. *Authority and Political Culture in Shi'ism.* Albany: SUNY Press, 1988.

Armstrong, Karen. *Islam: A Short History.* New York: Modern Library, 2000.

———. *Muhammad: A Biography of the Prophet.* San Francisco: HarperSanFrancisco, 1992.

Asin Palacios, Miguel. *La escatologia musulmana en la Divina comedia.* 2nd ed. Madrid. Publicaciones de las escuelas de estudios arabes de Madrid y Granada, 1943.

Athar, Ali. *The Mughal Nobility under Aurangzeb.* Bombay: Asia Publishing House, 1966.

Ayoub, Mahmoud M. *Redemptive Suffering in Islam: A Study of the Devotional Aspects of "Ashura" in Twelver Shi'ism.* The Hague: Mouton, 1978.

Badran, Margot. *Feminists, Islam, and Nation: Gender and the Making of Modern Egypt.* Princeton, N.J.: Princeton University Press, 1995.

Badran, Margot, and Miriam Cooke, eds. *Opening the Gates: A Century of Arab Feminist Writing.* Bloomington: Indiana University Press, 1990.

Bakhash, Shaul. *Iran: Monarchy, Bureaucracy, and Reform under the Qajars, 1858–1896.* London: Ithaca, 1978.

———. *The Reign of the Ayatollahs: Iran and the Islamic Revolution.* New York: Basic Books, 1986.

Baldick, Julian. *Mystical Islam: An Introduction to Sufism.* New York: New York University Press, 1989.

Bannerman, Patrick. *Islam in Perspective: An Introduction to Islamic Society, Politics and Law,* London: Routledge, 1988.

Banuazizi, Ali, and Myron Weiner, eds. *The State, Religion, and Ethnic Politics.* Syracuse, N.Y.: Syracuse University Press, 1986.

Basar, Hasmet, ed. *Management and Development of Awqaf Properties.* Jeddah, Saudi Arabia: Islamic Research and Training Institute, Islamic Development Bank, 1987.

Bassiouni, M. Cherif, ed. *The Islamic Criminal Justice System.* London: Oceana Publications, 1982.

Bat, Ye'or. *The Dhimmi: Jews and Christians under Islam.* Translated by David Maisel, rev. and enl. Rutherford, N.J.: Fairleigh Dickinson University Press, 1985.

———. *Islam and Dhimmitude: Where Civilizations Collide.* Translated by Miriam Kochan and David Littman. Madison, N.J.: Fairleigh Dickinson University Press, 2002.

Bayat, Mangol. *Mysticism and Dissent: Socioreligious Thought in Qajar Iran.* Syracuse, N.Y.: Syracuse University Press, 1982.

Beegle, Dewey M. *Moses: The Servant of Yahweh.* Ann Arbor, Mich.: Pryor Pettengill, 1979.

Betts, Robert B. *The Druze.* New Haven, Conn.: Yale University Press, 1988.

Binder, Leonard. *Islamic Liberalism: A Critique of Development Ideologies.* Chicago: University of Chicago Press, 1988.

Blyden, Edward Wilmot. *Christianity, Islam, and the Negro Race.* 2nd ed. Baltimore: Black Classic, 1994; orig. 1888.

Bosworth, Albert Brian. *Conquest and Empire: The Reign of Alexander the Great.* Cambridge: Cambridge University Press, 1988.

Bosworth, Clifford Edmund. *The Ghaznavids: Their Empire in Afghanistan and Eastern Iran 994–1040.* Edinburgh: Edinburgh University Press, 1963.

——. *The Islamic Dynasties.* Edinburgh: Edinburgh University Press, 1972.

——. *The Later Ghaznavids: Splendour and Decay—The Dynasty in Afghanistan and Northern India.* Edinburgh: Edinburgh University Press, 1977.

Bosworth, Clifford Edmund, and Carole Hillenbrand, eds. *Qajar Iran: Political, Social, and Cultural Change, 1800–1925.* Edinburgh: Edinburgh University Press, 1983.

Bright, John. *A History of Israel.* 3rd ed. Philadelphia: Westminster, 1981.

Brynen, Rex. *Sanctuary and Survival: The PLO in Lebanon.* Boulder, Colo.: Westview, 1990.

Burton, John. *An Introduction to the Hadith.* Edinburgh: Edinburgh University Press, 1994.

Cardini, Franco. *Europe and Islam.* Oxford: Blackwell, 2001.

Chabbi, Jacqueline. "ʿAbd al-Kadir al-Djilani, personnage historique." *Studia Islamica* 38 (1973): 75–106.

Chittick, William C., trans. *The Sufi Path to Love: The Spiritual Teachings of Rumi.* Albany: SUNY Press, 1993.

Chodkiewicz, Michel. *An Ocean without Shore: Ibn ʿArabi, the Book, and the Law.* Albany: SUNY Press, 1993.

Coats, George W. *Moses: Heroic Man, Man of God.* Sheffield: JSOT, 1988.

Cole, Juan R. I., and Nikkie R. Keddie, eds. *Shiʿism and Social Protest.* New Haven, Conn.: Yale University Press, 1986.

Cooey, Paula M., William R. Eakin, and Jay B. McDaniel, eds. *After Patriarchy: Feminist Transformations of the World Religions.* Maryknoll, N.Y.: Orbis, 1991.

Cook, Michael. *Commanding Right and Forbidding Wrong in Islamic Thought.* Cambridge: Cambridge University Press, 2000.

——. *Muhammad.* Oxford and New York: Oxford University Press, 1983.

Coulmas, Florian. *The Writing Systems of the World.* Oxford and New York: B. Blackwell, 1991.

Coulson, Noel James. *A History of Islamic Law.* Edinburgh: Edinburgh University Press, 1964.

——. *Succession in the Muslim Family.* Cambridge: Cambridge University Press, 1971.

Daftary, Farhad. *The Ismaʿilis: Their History and Doctrines.* Cambridge: Cambridge University Press, 1990.

——. *A Short History of the Ismailis: Tradition of a Muslim Community.* Edinburgh: Edinburgh University Press, 1998.

Dalrymple, James Norman. *Law Reform in the Muslim World.* London: Athlone, 1976.

Daniel, Norman. *Islam and the West: The Making of an Image.* Edinburgh: Edinburgh University Press, 1966.

Davis, Joyce M. *Between Jihad and Salaam: Profiles in Islam.* New York: St. Martin's, 1997.

Dawe, Donald G., and John B. Carman, eds., *Christian Faith in a Religiously Plural World.* Maryknoll, N.Y.: Orbis Books, 1978.

Deeb, Marius K. *Militant Islamic Movements in Lebanon: Origins, Social Basis, and Ideology.* Washington, D.C.: Center for Contemporary Arab Studies, 1986.

Denny, Frederick Mathewson. *An Introduction to Islam.* 2nd ed. New York: Macmillan, 1994.

Donner, Fred McGraw. *The Early Islamic Conquests.* Princeton, N.J.: Princeton University Press, 1981.

———. *Narratives of Islamic Origins: The Beginnings of Islamic Historical Writings— Studies in Late Antiquity and Early Islam.* Vol. 14. Princeton, N.J.: Darwin, 1998.

Dresch, Paul. *Tribes, Government, and History in Yemen.* Oxford: Clarendon, 1989.

Driver, Godfrey Rolles. *Semitic Writing: From Pictograph to Alphabet.* Revised by S. A. Hopkins. London and New York: Oxford University Press, 1976.

Dussaud, René. *Histoire et religion des Nosairis.* Paris: E. Bouillon, 1900.

Eastman, Roger, ed. *The Ways of Religion.* San Francisco: Canfield, 1975.

Eickelman, Dale F., and James P. Piscatori, eds. *Muslim Travellers: Pilgrimage, Migration, and the Religious Imagination.* Berkeley: University of California Press, 1990.

Ellis, Kail C., ed. *The Vatican, Islam, and the Middle East.* Syracuse, N.Y.: Syracuse University Press, 1987.

Enayat, Hamid. *Modern Islamic Political Thought.* Austin: University of Texas Press, 1982.

Endress, Gerhard. *An Introduction to Islam.* Edinburgh: Edinburgh University Press, 1987.

Esin, Emel. *Mecca the Blessed: Madinah the Radiant.* New York: Crown, 1963.

Esposito, John L. *Islam: The Straight Path.* 3rd ed. Oxford and New York: Oxford University Press, 1998.

———. *Islam and Politics.* 4th ed. Syracuse: Syracuse University Press, 1998.

———. *The Islamic Threat: Myth or Reality?* 2nd ed. New York: Oxford University Press, 1995.

———. *Women in Muslim Family Law.* Syracuse, N.Y.: Syracuse University Press, 1982.

Esposito, John L., and John Obert Voll. *Islam and Democracy.* New York: Oxford University Press, 1996.

Fakhry, Majid. *A History of Islamic Philosophy.* New York: Columbia University Press, 1970.

Finkelstein, Israel. *Living on the Fringe: The Archaeology and History of the Negev, Sinai and Neighbouring Regions in the Bronze and Iron Ages.* Sheffield: Sheffield Academic Press, 1995.

Firestone, Reuven. *Journeys in Holy Lands: The Evolution of the Abraham-Ishmael Legends in Islamic Exegesis.* Albany: SUNY Press, 1990.

Firro, Kais M. *A History of the Druzes.* Leiden: E. J. Brill, 1992.

Fischer, Michael M. J. *Iran: From Religious Dispute to Revolution.* Cambridge, Mass.: Harvard University Press, 1980.

Fischer, Michael M. J., and Mehdi Abedi. *Debating Muslims: Cultural Dialogues in Postmodernity and Tradition.* Madison: University of Wisconsin Press, 1990.

Fluehr-Lobban, Carolyn. *Islamic Law and Society in the Sudan.* London: F. Cass, 1987.

Forward, Martin. *Muhammad: A Short Biography.* Oxford: Oneworld, 1997.

Freeman-Grenville, Greville Stewart Parker. *The Muslim and Christian Calendars.* London: Oxford University Press, 1963.

Friedlander, Shems. *The Whirling Dervishes.* 2nd ed. Albany: SUNY Press, 1992.

Friedman, Thomas. *From Beirut to Jerusalem.* London: Fontana, 1990.

Friedmann, Yohanan. *Prophecy Continuous: Aspects of Ahmadi Religious Thought and Its Medieval Background.* Berkeley: University of California Press, 1989.

Frye, Richard N. *The Heritage of Persia.* London: Weidenfeld & Nicolson, 1963.

Gaudeul, Jean-Marie. *Encounters and Clashes: Islam and Christianity in History.* 2 vols. Rome: Pontifical Institute, 1998.

Ghafuri, ʿAli. *The Ritual Prayer of Islam.* Translated by Laleh Bakhtiar and Mohammed Nematzadeh. Tehran: Hamdami Foundation, 1982.

al-Ghazali, Abu Hamid Muhammad. *The Foundations of the Articles of Faith.* Translated by Nabih Amin Faris. Lahore: Sh. Muhammad Ashraf, 1963.

——. *Freedom and Fulfillment: An Annotated Translation of al-Ghazali's al-Muniqidh min al-Dalal and Other Relevant Works of al-Ghazali.* Translated by Richard Joseph McCarthy. Boston: Twayne, 1980.

Gibb, Hamilton Alexander Rosskeen. *Islam: A Historical Survey.* Oxford: Oxford University Press, 1975.

——. *Mohammedanism.* 2nd rev. ed. Oxford: Oxford University Press, 1970.

Giorgis, Belkis Wolde. *Female Circumcision in Africa.* Addis Ababa: United Nations, Economic Commission for Africa, 1981.

Glubb, John Bagot. *The Life and Times of Muhammad.* London: Hodder and Stoughton, 1979.

Gohari, M. J. *The Taliban: Ascent to Power.* Oxford and New York: Oxford University Press, 2000.

Goldziher, Ignácz. *Introduction to Islamic Theology and Law.* Translated by Andras Hamori and Ruth Hamori. Princeton, N.J.: Princeton University Press, 1981.

——. *Muslim Studies.* Edited by S. M. Stern. Translated by C. R. Barker and S. M. Stern. Vol. 2. Chicago: Aldine Atherton, 1971.

Göle, Nilufa. *The Forbidden Modern: Civilization and Veiling.* Ann Arbor: University of Michigan Press, 1996.

Goodson, Larry P. *Afghanistan's Endless War: State Failure, Regional Politics, and the Rise of the Taliban.* Seattle: University of Washington Press, 2001.

Gresh, Alain. *The PLO: The Struggle Within—Towards an Independent Palestinian State.* London: Zed Books, 1985.

Griffin, Michael. *Reaping the Whirlwind: The Taliban Movement in Afghanistan.* London: Pluto Press, 2001.

Guillaume, Alfred. *Islam.* 2nd rev. ed. Harmondsworth: Penguin Books, 1968; orig. 1954.

——. *The Traditions of Islam: An Introduction to the Study of the Hadith Literature.* Salem, N.H.: Ayer, 1924, reprint 1987.

——, trans. *The Life of Muhammad: A Translation of Ibn Ishaq's Sirat Rasul Allah.* London and Karachi: Oxford University Press, 1955.

Haddad, Yvonne Yazbeck. *Contemporary Islam and the Challenge of History.* Albany: SUNY Press, 1982.

Haddad, Yvonne Yazbeck, and John L. Esposito, eds. *Islam, Gender and Social Change.* New York: Oxford University Press, 1997.

Haddad, Yvonne, and Wadi Z. Haddad, eds. *Christian-Muslim Encounters.* Gainesville, Fla.: University Press of Florida, 1995.

Haddad, Yvonne, and Jane Idleman Smith. *Mission to America: Five Islamic Sectarian Communities in North America*. Gainesville, Fla.: University Press of Florida, 1993.

———, eds. *Muslim Communities in North America*. Albany: SUNY Press, 1994.

Hanafi, Hansan. *Islam in the Modern World*. 2 vols. Cairo: Anglo-Egyptian Bookshop, 1995.

Hatcher, William S. *The Baha'i Faith: The Emerging Global Religion*. San Francisco: Harper & Row, 1985.

Heikal, Mohamed. *Illusions of Triumph: An Arab View of the Gulf War*. London: Harper-Collins, 1992.

al-Hibri, Azizah, ed. *Women and Islam*. New York: Pergamon, 1982.

Hillenbrand, Carole. *The Crusades: Islamic Perspectives*. Edinburgh: Edinburgh University Press, 1999.

Hiskett, Mervyn. *Some to Mecca Turn to Pray: Islamic Values and the Modern World*. St. Albans: Claridge, 1993.

Hitti, Philip K. *History of the Arabs*. 9th ed. New York: St. Martin's, 1966.

Hodgson, Marshall G. S. *The Order of Assassins: The Struggle of the Early Nizari Isma'ilis against the Islamic World*. The Hague: Mouton, 1955.

———. *The Venture of Islam*. 3 vols. Chicago: University of Chicago Press, 1974.

Hooker, Michael Barry. *Islamic Law in South-East Asia*. Singapore and New York: Oxford University Press, 1984.

Hourani, Albert Habib. *A History of the Arab Peoples*. London: Faber & Faber, 1991.

———. *Islam in European Thought*. Cambridge and New York: Cambridge University Press, 1991.

———. *Western Attitudes towards Islam*. Southampton: Southampton University Press, 1974.

Housley, Norman. *Crusading and Warfare in Medieval and Renaissance Europe*. Aldershot: Ashgate, 2001.

Hoyland, Robert G. *Arabia and the Arabs: From the Bronze Age to the Coming of Islam*. London and New York: Routledge, 2001.

———. "The Earliest Christian Writings on Muhammad: An Appraisal." In Harald Motzki, ed., *The Biography of Muhammad: The Issue of the Sources*, 276–97. Islamic History and Civilization: Studies and Text, vol. 32. Leiden: E. J. Brill, 2000.

———. *Seeing Islam as Others Saw It: A Survey and Evaluation of Christian, Jewish, and Zoroastrian Writings on Early Islam*. Princeton, N.J.: Darwin, 1997.

Hussain, Jassim. *The Occultation of the Twelfth Imam*. London: The Muhammadi Trust, 1982.

Ibn Babawayh, Muhammad. *A Shi'ite Creed*. Rev. ed., translated by Asaf A. A. Fyzee. Tehran: WOFIS, 1982.

Ibn Maja. *Sunan*. Cairo, 1930.

Ibn al-Ukhuwah, Muhammad ibn Muhammad. *The Ma'alim al-Qurba*. Edited by R. Levy. Gibb Memorial Series, vol. 12. London: Luzac, 1938.

Ibn Warraq. *Why I Am Not a Muslim*. Amherst, N.Y.: Prometheus Books, 1995.

al-Imad, Leila S. *The Fatimid Vizierate 969–1172*. Berlin: K. Schwarz, 1990.

Inalçik, Halil. *The Ottoman Empire: The Classical Age, 1300–1600*. Translated by Norman Itzkowitz and Colin Imber. London: Weidenfeld & Nicolson, 1973.

al-Isfahani, Abu Nu'aym. *Hilyat al-Awliya, wa-tabaqat al-asfiya'*. 10 vols. Cairo: Misr Makatabat al-Khanji, 1932–38.

Izutsu. Toshihiko. *God and Man in the Koran: Semantics of the Koranic Weltanschauung.* Studies in the Humanities and Social Relations, vol. 5. Tokyo: Keio Institute of Cultural and Linguistics Studies, 1964.

Jomier, Jacques. *The Bible and the Koran.* Translated by Edward P. Arbez. Chicago: Henry Regnery, 1967.

Kamal, Ahmad. *The Sacred Journey.* London: Allen & Unwin, 1964.

Kamali, Sabih Ahmad. *Incoherence of the Philosophers.* Lahore: Pakistan Philosophical Congress, 1958.

Kamm, Anthony. *The Romans: An Introduction.* London and New York: Routledge, 1995.

Kandiyoti, Deniz, ed. *Women, Islam, and the State.* Philadelphia: Temple University Press, 1991.

Karim, Wazir Jahan. *Women and Culture: Between Malay Adat and Islam.* Boulder, Colo.: Westview, 1992.

Kateregga, Badru David, and David W. Shenk. *Islam and Christianity: A Muslim and a Christian Dialogue.* Grand Rapids, Mich.: William B. Eerdmans, 1981.

Kelly, Marjorie, ed. *Islam: The Religious and Political Life of a World Community.* New York: Praeger, 1984.

Kemp, Barry J. *Ancient Egypt: Anatomy of a Civilization.* London and New York: Routledge, 1989.

Kennedy, Hugh. *The Prophet and the Age of the Caliphates: The Islamic Near East from the Sixth to the Eleventh Century.* London and New York: Longman, 1986.

Khan, Mohammad Zahir. *Islam.* London: Routledge & Kegan Paul, 1980.

al-Khuli, Amin. *Malik ibn Anas: Tarjamah Muharrarah.* 3 vols. Cairo: Dar Ihyaᶜal-Kutub al-ᶜArabiyah, 1951.

Khuri, Fuʾad Ishaq. *Imams and Emirs: State, Religion, and Sects in Islam.* London: Saqi, 1990.

Kramer, Martin. *Hezbollah's Vision of the West.* Washington, D.C.: Washington Institute for Near East Policy, 1989.

Kreyenbroek, Philip G., and Stephan Sperl, eds. *The Kurds: A Contemporary Overview.* London: Routledge, 1992.

Kuhrt, Amélie. *The Ancient Near East c.3000–330 BC.* 2 vols. London and New York: Routledge, 1995.

al-Kurdi, Muhammad Tahir. *Tarikh al-Qurʾan.* Jedda: Matbaᶜat al-Fath, 1946.

Kutty, Ahmad. *Islamic Funeral Rites and Practices.* Toronto: n.p. available, 1991.

Lapidus, Ira. *A History of Islamic Societies.* Cambridge and New York: Cambridge University Press, 1988.

Lateef, Shahida. *Muslim Women in India: Political and Private Realities, 1890s–1980s* Atlantic Highlands, N.J.: Zed Books, 1990.

Lee, Martha F. *The Nation of Islam: An American Millenarian Movement.* Syracuse, N.Y.: Syracuse University Press, 1996.

Lemche, Niels Peter. *The Canaanites and Their Land: The Tradition of the Canaanites.* JSOTS 110. Sheffield: JSOT, 1991.

Lev, Yaacov. *State and Society in Fatimid Egypt.* Leiden and New York: E. J. Brill, 1991.

Levonian, Lutfi. *Studies in the Relationship between Islam and Christianity.* London: George Allen & Unwin, 1940.

Lewis, Bernard. *The Arabs in History.* New York: Harper & Row, 1966.

———. *The Muslim Discovery of Europe.* London and New York: W. W. Norton, 1982.

———. *What Went Wrong? Western Impact and Middle Eastern Response.* Oxford and New York: Oxford University Press, 2002.

Lewis, Bernard, ed. *Islam: From the Prophet Muhammad to the Capture of Constantinople.* New York: Harper & Row, 1974.

Lewis, Ioan M., ed. *Islam in Tropical Africa.* 2nd ed. Bloomington: Indiana University Press, 1980.

Lewis, Naphtali. *Life in Egypt under Roman Rule.* New York: Oxford University Press, 1983.

Lewis, Philip. *Islamic Britain: Religion, Politics, and Identity among British Muslims.* London: I. B. Tauris, 1994.

Lincoln, C. Eric. *The Black Muslims in America.* 3rd ed. Grand Rapids, Mich.: W. B. Eerdsman, 1994.

Lings, Martin. *Muhammad: His Life Based on the Earliest Sources.* Rochester, Vt.: Inner Traditions, 1983.

———. *What Is Sufism?* Berkeley: University of California Press, 1977.

Long, David Edwin. *The Hajj Today: A Survey of the Contemporary Makkah Pilgrimage.* Albany: SUNY Press, 1979.

Mahmassani, Subhi Rajab. *The Philosophy of Jurisprudence in Islam.* Translated by Farhat J. Ziadeh. Leiden: Brill, 1961.

Mahmood, Syed Tahir. *Personal Law in Islamic Countries: History, Texts, and Analysis.* 2nd rev. ed. New Delhi: India and Islam Research Council, 1995.

Malcolm X. *Malcolm X Speaks.* Edited by George Breitman. New York: Grove, 1965.

Malcolm X and Alex Haley. *The Autobiography of Malcolm X.* New York: Grove, 1965.

Malti-Douglas, Fedwa. *Woman's Body, Woman's Word: Gender and Discourse in Arabo-Islamic Writing.* Princeton, N.J.: Princeton University Press, 1991.

Mannan, Muhammad Abdul. *The Making of an Islamic Economy: Islamic Dimensions in Economic Analysis.* Cairo: International Association of Islamic Banks, 1984.

Mansfield, Peter. *The Arabs.* 3rd ed. London: Penguin, 1985.

Marsden, Peter Richard Valentine. *The Taliban: War, Religion and the New Order in Afghanistan.* London: Zed Books; Karachi: Oxford University Press, 1998.

Marsh, Clifton E. *From Black Muslims to Muslims: The Transition from Separatism to Islam, 1930–1980.* Metuchen, N.J.: Scarecrow, 1984.

Marty, Martin E., and R. Scott Appleby, eds. *Fundamentalisms and the State: Remaking Polities, Economies, and Militance.* Chicago: University of Chicago Press, 1993.

Massignon, Louis. *The Passion of al-Hallaj: Mystic and Martyr of Islam.* Translated by Herbert Mason. 4 vols. Princeton, N.J.: Princeton University Press, 1982.

———. *Recueil de textes inedits concernant l'histoire de la mystique en pays d'Islam.* Paris: Librairie Orientaliste Paul Geuthner, 1929.

Mawdudi, Sayyid Abu'l-aᶜla. *Towards Understanding Islam.* Translated and edited by Khurshid Ahmad. Markfield, Eng.: The Islamic Foundation, 1981/1401 A.H.

Mayer, Ann Elizabeth. *Islam and Human Rights: Tradition and Politics.* 3rd ed. Boulder, Colo.: Westview, 1999.

McAuliffe, Jane Dammen. *Qurᵓanic Christians: An Analysis of Classical and Modern Exegesis.* Cambridge and New York: Cambridge University Press, 1991.

McLaren, James S. *Power and Politics in Palestine: The Jews and the Governing of Their Land.* Sheffield: JSOTS, 1991.

McNeil, William H., and Marilyn R. Waldman, eds. *The Islamic World.* Chicago: University of Chicago Press, 1983

Mernissi, Fatima. *Beyond the Veil: Male-Female Dynamics in Modern Muslim Society.* Rev. ed. Bloomington: Indiana University Press, 1987.

———. *Women and Islam: An Historical and Theological Inquiry.* Translated by Mary Jo Lakeland. Oxford: B. Blackwell, 1991.

Miller, James Maxwell, and John H. Hayes. *A History of Ancient Israel and Judah.* Philadelphia: Westminster, 1986.

Miller, Roland E. *Muslim Friends: Their Faith and Feeling—An Introduction to Islam.* St. Louis: Concordia, 1995.

Minai, Naila. *Women in Islam: Tradition and Transition in the Middle East.* New York: Seaview Books, 1981.

Mishal, Shaul. *The PLO under ʿArafat: Between Gun and Olive Branch.* New Haven, Conn.: Yale University Press, 1986.

Moghadam, Valentine M. *Modernizing Women: Gender and Social Change in the Middle East.* Boulder, Colo.: Lynne Rienner, 1993.

——, ed. *Identity Politics and Women: Cultural Reassertions and Feminisms in International Perspectives.* Boulder, Colo.: Westview, 1994.

Momen, Moojan. *An Introduction to Shiʿi Islam: The History and Doctrines of Twelver Shiʿism.* New Haven, Conn.: Yale University Press, 1985.

——. *Islam and the Bahaʾi Faith.* Oxford: George Ronald, 2000.

Morey, Robert. *The Islamic Invasion: Confronting the World's Fastest Growing Religion.* Eugene, Ore.: Harvest House, 1992.

Mottahedeh, Roy P. *The Mantle of the Prophet: Religion and Politics in Iran.* New York: Pantheon Books, 1985.

Motzki, Harald, ed. *The Biography of Muhammad: The Issue of the Sources.* Islamic History and Civilization: Studies and Text, vol. 32. Leiden: Brill, 2000.

Muhammad, Elijah. *How to Eat to Live.* Chicago: Muhammad Mosque of Islam, 1972.

——. *Message to the Blackman in America.* Chicago: Muhammad Mosque of Islam, 1965.

Muhammad, Warith Deen. *As the Light Shineth from the East.* Chicago: WDM, 1980.

Muhammad, Zakariya. *Virtues of Salaat: An English Translation of Fazail-i-Namaz.* New Delhi: Idarah Ishaat-e-Diniyat, 1966.

Muir, William. *The Caliphate: Its Rise, Decline and Fall.* Edinburgh: J. Grant, 1924.

Mumtaz, Khawar, and Farida Shaheed, eds. *Women of Pakistan: Two Steps Forward, One Step Back?* Atlantic Highlands, N.J.: Zed Books, 1987.

Munson, Henry, Jr. *Islam and Revolution in the Middle East.* New Haven, Conn.: Yale University Press, 1988.

Murata, Sachiko. *The Tao of Islam: A Sourcebook on Gender Relationships in Islamic Thought.* Albany: SUNY Press, 1992.

Nanji, Azim. *The Nizari Ismaili Tradition in the Indo-Pakistan Subcontinent.* New York: Caravan Books, 1978.

Nasir, Jamal J. *The Islamic Law of Personal Status.* 2nd ed. London and Boston: Graham & Trotman, 1990.

——. *The Status of Women under Islamic Law and Under Modern Islamic Legislation.* London: Graham & Trotman, 1990.

Nasr, Seyyed Hossein. *Ideals and Realities of Islam.* Boston: Beacon, 1972.

——. *Traditional Islam in the Modern World.* London: KPI, 1987.

——, ed. *Islamic Spirituality.* 2 vols. New York: Crossroad, 1987–1990.

Nasr, Seyyed Vali Reza. *Islamic Leviathan: Islam and the Making of State Power.* New York: Oxford University Press, 2001.

Nelson, Kristina. *The Art of Reciting the Qurʾan.* Austin: University of Texas Press, 1985.

Nicholson, Reynold Alleyne. *Literary History of the Arabs.* Cambridge: Cambridge University Press, 1930.

Nielsen, Jorgen S. *Muslims in Western Europe.* 2nd ed. Edinburgh: Edinburgh University Press, 1995.

Nigosian, S. A. *The Zoroastrian Faith: Tradition and Modern Research.* Montreal and Kingston: McGill-Queen's University Press, 1993.

Nissen, Hans J. *The Early History of the Ancient Near East 9000–2000 B.C.* Translated by Elizabeth Lutzeier, with Kenneth J. Northcott. Chicago: University of Chicago Press, 1988.

Norton, Augustus Richard. *Amal and the Shiʿa: Struggle for the Soul of Lebanon.* Austin: University of Texas Press, 1987.

Nurbakhsh, Javad. *Sufi Women.* 2nd ed. London and New York: Khaniqahi-Nimatullahi Publications, 1990.

O'Leary, De Lacey. *A Short History of the Fatimid Khaliphate.* London: Kegan Paul, 1923.

Onon, Urgunge. *The Secret History of the Mongols: The Life and Times of Chinggis Khan.* Richmond, U.K.: Curzon, 2001.

Padwick, Constance Evelyn. *Muslim Devotions: A Study of Prayer-Manuals in Common Use.* London: SPCK, 1961.

Parrinder, Geoffrey. *Mysticism in the World's Religions.* New York: Oxford University Press, 1976.

Pearl, David. *Muslim Family Law.* 3rd ed. London: Sweet & Maxwell, 1998.

Perry, Bruce. *Malcolm: The Life of a Man Who Changed Black America.* Barrytown, N.Y.: Station Hill, 1991.

Peteet, Julie M. *Gender in Crisis: Women and the Palestinian Resistance Movement.* New York: Columbia University Press, 1991.

Peters, Francis E. *Children of Abraham.* Princeton, N.J.: Princeton University Press, 1982.

———. *The Hajj: The Muslim Pilgrimage to Mecca and the Holy Places.* Princeton, N.J.: Princeton University Press, 1994.

———. *Muhammad and the Origins of Islam.* Albany: SUNY Press, 1994.

Pipes, Daniel. *The Rushdie Affair: The Novel, the Ayatollah, and the West.* New York: Carol Publishing Group, 1990.

Pritchard, James B. ed. *Ancient Near Eastern Texts Relating to the Old Testament.* 2nd ed. Princeton, N.J.: Princeton University Press, 1955.

Pullapilly, Cyriac K., ed. *Islam.* Notre Dame, Ind.: Crossroads Books, 1980.

al-Qasimi, Jamal al-Din. *Mawʿizat al-Muʿminin min Ihya ʿUlam al-Din.* Cairo: Matbaʿat Walidat ʿAbbas al-Awwal, 1912.

Qureshi, Mohammed Ahmad. *Waqfs in India: A Study of Administrative and Legislative Control.* New Delhi: Gian, 1990.

Rahman, Fazlur. *Islam.* New York: Holt, Rinehart & Winston, 1966.

———. *Islam and Modernity: The Transformation of an Intellectual Tradition.* Chicago: University of Chicago Press, 1982.

———. *Major Themes of the Qurʾan.* 2nd ed. Minneapolis: Bibliotheca Islamica, 1994.

———. *Prophecy in Islam: Philosophy and Orthodoxy.* London: Allen & Unwin, 1958.

Rashid, Ahmed. *Jihad: The Rise of Militant Islam in Central Asia.* New Haven, Conn.: Yale University Press, 2002.

———. *Taliban: Militant Islam, Oil, and Fundamentalism in Central Asia.* New Haven, Conn.: Yale University Press, 2000.

Reeves, Edward B. *The Hidden Government: Ritual, Clientelism, and Legitimation in Northern Egypt.* Salt Lake City: University of Utah Press, 1990.

Renard, John. *Seven Doors to Islam: Spirituality and the Religious Life of Muslims.* Berkeley: University of California Press, 1996.

Richard, Jean. *The Crusades c. 1071–c. 1291.* Translated by Jean Birrell. Cambridge and New York: Cambridge University Press, 1999.

Riesebrodt, Martin. *Pious Passion: The Emergence of Modern Fundamentalism in the United States and Iran.* Translated by Don Reneau. Berkeley: University of California Press, 1993.

Rippin, Andrew. *Muslims: Their Religious Beliefs and Practices.* 2nd ed. London and New York: Routledge, 2001.

Rizvi, Saiyid Athar Abbas. *A History of Sufism in India.* 2 vols. New Delhi: Munshiram Manoharlal, 1978–1983.

Robinson, Francis. *Atlas of the Islamic World since 1500.* Oxford: Phaidon, 1982.

Rodinson, Maxime. *The Arabs.* Chicago: University of Chicago Press, 1981.

———. *Mohammed.* Translated by Anne Carter. New York: Vintage Books, 1974.

———. "The Western Image and Western Studies of Islam." In Joseph Schacht and Clifford Edmund Bosworth, eds., *The Legacy of Islam,* 2nd ed., 9–62. Oxford: Clarendon Press, 1974.

Roux, Georges. *Ancient Iraq.* 3rd ed. London and New York: Penguin, 1992.

Ruthven, Malise. *Islam and the World.* London: Penguin, 1984.

Sachedina, Abdulaziz Abdulhussein. *Islamic Messianism: The Idea of Mahdi in Twelver Shiʿism.* Albany: SUNY Press, 1981.

———. *The Just Ruler (al-sultan al-ʿadil) in Shiʿite Islam: The Comprehensive Authority of the Jurist in Imamite Jurisprudence.* New York: Oxford University Press, 1988.

al-Saʿdawi, Nawal. *The Hidden Face of Eve: Women in the Arab World.* Translated and edited by Sherif Hetata. London: Zed Books, 1995.

Sahliyeh, Emile F. *The PLO after the Lebanon War.* Boulder, Colo.: Westview, 1986.

———, ed. *Religious Resurgence and Politics in the Contemporary World.* Albany: SUNY Press, 1990.

Salih, Al-Tayyib. *The Wedding of Zein and Other Stories.* Translated by Denys Johnson Davies. London: Heineman, 1968.

Savory, Roger, ed. *Introduction to Islamic Civilization.* Cambridge: Cambridge University Press, 1976.

———. *Iran under the Safavids.* Cambridge and New York: Cambridge University Press, 1980.

Schacht, Joseph. *An Introduction to Islamic Law.* Oxford: Clarendon, 1964.

Schacht, Joseph, and Clifford Edmund Bosworth, eds. *The Legacy of Islam.* 2nd ed. Oxford: Clarendon, 1974.

Schimmel, Annemarie. *And Muhammad Is His Messenger: The Veneration of the Prophet in Islamic Piety.* Chapel Hill: University of North Carolina Press, 1985.

———. *Mystical Dimensions of Islam.* Chapel Hill: University of North Carolina Press, 1975; reprint 1983.

Schubel, Vernon James. *Religious Performance in Contemporary Islam: Shiʿi Devotional Rituals in South Asia.* Columbia: University of South Carolina Press, 1993.

Schuler, Margaret, ed. *Freedom from Violence: Women's Strategies from Around the World.* Washington, D.C.: WLD International, 1992.

Schuon, Frithjof. *The Transcendent Unity of Religions.* Translated by P. Townsend. New York: Pantheon, 1953.

———. *Understanding Islam.* Translated by D. M. Matheson. London: Allen and Unwin, 1963.

Seale, Morris S. *Muslim Theology.* 2nd ed. London: Luzac and Co., 1980.

Shah, Idries. *The Sufis.* Garden City, N.Y.: Doubleday and Co., 1971.

Shaʿrani, ʿAbd al-Wahib ibn Ahmat. *Mukhtasar al-Tadhkirah.* Cairo: Maktabat al-Thaqafah al-Diniyah, 1986.

Sharawi, Huda. *Harem Years: The Memoirs of an Egyptian Feminist.* Translated by Margot Badran. London: Virago, 1986.

Sharon, Moshe. *Black Banners from the East.* Leiden: E. J. Brill, 1983.

Shaw, Stanford J. *Between Old and New: The Ottoman Empire under Sultan Selim III, 1789–1807.* Cambridge, Mass.: Harvard University Press, 1971.

———. *The History of the Ottoman Empire and Modern Turkey.* 2 vols. London and New York: Cambridge University Press, 1976–1977.

Shell-Duncan, Bettina, and Ylva Hernlund, eds. *Female "Circumcision" in Africa: Culture, Controversy, and Change.* Boulder, Colo.: Lynne Rienner, 2000.

Siddiqi, Muhammad Z. *Hadith Literature: Its Origin, Development, Special Features, and Criticism.* Calcutta: Calcutta University, 1961.

Smith, Charles. *Palestine and the Arab-Israeli Conflict.* New York: St. Martin's, 1988.

Smith, Jane I., ed. *Women in Contemporary Muslim Societies.* Lewisburg, Pa.: Bucknell University Press, 1979.

Smith, Jane Idleman, and Yvonne Yazbeck Haddad. *The Islamic Understanding of Death and Resurrection.* Albany: SUNY Press, 1981.

Smith, Peter. *The Babi and Baha'i Religions: From Messianic Shi'ism to a World Religion.* New York: Cambridge University Press, 1987.

Snell, Daniel C. *Life in the Ancient Near East 3100–332 B.C.E.* New Haven, Conn.: Yale University Press, 1997.

Soggin, J. Alberto. *A History of Israel.* London: SCM, 1984.

Southern, Richard William. *Western Views of Islam in the Middle Ages.* Cambridge, Mass.: Harvard University Press, 1962.

Surty, Muhammad Ibrahim H. I. *A Course in the Science of Reciting the Qur'an.* Leicester: Islamic Foundation, 1988.

al-Suyuti, Jalal al-Din. *al-La'ali' al-masnu'ah fi al-ahadith al-mawdu'ah.* 2 vols. Cairo: al-Maktabah al-Tijariyah al-Kubra, 1933.

Sweetman, James Windrow. *Islam and Christian Theology.* 3 vols. London: Lutterworth, 1945–1955.

al-Tabari, Abu Ja'far Muhammad ibn Jarir. *Ta'rikh al-rusul wa'l-muluk* (The History of the Prophets and the Kings). Vol. I. Leiden: E. J. Brill, 1881.

Tabataba'i, Hossein Modarressi. *An Introduction to Shi'i Law: A Bibliographical Study.* London: Ithaca, 1984.

Thompson, Thomas L. *The Historicity of the Patriarchal Narratives.* Berlin and New York: Walter de Gruyter, 1974.

al-Tirmidhi, Muhammad ibn 'Isa. *Al-Jami' al-Sahih.* Cairo: Mustafa al-Babi al-Halibi, 1937.

Trimingham, John Spencer. *The Influence of Islam upon Africa.* 2nd ed. London and New York: Longman, 1980.

———. *The Sufi Orders in Islam.* Oxford: Clarendon, 1971.

Van Seters, John. *Abraham in History and Tradition.* New Haven, Conn.: Yale University Press, 1975.

———. *The Life of Moses: The Yahwist as Historian in Exodus-Numbers.* Louisville, Ky.: Westminster John Knox, 1994.

Voll, John Obert. *Islam, Continuity and Change in the Modern World.* 2nd ed. Syracuse: Syracuse University Press, 1994.

Von Grunebaum, Gustave Edmund. *Medieval Islam.* Chicago: University of Chicago Press, 1953.

———. *Muhammadan Festivals.* New York: Henry Schuman, 1958.

Wadud-Muhsin, Amina. *Qur'an and Woman.* Kuala Lumpur: Penerbit Fajar Bakti Sdn. Bhd., 1992.

Wagtendonk, Kees. *Fasting in the Koran.* Leiden: E. J. Brill, 1968.

Waines, David. *An Introduction to Islam.* Cambridge: Cambridge University Press, 1995.

Wansbrough, John. *Qur'anic Studies: Sources and Methods of Scriptural Interpretation.* London Oriental Series 31. Oxford: Oxford University Press, 1977.

Watt, William Montgomery. *Free Will and Predestination in Early Islam.* London: Luzac, 1948.

——. *Islam and Christianity Today.* London: Routledge and Kegan Paul, 1983.

——. *Muhammad: Prophet and Statesman.* London: Oxford University Press, 1961.

——. *Muslim-Christian Encounters: Perceptions and Misperceptions.* London and New York: Routledge, 1991.

Weiss, Bernard G., and Arnold H. Green. *A Survey of Arab History.* Cairo: The American University in Cairo Press, 1985.

Wellhausen, Julius. *The Arab Kingdom and Its Fall.* Translated by Margaret G. Weir. Calcutta: University of Calcutta, 1927; reprint, Beirut: Khayats, 1963.

Wensinck, Arent Jan. *The Muslim Creed: Its Genesis and Historical Development.* London: Frank Cass, 1956.

Williams, John Alden, ed. *The World of Islam.* Austin: University of Texas Press, 1994.

Wittek, Paul. *The Rise of the Ottoman Empire.* London: Royal Asiatic Society, 1938; New York: B. Franklin, 1971.

Al-Yassini, Ayman. *Religion and State in the Kingdom of Saudi Arabia.* Boulder, Colo.: Westview, 1985.

Zakaria, Rafiq. *Muhammad and the Quran.* New York: Penguin, 1991.

Ziadeh, Farhat. *Lawyers, the Rule of Law, and Liberalism in Modern Egypt.* Stanford, Calif.: Stanford University Press, 1968.

Index

for emigration, 10; term for messenger of God, 9; term for successor, 18; term for veil, 91; term for wool, 55; translations, 45; Yezidi books in, 62

Arafat, Yasser, xviii

Armenia, 24, 31

Armenian, 6

Articles of Faith, 93–102

Ascetic, 25, 55, 56, 116

Asia, 91; converts in, 47; extent or spread of Islam in, xv, xvi, 24, 32; Khojas in, 54; Minor, 32, 36; missionaries in, 41; and Mongols, 33; Nizari communities in, 54; Ottoman forces in, 36; partitioning of, 38; Shafiʿi principles in, 87; Shiʿi communities in, 49; Sufis in, 56; Yezidi in, 61

Asia Minor, 32, 36

Assassin, 31, 53

Assassination, 21, 29, 31, 53, 54; of ʿAli, 21, 126; of the Bab, 62; of Caliph ʿUthman, 21, 44; of Murad I, 36

Attaurk, Mustafa Kemal, 39

Aurangzeb I, 34

Authority, xvii, 77, 123; of ʿAli, 21; of Abu Hanifa, 87; of caliph, 27, 30, 31, 39; of Christian scriptures, 73; of Greek patriarch, 37; of Hadith, 83; of Harun al-Rashid, 28; of imam, 48, 49, 88; of Jewish scriptures, 73; legal, 88; of medieval schools, 46; of Muhammad I, 37; of Nuʿman ibn Thabit, 87; of prophet Muhammad, 66, 68, 82; of Qurʾan, 7, 70, 73, 75, 78, 85; of religious leaders, 29; of sultan, 30, 38; of az-Zubyar, 23

Averroes (Avicenna), 45

al-Azhar, 64

Bab, 62, 63

Babak, 29

Babar, 33

Badr, 10

Baghdad, 27, 28, 29, 31, 33, 56, 57, 58, 62, 86, 87

Bahadur II, Emperor, 35

Bahaʾi, 59, 62–63

Bahaʾuʾllah, 62–63

Bangladesh, 35

Baptism, 41, 62

Battle, xvi, 10, 11, 15, 24, 37, 51, 113, 114; of Angora (Ankara), 36; of the Camel, 21; of Karbala, 22, 23; of Kossovo, 36; of Manzikert, 32

Bayazid I, 36

Baybars, 54

Baybars I, 33

Bedouin, 2, 80

Belief, 1, 48, 51, 56, 61, 62, 63, 66, 93, 100, 129; in ʿAli, 60; in God, 49, 59, 107; in imam, 49, 50; in jinn, 97–98; in life after death, 124; in prophet Muhammad, 49, 60; in Qurʾan, 99; in Salman, 60; in scriptures, 99; in Trinity, 94

Bible, xv, 16, 64, 68, 73; and Qurʾan, 73–79

Birth, 44, 50, 62, 95, 111, 120, 123; of Jesus, 76; of prophet Muhammad, 7–8

Black Book, 62

Black Muslims, 41, 59, 63–64

Black Stone, 4, 12, 30, 111

Blair, Tony, xix

Bosnia, 36, 37

Brethren of Purity, 54

British, 35

Brotherhood, 15, 57

Buddhist, 44, 46

Bukhara, 24, 32

al-Bukhari, 82, 83

Bulgaria, 36

Burial, 123, 124; of Husayn, 127; of prophet Muhammad, 18

Bursa, 36

Bush, George W., xix

Buyids, 30, 31

Byzantine, 12, 28, 32, 36, 37; emperor, 32, 36, 37; Empire, 4, 19, 23, 36, 37

Byzantium, 25, 29, 31, 32

Calendar, 10, 81, 110, 125

Caliph(s), 18–39, 47, 53, 54, 61, 75; Abu Bakr, 18, 21, 51; ʿAli, 18, 21, 85; Harun ar-Rashid, 86, 127; Marwan ibn al-Hakam, 23; al-Mustansir, 52; ʿUmar, 18; ʿUthman, 18, 19, 23, 44, 68; az-Zubayr, 23

Caliphate, 13, 18, 21–39, 44, 47, 48, 68, 85, 94; ʿAbbasids, 26–30; Mughals, 33–35; Ottomans, 36–39; Qajars, 35–36; rival dynasties, 30–33; Safavids, 35; Ummayads, 22–26

Celibacy, 60, 121

Charity, 15, 76, 116

China, 22, 24, 25, 32, 33, 40

Christ, 74, 75, 76, 77. See also Jesus

Christian(s), 44, 62, 68, 71, 102; Anatolia, 32; calendar, 110; Church of Saint Sophia, 37; colonial, 40; Coptic, xix; Emperor John Cantacuzene, 36; Europe, 32; faith, 41, 73, 75, 77, 94; festivals, 61; and Jewish, 5, 6, 13, 16, 29, 70, 73, 74, 83, 113, 121; monk Bahirah, 8; and Muslim, 63, 74, 93, 94; priest Waraqa ibn Qusayy, 8; and prophet

Muhammad, 94; rule, 32; scriptures, 75, 78–79
Christianity, xv, 5, 70, 73, 75, 77, 104
Church, 37, 114
Circumcision, 62, 120
Civilization, 16, 63; changes in, 1; Islamic, 28, 32, 33, 43; Spanish, 31; Western, xix, 41, 90; of Yemen, 4
Community, 98, 100
Community, Islamic, 22, 59, 84, 102, 104 (*see also Ummah*); of agha khan, 54; almsgiving in, 107; apostasy in, 94; challenge of, 41; changing religion in, 103; consensus of, 45; consolidating, 13; cut ties with, 47; differences within, 18, 19, 50, 54, 86, 93; of Druzes, 61; early, 6; of Egypt, 87; expansion of, 55; feminist movements in, 91; founder of, 7, 80; head or leader of, 21, 48, 60; *imams* of, 27; in India, 33; less privileged, 25; membership in mystical, 57; non-members of, 27; in the Ottoman Empire, 38; as political and religious, xvi, 44; protecting, 31; religious head of, 23; social services in, 58; strict elements of, 58
Companion(s), 81, 128; fate of, 62; Medinese, 12; of prophet Muhammad, 15, 18, 19, 46, 80, 82, 83
Concealment, 48, 49, 61
Conduct, 9, 83, 98, 114, 116, 120, 123, 124
Confederation, 10, 13, 15, 30
Conquest, xvi, 19, 24, 25, 32, 115
Consensus, 22, 38, 45, 48, 51, 82, 85, 86
Constantine IX, Emperor, 37
Constantinople. See Istanbul
Contemplation, xv, 8, 55, 56, 58
Cosmology, xvii, 80
Creation, xv, 40, 62, 71, 95, 97, 127
Creed, 102
Crete, 37
Crucifixion, 73, 77
Crusade, 32, 37
Cyprus, 37

Dancing, 5, 56, 57, 64
Dar al-Harb, xvi
Dar al-Islam, xvi, xvii
Dar al-Sulh, xvi
David, 65, 73, 99, 100
Death, 49, 97, 101, 120, 128; of Abu Bakr, 18; of Abu Talib, 9; of ʿAli, 22, 129; custom associated with, 123–125; doctrine of, 102; of Elijah Muhammad, 64; God as source of, 96; of Harun ar-Rashid, 28; of Hasan, 129; of Hisham, 26; of Husayn, 23, 48, 126,

127; of Jesus, 73, 76; of Khadijah, 7, 9; of al-Mahdi, 28; of Marwan, 23; as metempsychosis, 61; of Mirza Ghulam Ahmed, 47; of Muhammad ibn al-Hanafiya, 48; of Murad I, 36; mystery of, 5; persons targeted for, 54; of prophet Muhammad, 6, 9, 13, 18, 21, 24, 67, 82, 84, 93, 99, 102; as punishment, 62, 103, 118; of Shah Nadir, 35; of Sulayman, 38; of ʿUmar, 19; of ʿUmar II, 25; of ʿUthman, 21; of Yazid I, 23
Defeat, xvi, 10, 11, 19, 22, 32, 36, 37, 48, 113
Delhi, 32, 33, 34
Devil, 61, 72, 97
Devotion, xvi, 57, 58, 87, 96, 104, 116, 127
Dhikr, 57
Dhimmi, xvi
Disbelievers, 74, 113
Dissimulation, 49, 61
Divine, 1, 15, 62, 76, 77, 101, 104; apparition, 8; attributes, 49; authority, 75; beings, 59; blessing, 5; command, 70, 128; essence, 60; favor, 86; gift(s), 55; incarnation, 61; injunction, 69; intervention, 84; knowledge, 49; law, 55; light, 23, 49, 51; message(s), 70–73, 75, 76, 99; omnipotence, 45; person, 48; prerogatives, 95; revelation(s), 9, 15, 17, 65–66, 67, 88, 99; vindication, 10; will, 85, 90
Divorce, xvi, 72, 88, 90, 121, 122
Doctrine, xvii, 25, 44, 46, 47, 52, 53, 59, 82, 103; of angels, 97; Christian, 73, 75, 76, 77, 94; of God, 93–97; of the Guided One, 101; of heaven and hell, 101; Imami, 51; of intercession, 102; Ismaʿili, 54, 60; of Last Day, 100; of life after death, 124; Maliki, 87; mystical, 56; Nusayri, 61; of predestination, 116; of prophets, 98, 99; of scriptures, 99; Shiʿi, 48, 49; Sunni, 45; Zaydi, 51
Dome of the Rock, 23
Dowry, 121, 122
Dream, 11, 128
Druze, 59, 61

Ecstasy, 53, 55, 57, 58
Education, xvii, xviii, 13, 88
Egypt, 40; authority of az-Zubayr in, 23; Cairo, capital of, 31; Copts in, xix; Fatimid dynasty in, 52; Hanafi school in, 87; Islamic conquest of, 19; Khalwati order in, 58; King Faruk of, 39; Maliki school in, 87; Mamluk rulers of, 33, 37, 54; Marwan killed in, 26; modern Islamic government of, 86, 90; Nizaris spread from, 54; rebellion and unrest in, 28; Roman, 4
Elijah Muhammad, 63–64

Hindu, 34, 46, 47, 54
Hisham, 6, 25, 26
Holy Book, 9, 13, 15, 63, 65, 68, 78, 79, 100
Holy Family, 50
Holy Spirit, 76
Holy War. *See Jihad*
Hulaga Khan, 33
Humanity, 65, 70, 73; and angels, 97; creation of, 98; God's message to, 15, 17, 65, 72, 76, 77, 98, 116; guidance of, 100; idol worship of, 76; and jinns, 98; judgment of, 9; and original sin, 77; the Qur'an for, 71; welfare of, 50; will of God to, 52
Humankind, 63, 75
Hungary, 36, 37
Husayn, 22, 23, 30, 47, 48, 50, 51, 126, 127, 129
Hussein, Saddam, xviii

'Ibadi, 60
Ibadis (Abadis), 22
Iblis, 97
Ibn Khaldun, 101
Ibn Rushd, 45
Ibn Saud, 46
Ibn Sina, 45
Idol, 5, 12, 74, 76, 80, 111
Idolaters, 74, 101, 113
Idolatry, 9, 117, 127
Idrisid(s), 31
Ijma', 45, 48, 85, 86
Imam, 23, 29, 30, 49, 50, 51, 52, 54, 60, 88, 100; descendant of prophet Muhammad, 50; disappearance of or hidden, 30, 50, 51, 52, 101; divinely determined, 50; doctrine of, 49; human being, 51; long-awaited, 62; of Nizaris, 54; possessing superhuman knowledge, 46, 49; possessing unlimited authority, 88; sinless and infallible, 46, 49, 51; spiritual head or religious leader, 27, 48, 49, 103, 104, 123; tomb of, 49
Imami Group, 49, 50–51, 52, 54, 86, 101
Imami School, 88
Immorality, 64, 123
Immortality, 63
Incarnation, 47, 61
India, 76; breakdown of Mughal rulers in, 35; British rule in, 35; Hanafi school in, 87; Imami communities in, 51; Islamic civilization in, xvi, 22, 24, 30; Mongol invasion of, 33; Nizaris in, 54; partitioning of, 38, 47; Shi'i communities in, 34, 49; spices of, 4; Sufi orders in, 58; sultanate in Delhi, 32; Tomb of Taj Mahal, 124
Indonesia, 32, 87, 126, 129

Infallible, 17, 46, 48, 49, 50, 51, 62, 65, 79
Infidel, 21, 29, 31, 32, 61, 71, 76, 80, 113, 115
Inheritance, 29, 34, 47, 72, 85, 88, 89, 90
Iran, xvi, xviii, xix, 24, 31, 32, 35, 49, 51, 54, 61, 62
Iranian(s), 36, 62, 88, 102, 111, 118
Iraq, 19; 'Abbasid caliphs in, 26, 27; authority of az-Zubayr in, 23; battle of Karbala in, 22; as center of caliphate, 21; defiant acts by, xviii, xix; founder of Hanafi school in, 87; Husayn's martyrdom in, 48, 126; Imamis in, 51, 88; Nizaris in, 54; observatory in, 28; raids from mountaintops in, 31, 46; Shi'i communities in, 49; Sufi ascetics in, 55–58; Yezidis in, 61
Isaac, xv, 73, 98, 125
Isfahan, 35
Ishmael, xv, 4, 5, 73, 98, 112, 125
Isma'il, 30, 52, 82, 83, 100
Isma'il I, 35
Isma'ili(s), 31, 33, 49, 52, 53, 54, 60, 100
Israel, xviii, xix
Israeli, xviii, xix, 91
Israelite(s), 68
Istanbul, 32, 37

Jacob, 16, 73, 81, 98
Ja'far al-Sadiq, 50, 52
Jalal ad-Din ar-Rumi, 57
Janissary Corps, 38
Jerusalem, xviii, 23, 39, 81, 127, 128
Jesus: claim of, 56; crucifixion of, 47; disappearance of, 50; divinity of, 73, 76–77; gospel entrusted to, 78, 100; Holy Book revealed to, 65; invocation of, 16; as prophet, 17, 52, 63, 73, 81, 99, 100, 128; Qur'anic presentation of, 79; resurrection of, 73; as second person in godhead, 75; son of Mary, 74, 81, 99
Jew(s), xv, 7, 11, 17, 74, 76, 94, 99, 113, 121; and Christian(s), 13, 16, 29, 73, 74, 79; messiah of, 76
Jewish, 62; and Christian, 5, 6, 70, 73, 74, 83; clan or tribe, 11, 77; covenant, 74; holy book, 78; scripture, 17
Jihad, 22, 28, 31, 32, 51, 102, 109, 113–116
Jihan I, 33
al-Jilani, 57, 58
Jinn, 97, 98
Job, 99
John Cantacuzene, Emperor, 36
John the Baptist, 17, 128
Jordan, 19, 87
Joseph, 81, 98, 128

Index 173

S. A. NIGOSIAN, Ph.D., is a historian of religion, specializing in Near Eastern religions. He is a frequent contributor to scholarly journals and his numerous books include *Judaism: The Way of Holiness; The Zoroastrian Faith: Tradition and Modern Research; Occultism in the Old Testament;* and *World Religions: A Historical Approach.* Currently, Dr. Nigosian is Research Associate at Victoria College, University of Toronto. He received the Excellence in Teaching Award from the University of Toronto, School of Continuing Studies.